THE TEXTUAL HISTORY
OF THE
LETTER TO THE ROMANS

STUDIES AND DOCUMENTS

Founded by Kirsopp and Silva Lake

EDITED BY

IRVING ALAN SPARKS

in Collaboration With

J. NEVILLE BIRDSALL   ELDON J. EPP
SEBASTIAN P. BROCK   GORDON D. FEE
†ERNEST CADMAN COLWELL

VOLUME 42

GRAND RAPIDS, MICHIGAN
Wm. B. EERDMANS
1977

THE TEXTUAL HISTORY
OF THE
LETTER TO THE ROMANS

A Study in Textual and Literary Criticism

BY

HARRY GAMBLE, JR.

University of Virginia

GRAND RAPIDS, MICHIGAN

Wm. B. EERDMANS

1977

To my mother and father,
in gratitude

Library of Congress Cataloging in Publication Data

Gamble, Harry, 1941–
   The textual history of the letter to the Romans.

   A revision of the author's thesis, Yale, 1970.
   Includes bibliographical references.
   1. Bible. N.T. Romans—Criticism, Textual.
I. Title.
BS2665.2.G35 1976   227'.1'04   76-44484
ISBN 0-8028-1670-3

PREFACE

This study was conceived in a seminar on the canon and text of the New Testament conducted by Professor Nils A. Dahl at Yale University, during which a preliminary foray was made into the topic. The present form represents a revision of my dissertation, submitted to the Graduate School of Yale University. To Professor Dahl I wish to express appreciation for uncounted thoughtful criticisms and suggestions. I would also thank Professor Paul Minear and the late Professor Paul Schubert, both of whom took an interest in the project and offered useful insights. In revising the study I have benefited especially from some suggestions of Professor Abraham Malherbe, as well as from lively discussions in the Seminar on the Pauline Letters of the Society of Biblical Literature.

I am grateful to Professor Sparks and the editorial board for their willingness to publish this work in *Studies and Documents,* and to the University of Virginia for financial assistance in the preparation of the manuscript for publication.

Harry Gamble, Jr.
University of Virginia
Charlottesville

CONTENTS

TABLE OF ABBREVIATIONS

ATR	*Anglican Theological Review*
AusBR	*Australian Biblical Review*
BBB	Bonner biblische Beiträge
BGU	*Berliner griechische Urkunden*
BR	*Biblical Research*
BVL	Beuron Vetus Latina
BWANT	Beiträge zur Wissenschaft vom Alten und Neuen Testament
BZNW	Beihefte zur ZNW
CBQ	*Catholic Biblical Quarterly*
CSEL	Corpus scriptorum ecclesiasticorum latinorum
CQR	*Church Quarterly Review*
EBib	Etudes bibliques
ETL	*Ephemerides theologicae lovanienses*
EvT	*Evangelische Theologie*
Expos	*Expositor*
ExpT	*Expository Times*
FRLANT	Forschungen zur Religion und Literatur des Alten und Neuen Testaments
HNT	Handbuch zum Neuen Testament
HTR	*Harvard Theological Review*
HTS	Harvard Theological Studies
ICC	International Critical Commentary
IEJ	*Israel Exploration Journal*
Int	*Interpretation*
JBL	*Journal of Biblical Literature*
JTS	*Journal of Theological Studies*
Jud	*Judaica*
Meyer	H. A. W. Meyer, Kritisch-exegetischer Kommentar über das Neue Testament
NovT	*Novum Testamentum*
NTAbh	Neutestamentliche Abhandlungen
NTD	Das Neue Testament Deutsch
NTS	*New Testament Studies*
NTSMS	New Testament Studies Monograph Series
PG	J. Migne, *Patrologia graeca*
PL	J. Migne, *Patrologia latina*
RAC	*Reallexikon für Antike und Christentum*
RB	*Revue biblique*
RBen	*Revue bénédictine*
RGG	*Religion in Geschichte und Gegenwart*
SBT	Studies in Biblical Theology
SEA	*Svensk exegetisk Årsbok*
ST	*Studia theologica*
TDNT	G. Kittel and G. Friedrich (eds.), *Theological Dictionary of the New Testament*

TLZ	*Theologische Literaturzeitung*
TU	Texte und Untersuchungen
TZ	*Theologische Zeitschrift*
VD	*Verbum domini*
WMANT	Wissenschaftliche Monographien zum Alten und Neuen Testament
ZNW	*Zeitschrift für die neutestamentliche Wissenschaft*

INTRODUCTION

The early history of the Pauline letters is a continuing enigma in NT scholarship. Despite a great expenditure of effort over the past century, we are able today to claim very few assured conclusions and cannot describe with any confidence the process by which the individual letters of the Apostle were gathered into a collection and came to form a substantial part of the NT canon.

The task of clarifying this process has traditionally fallen to that discipline called "the history of the NT canon," and specialists in this field have recovered and examined in detail the relevant external evidence, that is, ancient canon lists, patristic testimony and the contents of MSS.[1] But textual criticism also has a role to play here, insofar as the history of the NT canon cannot and ought not be completely distinguished from the history of the NT text. To that extent it is the responsibility of the textual critic not merely to seek out the "original readings" but also to inquire what texts belonged to the canon at different times and places, and why.[2] Thus the history of MSS and of text-types comprises an important aspect of the history of the canon.

The question of the early history of the Pauline letters has also been raised, and as a concern of more immediate importance, from still another point of view, namely, the criticism of the letters themselves. It has been a strong and growing conviction among many critics that the transmitted texts of at least some of the letters of Paul do not correspond in form to the letters actually written by Paul, but are to be regarded as "editorial products" in which originally independent pieces of Paul's correspondence are conflated. Such a conviction has obvious importance for the exegetical task: if a given letter's unity is thought to be imposed and artificial, then the interpreter is obliged by the methods of historical criticism to treat it in terms of its constituent parts, discovering the proper historical setting, occasion and purpose for each. The literary-critical judgment that a given letter is a composite of originally independent elements has little to do, at the level of evidence and method,

---

[1]Theodor Zahn's massive study, *Geschichte des neutestamentlichen Kanons* (2 vols.; Erlangen, 1888–92), has yet to be surpassed as a collection of the evidence available at that time, even though many of his interpretations may be rejected. For a recent discussion of the whole question see Hans von Campenhausen, *The Formation of the Christian Bible* (Philadelphia, 1972).

[2]The "original text" which textual criticism has traditionally sought to recover is not necessarily to be equated with the canonical text. The discipline of textual criticism needs to develop and apply a method analogous to form criticism which will allow the text of the NT to be studied within the ongoing life of the church. The question of originality ("authenticity") should not preempt the question of the process of the textual tradition and the relation of textual tradition to ecclesiastical tradition. The history of the text is, after all, an aspect of church history. There is room for many studies on the order of Eldon J. Epp's *The Theological Tendency of Codex Bezae Cantabrigiensis in Acts* (NTSMS 3; Cambridge, 1966).

with the history of the canon or with textual criticism, since it is based on phenomena internal to the letter itself which call its integrity into question. But by implication it inevitably raises important questions about the early history of the Pauline letters and their transmission in the early church.

The unity of every one of the authentic letters of Paul has been disputed, with the single exception of the small letter to Philemon.[3] Not all theories have found acceptance, but there appears to be a far-reaching consensus of critical judgment against the integrity of several letters, especially Romans, 2 Corinthians and Philippians. Whatever position may be taken on the integrity of any individual letter, it is generally granted as a firm critical principle that the form of the transmitted text of any letter should not be assumed, without further ado, to represent the original form of the Pauline correspondence.

In the establishment of this literary-critical principle the letter to the Romans has played an important part. In the case of Romans, the critic is able to rely not only upon internal (literary-critical) evidence against its unity but also upon clear signs in the textual tradition itself that this letter was transmitted in several forms in the early church, and thus the evidential base is broader. The availability of textual evidence in addition to the literary-critical evidence in Romans has served to justify the development of partition theories for other letters, even though in other letters text-critical evidence is not available.[4] Nevertheless, the strength of the internal evidence in other letters is often found to be compelling.[5] In any case, it is a legitimate principle of criticism that the integrity of the transmitted text of any letter may not be presupposed.

The present study is focused on the Roman letter itself and the problem of its textual history. The title *The Textual History of the Letter to the Romans* is broadly construed to embrace the question of the origin and development of the several forms of the text attested in the tradition. We therefore concentrate on two primary issues: (a) the original address and extent of the letter, and (b) the derivation of the deviant forms. Such an investigation is necessary and important for our understanding of the Roman letter itself. But our approach to this particular problem is conceived also with regard to the more general concerns noted above, the early history of the Pauline letters, and the methodology of the literary criticism of the epistles. Hopefully, this study will illumine those areas as well.

The problematic character of the textual history of Romans is expressed, on the one hand, by a limited number of textual variants relating to the address (1:7, 1:15), to the position of the doxology (16:25–27 in modern editions), and to the concluding benedictions (variously placed at 16:20b, 16:24 and 16:28). The variants encountered at these points, with supporting documentary evidence, reveal that at an early date the letter was current in several forms of differing length and that the Roman address was not consistently maintained in each. The question of the history

[3]Galatians enjoyed exemption, along with Philemon, until recently. See now J. C. O'Neill, *The Recovery of Paul's Letter to the Galatians* (London, 1972), in which its unity is disputed.

[4]We are not suggesting that the first "partition theory" was developed for the Roman letter, but only that the availability there of textual evidence helped establish the principle that the transmitted form of the text may not be assumed to be original, even where textual evidence does not impugn integrity.

[5]The nature of such internal evidence and its probative force needs to be analyzed. We do this for the Roman letter in the present study, and make a beginning in a critical evaluation of the methodology of literary-critical theories generally (below, Chapter V).

of the text is raised, on the other hand, by the literary criticism of the letter. Many have been led to deny the integrity of the transmitted text by purely internal features of the letter—certain anomalies of content, style, and tone—which seem to be best explained by differentiating ch. 16 as having had an address different from that of the rest of the letter and/or by supposing that a general letter of multiple address lies behind the transmitted text. Thus from different points of view, and for different reasons, the same questions arise: what is the "original" form of the text, and how did the other attested forms emerge?

The problem of the textual history of Romans, thus posed, was once described by the Benedictine scholar, Donatien de Bruyne, as "the most debated and yet, for all that, the most obscure of the entire New Testament."[6] In the decades since he wrote the debate has continued, but the obscurity has not been relieved. If anything, the situation is even more beclouded now with the addition of new evidence and a proliferation of hypotheses. Perhaps Hans Lietzmann was right when he ventured that for this problem "a completely satisfying explanation . . . is not available."[7] If the complexity of the problem cannot be gainsaid, the possibility of its solution can be estimated only by means of a comprehensive study. But just this has been lacking. No satisfactory solution has emerged precisely because the problem has been treated in piecemeal fashion.[8] The textual critic, for example, has usually been content to work strictly with the textual evidence and standard text-critical methods. While it is absolutely necessary to exploit this approach, the problem yields relatively little to textual criticism alone, and text critics have been reluctant to move on from their assessments of the facts of the tradition to view the problem from other, possibly illuminating, perspectives. The literary critic, for his part, approaches the problem differently. He may refer to the textual evidence, but it is ordinarily used only as a point of departure which serves to raise the question, or to justify posing the question on other grounds. Rarely is the textual evidence permitted to control or positively to inform the search for a solution. Yet the internal evidence used by the literary critic is in itself sufficiently ambiguous to preclude a solution on that basis alone. It is largely because of a failure to correlate closely textual and literary criticism that the textual history of Romans has continued to be debated along the same lines without measurable progress.

It is clear, then, that a serious effort to clarify the textual history of the letter must garner and integrate all the relevant evidence and discipline various methodological approaches into effective cooperation. Only so will the full dimensions of the problem and an adequate solution be grasped. Consequently, the unity of this study is furnished by the subject matter, not by a particular method. We have freely drawn upon textual and literary criticism, but also upon other methods, in the hope that these various approaches, once brought together, will allow us to proceed beyond the current impasse.

We begin with a thorough assessment of the textual problem as such,

---

[6]"Les deux derniers chapitres de la lettre aux Romains," *RBen* 25 (1908) 423.

[7]*An die Römer* (HNT; 1st ed.; Tübingen, 1907) 77.

[8]To our knowledge there has been only one monograph devoted to the subject, the slim volume of Rudolf Schumacher, *Die beiden letzten Kapitel des Römerbriefes. Ein Beitrag zu ihrer Geschichte und Erklärung* (NTAbh 14/4; Münster, 1929). The study is primarily a (now dated) survey of opinion which seems to make no advance over previous research.

dealing with the evidence of the MS tradition and the pertinent materials in the patristic literature (Chapter I). This serves to raise the salient issues and provides a firm footing for the remainder of the study. We turn next to the question of the integrity of the transmitted text, discussing the problems and possibilities from a literary-critical point of view (Chapter II) and offering a solution (Chapter III). We then proceed to consider the subsequent development of the textual tradition, its causes and effects (Chapter IV). In conclusion, we add some reflections on the significance of our results for the related concerns of the literary criticism of the letters generally and of the purpose of the Roman letter (Chapter V).

CHAPTER I

THE TEXTUAL EVIDENCE

It has long been recognized that various aspects of the textual tradition of Romans suggest the currency, at one time or another, of as many as three basic forms of the letter, characterized primarily by differences of length, but also by other features. Though the textual evidence for these forms is well known in its general outlines, a detailed critical presentation of it is essential in order to pose the problems clearly and to provide a sound basis for their solution.

The fundamental data of the textual tradition of Romans were brought to light for the most part by several scholars of the late nineteenth and early twentieth centuries, above all J. B. Lightfoot, F. J. A. Hort, Eduard Riggenbach, Donatien de Bruyne and Peter Corssen.[1] Their studies of the text of Romans are essential even today for a firm grasp of the textual phenomena, even if their interpretive conclusions are often open to doubt, and every modern statement of the evidence must consist largely of a collation and review of their results. To this must be added, of course, more recent evidence which was not accessible to them. This further evidence is not extensive, but adds a new and important dimension to the problem. Our present aim, then, is to provide a comprehensive and precise survey of the attestation for the various forms of the letter. For the moment we are concerned strictly with the facts of the textual tradition. Only later will we undertake to interpret these facts and integrate them into a coherent explanatory scheme.[2]

---

[1]The studies by Lightfoot and Hort appeared originally as follows: J. B. Lightfoot, "M. Renan's Theory of the Epistle to the Romans," *Journal of Philology* 2 (1869) 264–295; F. J. A. Hort, "On the End of the Epistle to the Romans," *Journal of Philology* 3 (1871) 51–80; J. B. Lightfoot, "The Epistle to the Romans," *Journal of Philology* 3 (1871) 193–214. These three pieces were made available together under the heading "The Structure and Destination of the Epistle to the Romans," in J. B. Lightfoot, *Biblical Essays* (London, 1893) 285–374. All following references are to the pagination of the latter. For the rest: E. Riggenbach, "Die Textgeschichte der Doxologie Röm. 16,25–27 im Zusammenhang mit den übrigen, den Schluss des Römerbriefs betreffenden, textkritischen Fragen," *Neue Jahrbücher für deutsche Theologie* 1 (1892) 526–605 (hereinafter "Textgeschichte"); idem, "Die Kapitelverzeichnisse zum Römer- und Hebräerbrief im Codex Fuldensis der Vulgata," *Neue Jahrbücher für deutsche Theologie* 3 (1894) 350–363 (hereinafter "Kapitelverzeichnisse"); D. de Bruyne, "Les deux derniers chapitres de la lettre aux Romains," *RBen* 25 (1908) 423–430 (hereinafter "Derniers chapitres"); idem, "La finale marcionite de la lettre aux Romains retrouvée," *RBen* 28 (1911) 133–142 (hereinafter "La finale marcionite"); P. Corssen, "Zur Überlieferungsgeschichte des Römerbriefes," *ZNW* 10 (1909) 1–45 (hereinafter "Überlieferungsgeschichte"); idem, "Zur Überlieferungsgeschichte des Römerbriefes, Nachtrag," *ZNW* 10 (1909) 97–102 (hereinafter "Nachtrag").

[2]See below, Chapters IV–V.

The Fourteen-Chapter Form[3]

Although it is preserved by no extant MS, diverse types of evidence show conclusively, if indirectly, that at one time the letter to the Romans was current in a form consisting of only fourteen chapters.

Part of the oldest documentary evidence for the fourteen-chapter text is furnished by the *capitula* or *breves* found in many Vulgate MSS.[4] These systems of text division provide a brief précis for each segment of the text, and so function in the manner of "tables of contents" for the letters. Two different *capitula* systems attest a text of Romans in fourteen chapters.

The oldest MS preserving the first system completely is Codex Amiatinus (vg^A) of the eighth century. Here we find the text of Romans divided into fifty-one parts, with a brief summary allotted to each. For our purposes it is necessary to cite only the last two of these *capitula*:[5]

> L. *De periculo contristante fratrem esca sua et quod non sit regnum Dei esca et potus sed iustitia et pax et gaudium in spiritu sancto.*
> Concerning the danger of grieving a brother by one's food, and that the kingdom of God is not food and drink, but righteousness and peace and joy in the Holy Spirit.
> LI. *De mysterio domini ante passione in silentio habito post passione vero ipsius revelato.*
> Concerning the mystery of the Lord kept in silence before the passion, his truth having been revealed after the passion.

Capitulum L refers specifically to Rom 14:15, 17. Equally clearly, *capitulum* LI, the last of the series, refers to the doxology, 16:25–27 in modern editions. At the most, *capitulum* L could denote the line of thought through 14:23, and so we have here no *capitula* for chs. 15 and 16 of Romans.[6] Given the method of the Amiatine system, it is impossible that its author would have passed over two entire chapters in silence had they been present in the text he employed, for elsewhere texts of such length are accorded many summaries. This anomaly is, then, a clear sign that the

---

[3]Throughout this study Greek MSS are designated by the numbers of Gregory. For Greek MSS of particular importance for the topic we have sometimes added, in parentheses following Gregory's number, other sigla occasionally used in the pertinent literature. Traditional designations of the Old Latin MSS are supplemented with the sigla used in the Beuron edition of the Old Latin Bible, as listed in Bonifatius Fischer, *Vetus Latina. Die Reste der altlateinischen Bibel nach Petrus Sabatier neu gesammelt und herausgegeben von der Erzabtei Beuron, I/1: Verzeichnis der Sigel für Handschriften und Kirchenschriftsteller* (2nd ed.; Freiburg, 1963). We preface these sigla with BVL (Beuron Vetus Latina). Vulgate MSS are designated with the sigla used by J. Wordsworth, H. J. White, *et al.*, eds., *Novum Testamentum Domini nostri Iesu Christi Latine secundum editionem sancti Hieronymi* (3 vols.; Oxford, 1889–1954). Whenever the designations of Latin MSS in the Beuron edition differ from those of Wordsworth and White, the Beuron sigla also are given, preceded by BVL.

[4]The importance of this material for the textual question was first perceived by J. J. Wettstein, *Novum Testamentum Graecum* (2 vols.; Amsterdam, 1751–52) II, 91. His observation was taken up, clarified and developed first by Hort, *Biblical Essays*, 337–38.

[5]For the full text in synoptic presentation with other systems see J. Wordsworth and H. J. White, *Novum Testamentum Domini nostri Iesu Christi Latine secundum editionem sancti Hieronymi*, II, "Epistulae Paulinae" (with A. Ramsbotham, H. F. D. Sparks and C. Jenkins; Oxford, 1913–41) 44–60 (hereinafter Wordsworth and White, *Novum Testamentum Latine*); also D. de Bruyne, *Sommaires, divisions et rubriques de la Bible latine* (Namur, 1914) 314–18.

[6]The position of the *capitulum* number in the margin of the text of Amiatinus is at 15:4, but such imprecision is common in the MSS.

16

final two chapters were absent from the text of Romans on which the system is based. The form of the text presupposed is 1:1–14:23+16:25–27.

The *capitula* system of Codex Amiatinus is not a peculiar and isolated witness, for the same system or apparent remnants of it is found in many other Vulgate MSS.[7] Interestingly, a portion of the Amiatine system is found appended to another *capitula* system in Codex Fuldensis (vg^F), also of the sixth century, the only known witness to the second system. Here *capitula* I–XXIII describe Rom 1–14. To these have been added *capitula* XXIV–LI of the Amiatine system. The last *capitulum* of the specifically Fuldensian series reads:[8]

> XXIII. *Quod fideles Dei non debeant invicem iudicare cum unusquisque secundum regulas mandatorum ipse se debeat divino iudico praeparare ut ante tribunal Dei sine confusione possit operum suorum praestare rationem.*
>
> That those who have faith in God ought not judge each other since each must prepare for the divine judgment according to the dictates of his own conscience, so that before the judgment seat of God he may be able to give account of his work without difficulty.

This obviously relates to Rom 14:1–23. But this *capitulum* is followed by the Amiatine *capitulum* XXIV, which refers to Rom 9. The result of the combination is that chs. 9–14 are described twice (*capitula* XVII–XXIII and XXIV–L).

This peculiarity can be variously estimated. It may be that an exemplar of Codex Fuldensis lacked a leaf containing the Amiatine *capitula* I–XXIII, and that the scribe (editor?) compensated for this by excerpting the missing number of *capitula* from another MS with a different apparatus, not noticing the duplication involved in the process. Something of the sort is suggested by the presence of the Amiatine system in the other epistles of Fuldensis, and even in Romans the text is divided, according to the Amiatine pattern, into fifty-one sections.[9] Alternatively, we might suppose that the uniquely Fuldensian series was secondarily augmented by the addition of part of the Amiatine series. In this case we would presume that the scribe (editor?) of Fuldensis observed the discrepancy between the twenty-three *capitula* and the fifty-one sections in the text, and brought the *capitula* into conformity by deriving more *capitula* from the Amiatine apparatus.[10] We cannot in fact determine the cause of the combination of two distinct systems in Fuldensis,[11] and

---

[7]MSS containing the Amiatine *capitula* are partially enumerated by S. Berger, *Histoire de la Vulgate pendant les premiers siècles du moyen âge* (Paris, 1893) 357. The major representatives, in addition to Amiatinus, are F K M O V Z (BVL: F φ^G M O φ^V Z^H).

[8]For the full text see Wordsworth and White, *Novum Testamentum Latine*, II, 45–53; de Bruyne, *Sommaires, divisions et rubriques de la Bible latine*, 315–17.

[9]Thus Riggenbach, "Kapitelverzeichnisse," 355–56, and Theodor Zahn, *Introduction to the New Testament* (3 vols.; New York, 1909) I, 398 (hereinafter *Introduction*). It is not necessary of course to think of the scribe (editor?) of Fuldensis as the agent here, since the anomaly may have been present already in an exemplar.

[10]Thus Hort, *Biblical Essays*, 351 n. 1; Lightfoot, ibid., 360; and Corssen, "Überlieferungsgeschichte," 30–31. This explanation must come to terms with the use elsewhere in Fuldensis of the Amiatine system. It might be posited, for example, that in an exemplar of Fuldensis, or somewhere in the ancestry of an exemplar, the Amiatine *capitula* were given in full for Romans, but were then lost for this letter. They might then have been replaced by the Fuldensian system, which in turn was augmented by a portion of the Amiatine system.

[11]The presence in Fuldensis of this indiscriminate conflation of distinct systems is the more remarkable because Fuldensis is nothing less than a careful edition commissioned by Victor of Capua and revised by Victor himself. See Bonifatius Fischer, "Bibelausgaben des frühen Mittelalters," *La Bibbia*

without knowing the cause the relevance of the Fuldensian *capitula* as evidence for the fourteen-chapter text is uncertain. If the non-Amiatine *capitula* in Fuldensis are merely a compensating addition, then they may have been only a partial appropriation of a system which also embraced chs. 15 and 16 of Romans. But the fact that the text covered by the Fuldensian series is precisely Rom 1–14 constitutes at the least a remarkable coincidence in view of the assured existence of a fourteen-chapter text. If the Fuldensian *capitula* attest such a form of the text, it is different from that suggested by the Amiatine system, for it does not allude to the doxology. The text implied would be 1:1–14:23, but without the doxology.[12]

While these *capitula* systems are to be found only in Vulgate MSS, it is beyond doubt that they antedate the Vulgate itself. There are many indications that they were patterned closely upon an Old Latin text.[13] Thus they constitute early testimony to a fourteen-chapter text of Romans.[14]

A further witness to a text of Romans in only fourteen chapters is the so-called *Concordia epistularum Pauli,* a concordance to the Pauline letters found in partial form in a number of Vulgate MSS. The method of this work is to list under various subject headings, drawn successively from each letter, the pertinent Pauline texts, and these texts are referred to by means of the numbers of the Amiatine *capitula* system. There are two versions of this concordance, a shorter and widely attested one comprising fifty-six subject headings and containing only one reference to Romans, this under the last heading,[15] and a longer one extant only in Codex Morbacensis of the Murbach monastery and comprising one hundred subject headings with copious references to Romans.[16]

---

nell' Alto Medioevo (Spoleto, 1963) 545–557. This edition drew upon both a mixed text with many Old Latin readings and a Vulgate text. Possibly the combination of *capitula* systems in Romans is to be explained with reference to the texts used for this edition; did the mixed text lying behind Fuldensis, or perhaps one of its ancestors, have a short text of Romans with the non-Amiatine *capitula* to the same effect?

[12]This form of the text (fourteen chapters without the doxology) is elsewhere attested in the Old Latin. See further below.

[13]This was first suggested by Lightfoot (*Biblical Essays,* 362), who offered as evidence, however, only one Old Latin reading, viz., *de tempore serviendo* in *capitulum* LXII, referring to Rom 12:11 and presupposing a reading explicitly rejected by Jerome, Ep. XXVII (*Ad Marcellam*), PL XXII, 432. This slim evidence was greatly enlarged by Riggenbach, "Textgeschichte," 534–39, and Corssen, "Überlieferungsgeschichte," 27–29, putting the matter beyond doubt.

[14]It was objected by Riggenbach ("Textgeschichte," 586–87) and by Zahn (*Introduction,* I, 399–400) that even the Amiatine *capitula* provide no basis for this assumption. They contended that the Amiatine *capitula* system as witnessed in extant MSS is defective, and that the system originally contained further *capitula* after the fifty-first covering chapters 15 and 16. On this view the Amiatine *capitula* would testify not to a short text, but only to a text in which the doxology had been transposed to the position after chapter 14, without any omission of the final two chapters. The Amiatine *capitula* system would then attest in Latin a form of the text parallel to the Byzantine text in Romans, 1:1–14:23, 16:25–27, 15:1–16:23 (24). But the wide dispersion of the Amiatine system in its present form speaks decisively against the theory of a mutilated archetype, as does the dependence of the *Concordia epistularum* on these *capitula*. In some late MSS first noted by Lightfoot (*Biblical Essays,* 358–59) the Amiatine system has been variously expanded to produce conformity with the sixteen-chapter text, thus, e.g., in Mus. Br. Reg. I. E. VIII (see Wordsworth and White, *Novum Testamentum Latine,* II, 44–61). Such alterations are clearly late developments which are irrelevant for the early form of the *capitula* system.

[15]Text in Wordsworth and White, *Novum Testamentum Latine,* II, 12–16, and D. de Bruyne, *Préfaces de la Bible latine* (Namur, 1920) 220–23.

[16]Text available in A. F. Vezzosi, ed., *Josephi Mariae Thomasii, Opera Omnia* (Rome, 1747) I, 489–495.

Naturally it is a question which of these versions of the concordance is original and which a later development, but there are good reasons to suppose that the longer form is original. The concordance is drawn up in such a way that, as the subject headings are derived consecutively from the letters, texts from the preceding letters are not cited. Thus under the headings taken from Galatians there are no references to the Corinthian letters. It is quite surprising that Romans plays no role in the shorter version, and such a situation can hardly be original. In the longer version the concordance begins with forty-three headings drawn from Romans. Given the principle of citation which is followed, it must be assumed that there is no allusion to Romans in the shorter version simply because that version is fragmentary, beginning only with Corinthians, and that Romans is properly represented in the longer form. The headings drawn from Romans give no indication of having been secondarily composed, but correspond very well with the other headings. Thus the longer version may be taken as primary, the shorter as a consequence of the tradition.[17]

Two subject headings of the longer version are important for our question:

XLII. *Quod regnum Dei non sit esca et potus, ad Rom. L, ad Cor. prima XI.*
That the kingdom of God is not food and drink, in Rom (section) L, in I Cor (section) XI.

XLIII. *De abscondito sacramento a saeculo, ad Rom. LI, ad Eph. IX, ad Col. III, ad Tit. I, ad Heb. II.*
Concerning the mystery hidden for ages, in Rom (section) LI, in Eph (section) IX, in Col (section) III, in Tit (section) I, in Heb (section) II.

The reference of heading XLII to Rom 14:17ff. is clear, and so is that of XLIII to the doxology. Thus the concordance applies to a text of Romans extending only to 14:23, with the doxology following.[18]

Evidence for the fourteen-chapter form of the text is also provided by the allegedly Marcionite prologues to the Pauline letters, specifically by the prologue to Romans.[19] These prologues provide brief notes for each letter, indicating its recipients, their location, the occasion and purpose of the letter, and the place of composition. In the prologue to Romans some MSS designate as the place of composition *a Corintho,* but others read here *ab Athenis.* Most likely, the latter is the original reading: how could it have originated if *a Corintho* were primary? The idea that Romans was written "from Athens" could not easily have been fostered if chs. 15

---

[17]Thus Berger, *Histoire de la Vulgate pendant les premiers siècles du moyen âge,* 209; Riggenbach, "Textgeschichte," 545-49; Corssen, "Überlieferungsgeschichte," 22-24. For the opposite view see Donatien de Bruyne, "Une concordance biblique d'origin Pelagienne," *RB* 5 (1908) 75-83, and Wordsworth and White, *Novum Testamentum Latine,* II, 12. Apart from the problem of attestation, the difficulty in regarding the longer version as primary is posed by the fact that it contains references to Hebrews, which the shorter version does not, and some take this as a sign of lateness. But it is possible to hold the longer version as primary while allowing that the citations of Hebrews are later additions.

[18]It cannot be said that the concordance is based only on the Amiatine *capitula* and thus is not to be treated as an independent witness, for Corssen showed ("Überlieferungsgeschichte," 23-24) that although a number of the subject headings in the concordance are derived directly from the *capitula,* others are taken from the biblical text itself, whereas still others which clearly depend on the *capitula* are slightly recast by reference to the biblical text. For example, in heading XLIII, mentioned above, the *mysterio* of the Amiatine *capitulum* is replaced with *sacramento.*

[19]See Wordsworth and White, *Novum Testamentum Latine,* II, 41-42. On these prologues see further below, 111-13.

and 16 belonged to the text used by the author of the prologues, since in these chapters Corinth stands out rather obviously as the place of writing (15:25–27; 16:1).[20]

Moreover, the order of the Pauline letters with Galatians in first place, followed by the Corinthian letters and Romans—an order presupposed by the prologues, attested for Marcion, and attested for the Old Syriac by Ephraem and the *Catalogus Sinaiticus*—may well be the result of an effort to order the letters chronologically, that is, according to the time of their composition.[21] If this order is chronologically intended, it must rest on a text of Romans without the last two chapters. Only so could Romans not be placed in the final position, but given after the Corinthian and before the Thessalonian letters, inasmuch as ch. 15 makes it unmistakably clear that the letter was written quite late in Paul's career.

Patristic testimony is of greater than usual significance for the textual history of Romans and is relatively abundant, though difficult to evaluate. Some of this testimony is composed only of arguments from silence. The probative force of such arguments is notoriously problematic, but the uncertainty can be relieved somewhat if we rely on the following principles of evaluation: (a) an argument from silence based on a single author is of little or no value, but the lack of a citation of a given text by several authors is valuable, and this value increases with the number of such authors; (b) the force of an argument from silence depends to some extent on the importance of the text in question (i.e., it is not so important that a text is not quoted, but that it is not cited in contexts where it would have required consideration); (c) the force of an argument from silence depends also on the extent of the text in question (silence on a single verse may result from mere oversight, but the longer the text the less likely unintentional neglect).

With these considerations in view, we observe first that three fathers, Irenaeus, Cyprian and Tertullian, do not quote at all from Rom 15–16. Regarding Irenaeus we can do little more than state his neglect of these chapters,[22] but more may be said of Cyprian and Tertullian.

In his *Testimonia adversus Judaeos* Cyprian provides a collection of widely scattered texts arranged according to their dogmatic import. In *Testimonia* iii.68, 78 and 95 he brings together texts which encourage the avoidance of heretics.[23] The exhortation of Rom 16:17–19, despite its pertinence, is not cited in any instance. What is more, there is no reference to chs. 15 and 16 throughout the work. This can only mean that Cyprian employed a fourteen-chapter text of the letter.[24]

That Tertullian never makes citations from Rom 15–16 does not in itself mean much, but Tertullian seems to confirm for us his knowledge of a form of

---

[20]It is also to be noted that the prologue to Romans says nothing about the letter carrier, even though an inference could have been made on the basis of 16:1–2 if these verses were at hand. Carrier notices are found in the prologues to Philippians and Corinthians.

[21]On this order of the letters, see below, 111–12.

[22]See W. Sanday, C. H. Turner and A. Souter, eds., *Novum Testamentum Sancti Irenaei Episcopi Lugdunensis* (Old Latin Biblical Texts 7; Oxford, 1923) 168. This neglect should, however, be brought into connection with the marked agreement of the Greek quotations of Irenaeus with Western witnesses, especially D, and of his Latin quotations with g, especially when g stands alone (cf. ibid., clxv–clxvi). On the importance of these witnesses for the problem, see further below.

[23]*PL* IV, 800B, 802B, 805A.

[24]See Hans von Soden, ed., *Das lateinische Neue Testament in Afrika zur Zeit Cyprians nach Bibelhandschriften und Vaterzeugnissen* (TU 33; Leipzig, 1909) 592.

Romans ending with ch. 14. In *Adversus Marcionem* v.14 he writes: *Bene autem quod et in clausula epistolae tribunal Christi comminatur. . . .*[25] ("It is well, however, that in the conclusion of the letter he threatens us with 'the judgment seat of Christ'. . . .") The allusion here is to Rom 14:10 (τῷ βήματι τοῦ Χριστοῦ), said to occur *in clausula,* that is, in the closing section of the letter; and immediately after this statement Tertullian turns to a consideration of the Thessalonian letters. The phrase *in clausula* is somewhat imprecise, certainly, and need not mean "at the very end," but that these words would have been used with two and a half chapters remaining beyond Rom 14:10 is extremely improbable.[26] Yet they would have been appropriate if Tertullian's text of Romans ended with ch. 14. We cannot be absolutely certain whether at this point Tertullian is referring to his own text or to Marcion's text or indeed to both.[27] Although his custom was to refute Marcion on the basis of the heretic's own text, he also took it upon himself to point out the excisions and other alterations which Marcion had made.[28] Since no mutations are here imputed to Marcion, and since Tertullian himself never cites from chs. 15 and 16, it is virtually assured that Tertullian himself employed a fourteen-chapter text of Romans.[29]

We observe, furthermore, that with one exception there is in the West no clear reference to the last two chapters of Romans until the pseudo-Cyprianic tract *De singularitate clericorum,* dated about the middle of the fourth century.[30] After this, random allusions to these chapters frequently appear. Assuming the principles stated above, the cumulative *argumentum e silentio* is quite strong: there is a consensus of Western writers through the third century, no part of the text is quoted even when its appropriateness is obvious, and the extent of the text is such that silence on it can have but one explanation: chs. 15 and 16 of the Roman letter were not generally known in the West for a long time.

An exception to this judgment is probably to be seen in the Muratorian Canon, whose Roman provenance is ordinarily conceded. The Canon reports that in Acts Luke dealt only with the things of which he had been an eyewitness, and that this is shown in that Luke does not mention the martyrdom of Peter or the journey of Paul to Spain.[31] It is important here not merely that the author of the Muratorian Canon knows of a journey of Paul to Spain, but that he speaks of a journey from Rome and instead of the customary term for Spain, *Iberia,* or *Hispania,* he

---

[25]*PL* II, 541A.

[26]Hort (*Biblical Essays,* 335–36) wished to understand the words in the widest possible sense as embracing the section 14:10–16:27. See the full discussion by Theodor Zahn, *Geschichte des neutestamentlichen Kanons* (2 vols.; Erlangen, 1888–92) II, 520–21 (hereinafter *Geschichte*), who did not suppose that the words necessarily mean that even Marcion's text ended with ch. 14.

[27]Cf. *Adv. Marc.* v.1 (*PL* II, 502B). If Tertullian were here using his own text in addition to Marcion's then it could also be urged that Tertullian would have found useful polemical matter in Rom 15–16, and that his failure to cite it shows he did not know it. But the premise is uncertain.

[28]The large omission by Marcion of perhaps all of Rom 9 is carefully marked by Tertullian, *PL* II, 539B. See Zahn, *Geschichte,* II, 518, and Adolf von Harnack, *Marcion: das Evangelium vom fremden Gott. Eine Monographie zur Geschichte der Grundlegung der katholischen Kirche* (2nd ed. rev.; TU 45; Leipzig, 1924) 108* (hereinafter *Marcion*).

[29]See, among others, Corssen, "Überlieferungsgeschichte," 14 n. 1, and cf. H. Rönsch, *Das Neue Testament Tertullians* (Leipzig, 1871) 320–21, 350.

[30]*PL* IV, 911B ff., citing Rom 15:2 and 16:17.

[31]Lines 40–48; lines 45–48 read: . . . *sicut et remote passionem Petri evidentur declarat, sed et profectionem Pauli ab urbe ad Spaniam proficiscentis.*

employs the less usual *Spania* (Σπανία), which is also found in Rom 15:24 and 28 in Paul's discussion of his intention to go on to Spain. The natural inference is that the author of the Muratorian Canon was acquainted with Rom 15.[32]

Of all the fathers, Origen provides the most explicit and extensive testimony on the textual history of Romans. In his *Commentaria in epistolam ad Romanos* Origen remarks apropos Rom 16:25–27:

> Caput hoc Marcion a quo scripturae evangelicae atque apostolicae interpolatae sunt de hac epistula penitus abstulit; et non solum hoc sed et ab eo loco ubi scriptum est 'omne autem quod non est ex fide peccatum est' usque ad finem cuncta dissecuit. In aliis vero exemplaribus id est in his quae non sunt a Marcione temerata, hoc ipsum caput diverse positum invenimus. In nonnullis etenim codicibus post eum locum quem supra diximus, hoc est 'omne quod non est ex fide peccatum est,' statim cohaerens habetur, 'ei autem qui potens est vos confirmare'; alii vero codices in fine id, ut nunc est positum, continent.

> Marcion, by whom the evangelical and apostolic writings were falsified, completely removed this section [i.e., 16:25–27] from this letter; and not only this, but also from that place where it is written 'all that is not of faith is sin' he cut it away up to the end. Indeed, in other copies, that is, in those which are not contaminated by Marcion, we find this same section differently placed. For in some manuscripts, following the place which we mentioned above, that is, 'all that is not of faith is sin' [the words] 'now to him who is able to strengthen you' have a consistent position; yet other manuscripts have this at the end, as it is now placed.[33]

This notice is transmitted to us only in the Latin version of the commentary made by Rufinus *ca.* 405. Though there is considerable uncertainty as to how Rufinus handled the commentary, there is every reason for us to believe that these remarks are Origen's own.[34] For him Marcionism was still a real concern, as it was not for Rufinus, who in any case can have known little or nothing of Marcion's biblical text.

Origen, then, clearly informs us that Marcion completely removed (*abstulit*) the doxology. Beyond this there has been much debate over the precise

[32]Thus Schumacher, *Letzten Kapitel,* 11, and Nils A. Dahl, "Welche Ordnung der Paulusbriefe wird vom muratorischen Kanon vorausgesetzt?," *ZNW* 52 (1951) 46, following a number of older commentators. This conclusion has recently been disputed by H. J. Frede in his *Altlateinische Paulus-Handschriften* (Vetus Latina. Die Reste der altlateinischen Bibel. Aus der Geschichte der lateinischen Bibel 4; Freiburg, 1964) 154. Frede holds that the author of the Fragment relied here not on Rom 15 but on the apocryphal Acts of Peter. The Fragment does not itself mention the Acts of Peter but several scholars have presumed its use on the basis of the passage we have cited. But this assumption is disputed by W. Schneemelcher in E. Hennecke and W. Schneemelcher, eds., *New Testament Apocrypha* (2 vols.; Philadelphia, 1963–65) II, 260 (with literature). Schneemelcher holds that from the relevant passage it is to be supposed only that the author of the Fragment knew of these things "but had not found them in Acts because, in his opinion, Luke was not an eyewitness of these events. The source of his information cannot be discovered from his comment." Quite apart from the delicate question whether the Acts of Peter can be dated as early as the Muratorian Fragment, it is only to be asked whether the information about Paul's journey to Spain was not more likely to have been drawn from Rom 15 than from the Acts of Peter, especially in view of the verbal peculiarity.

[33]*PG* XIV, 1290AB.

[34]On the question of Rufinus' treatment of the commentary see especially the summary of the debate in M. M. Wagner, *Rufinus the Translator: A Study of His Theory and Practice as Illustrated in His Version of the Apologetica of St. Gregory Nazianzen* (Catholic University of America Patristic Studies 73; Washington, 1945) 1–11, and more recently Henry Chadwick, "Rufinus and the Tura Papyrus of Origen's Commentary on Romans," *JTS* n.s. 10 (1959) 10–42.

meaning of Origen's statement, especially of the term *dissecuit*. The natural sense of the passage is that Marcion, in addition to removing the doxology, "cut away" (*dissecuit*) everything following 14:23, which Origen quotes (*et ab eo loco* [14:23]... *usque ad finem cuncta dissecuit*).[35] This interpretation has not been unanimous, as some have preferred to take *dissecuit* in the sense "mutilated" (through various omissions).[36] But this meaning is impossible to sustain against the natural drift and syntax of the passage. Nor is there any reason to propose arbitrary grammatical emendations.[37] Origen is correctly understood to say that the form of Romans employed by Marcion concluded with 14:23 and lacked the doxology, and further that Marcion himself was the creator of this form of the letter. In addition, all catholic MSS known to Origen are said to contain the doxology, though not all at the same place: in some it stood after 14:23, in others at the end of ch. 16. Origen apparently preferred to read the doxology at the end of the letter, presumably at the end of ch. 16 (*ut nunc est positum*).[38] It will be necessary later for us to return to this important passage to determine what light it throws on the origin of this form of the letter.[39]

A fourteen-chapter form of Romans is to be inferred also from the MS tradition itself, chiefly on the basis of the wide variations in the position of the doxology which modern printed texts furnish at the end of ch. 16. There are five attested possibilities for its placement, listed here together with the major witnesses for each:

(a) doxology after 16:23 (24) and only there: ℵ B C D E 81 436 630 1739 1962 2127 syr[p] cop vg def ar gig Origen Ambrosiaster Pelagius;

(b) doxology after 14:23 and only there: L Ψ 181 326 330 451 460 614 1241 1877 1881 1984 1985 2492 2495 *et plur*.[40] syr[h] goth[41] Origen Chrysostom Cyril Theodoret John of Damascus pseudo-Theodulus pseudo-Oecumenius;

[35] So most commentators; see especially the arguments of Corssen, "Überlieferungsgeschichte," 13–14.

[36] E.g., Zahn, *Geschichte*, II, 520; *Introduction*, I, 397–98.

[37] Hort (*Biblical Essays*, 329–331) attempted to understand Origen's statement as applicable to the doxology alone, not to chs. 15–16. This he could do only by emending the text to read *et non solum hic sed in eo loco*, thus gaining the sense that Marcion removed the doxology only, and this from two places. But this interpretation was demolished by Lightfoot, *Biblical Essays*, 353–54. Cf. also Zahn, *Geschichte*, II, 519–520.

[38] The phrase *ut nunc est positum* is difficult to interpret with any assurance. Most take it to indicate Origen's preference. It could refer, however, to the position of the doxology in the MS used by Origen when he wrote the commentary, and might even mean that the position after 14:23 was dominant in the earlier tradition.

[39] See below, 101–107.

[40] The most recent review of the minuscules is provided by Kurt Aland in "Glosse, Interpolation, Redaktion und Komposition in der Sicht der neutestamentlichen Textkritik," *Studien zur Überlieferung des Neuen Testaments und seines Textes* (Arbeiten zur neutestamentlichen Textforschung 2; Berlin, 1967) 35–57, esp. 46–47. Of the 382 MSS containing Romans which had been collated at the time of writing, 362 read the doxology after 14:23 and only there.

[41] The Gothic evidence is fragmentary but sufficient to show that the doxology was placed after 14:23 and not at the end of ch. 16. This evidence was remarked upon by Hort (*Biblical Essays*, 340 n. 2) and Riggenbach ("Textgeschichte," 549–553). The bilingual Gothic-Latin palimpsest contained in Codex Carolinus (gue), which was first edited by C. von Tischendorf (*Anecdota sacra et profana ex oriente et occidente alta* [Leipzig, 1855]) and is available in the facsimile edition of H. Henning (*Der Wulfila der Bibliotheca Augusta zu Wolfenbüttel* [Hamburg, 1913]), preserves in the latter part of Romans only 14:9–20 (fol. 254v and 255r) and 15:3–13 (fol. 280r and 280v). Thus neither the end of ch.

(c) doxology after both 14:23 and 16:23 (24): A P 5 17 33 104 109 arm;
(d) doxology after 15:33 and only there: P[46];
(e) doxology completely absent: G F 629 g E 26 inf. (BVL: Γ[B]) Marcion (Origen) Jerome (Origen?) Priscillian.

The mere fact of such numerous placements of the doxology is significant, and shows that uncertainty as to its proper place, if any, was early and widespread. The position at the end of ch. 14 is very well attested in the Greek tradition but rare in the Latin.

It is generally and properly assumed that the doxology, by virtue of its tone and extent, must be regarded as a concluding element, and that it would therefore have stood at the end of the letter, wherever that might be.[42] On the basis of this assumption the presence of the doxology after 14:23 constitutes indirect testimony to the fourteen-chapter form of the text, even though all MSS which so place the doxology now contain the final two chapters. That the doxology in the position after 14:23 did indeed mark the conclusion of the letter is confirmed by several Latin MSS which offer the doxology here but just before it add a brief benediction. This phenomenon was first observed by de Bruyne in MS i-2/9 (BVL: 86; Monza, Biblioteca Capitolare) of the tenth century.[43] The MS is largely defective from Rom 10:2–15:11, but on the basis of a few remaining letters and the available space it is clear that after 14:23 there followed the words *gratia cum omnibus sanctis,* and only after this the doxology. De Bruyne subsequently discovered two other MSS, Clm 17040 and 17043, neither mutilated, with precisely the same reading.[44] He rightly observed the obvious: after such a benediction and the doxology nothing more could have followed.[45] No extant Greek text offers a corresponding peculiarity, but these Latin witnesses and the Greek witnesses which place the doxology after 14:23 are quite sufficient to attest in Greek the text form 1:1–14:23+16:25–27.

In the summary of the MS evidence for the placement of the doxology it is striking that some witnesses completely omit it. As we have seen, a fourteen-

---

14 nor of ch. 16 remains. But the MS was written colometrically according to a system very similar to that of Claromontanus (D) and so it is possible to calculate rather precisely that the doxology must have been present after 14:23. The final verses of Romans, 16:21–24, with subscription, are furnished by the palimpsest fragment Ambrosianus S. 36 of the sixth century, showing that the doxology did not stand at the conclusion. See W. Streitberg, ed., *Die Gotische Bibel* (5th ed.; Darmstadt, 1965), *ad loc.*

[42]This is a working assumption of all critics with the exception of Zahn (*Introduction,* I, 382–87; *Der Brief des Paulus an die Römer* [Kommentar zum Neuen Testament 6; Leipzig, 1910] 620–22). Zahn accepted the doxology as genuine and as having stood originally after 14:23, but with chs. 15–16 following. There is little to be said for this view since it is problematic enough whether the doxology is authentic. Zahn's appeal to stylistic traits of Paul, especially his use of benedictory and doxological phrases within his letters, comes to grief on the extent and self-contained character of the doxology, which make it unparalleled elsewhere in Paul. It is certainly correct, however, as we shall see, that the original position of the doxology was after 14:23, but only when the final chapters lacked.

[43]"Derniers chapitres," 426–28. Riggenbach ("Textgeschichte," 553–56) was the first to notice the relevance of this MS for the question, but he noted only the placement of the doxology after 14:23, not the benediction. His information about the MS was gained secondhand, however. A complete transcription of this MS has been given by Frede (*Altlateinische Paulus-Handschriften,* 179–286), who supports de Bruyne's reconstruction.

[44]"La finale marcionite," 133–34.

[45]Corssen ("Nachtrag," 102) disputed this conclusion and supposed that the benediction was a later insertion derived from the long text (16:24). Yet Corssen held that the other evidence was more than sufficient to show the existence of the short text with the doxology after 14:23. The real point of difference between de Bruyne and Corssen concerned the allegedly Marcionite conclusion, whether it comprised only the doxology after 14:23 (Corssen) or the doxology and the benediction (de Bruyne). On Marcion and the Marcionite form of the letter see below, 100–114.

chapter text lacking the doxology is imputed to Marcion by Origen. A text lacking the doxology but not the final two chapters is intimated by both Priscillian and Jerome.

Priscillian composed a concordance of the Pauline letters under ninety canons or headings, indicating under each those portions of the letters pertaining to it.[46] The letters, for their part, were divided into sections, Romans having 125.[47] The last of the sections in Romans is characterized only in terms of 16:21–23. If Priscillian had known the doxology it would probably have been allotted a new and separate section since as a rule the sections cover small amounts of text and take account of shifts in subject matters. That he did not know the doxology is shown as well by his failure to mention it under the two headings which would seem to demand reference to it:

> XV. *Quia sacramentum olim filiis hominum absconditum, nunc per apostolum sanctis manifestatum sit; et quod Christus sapientia nuncupetur quam nemo principium huius mundi cognovit.*
> That the mystery was always hidden to the sons of men, but has now been revealed by the holy apostle; and that Christ is proclaimed the wisdom which no ruler of this world recognized.
> XXIV. *Quia Deus ante saecula sapientiam in sacramento absconditam ad gloriam nostram praedestinavit eorum videlicit quos ante constitutionem mundi elegit.*
> That before the ages God foreordained the wisdom hidden in mystery to our glory, of those, namely, whom he chose before the creation of the world.

The final section of Romans is cited only under heading LXXVI:

> *Quia collegam habuerit Timotheum et Epafroditum coapostolum atque conmilitonem aliosque aditutores sive ministros.*
> That he has as colleagues Timothy and Epaphroditus, fellow-apostles as well as fellow-soldiers, and otherwise assistants or helpers.[48]

The complete absence of the doxology is attested also by Jerome in his *Commentariorum in epistolam ad Ephesios.* Commenting on Eph 3:5, he remarks in passing that the doxology of Rom 16:25–27 is to be found only *in plerisque codicibus.*[49]

This patristic testimony is buttressed by the MS tradition, and much more strongly than at first appears. The doxology is missing in Codex Bobbiensis (E 26 inf.; BVL: Γ[B], Milan, Biblioteca Ambrosiana) of the late ninth or early tenth century. The MS offers a mixed text, predominantly Vulgate but with strong Old Latin affinities.[50] Romans concludes with the grace-benediction at 16:24.

The omission of the doxology may be surmised also for the Freising fragment r (64) of the fifth or sixth century.[51] The fragment contains near the end of

---

[46]Prologue and text in Wordsworth and White, *Novum Testamentum Latine,* II, 18–32.

[47]Text of the *sectiones Priscilliani* in Wordsworth and White, ibid., II, 44–61.

[48]The testimony of Priscillian was first perceived by de Bruyne, ''Derniers chapitres,'' 29–30. See also G. D. Kilpatrick, ''Western Text and Original Text in the Epistles,'' *JTS* 45 (1944) 60–65.

[49]*PL* XXVI, 512D. This testimony will be examined in more detail below, 102–104.

[50]On this MS see Berger, *Histoire de la Vulgate pendant les premiers siècles du moyen âge,* 138–140. Notice of it was taken by Riggenbach, ''Textgeschichte,'' 556–57.

[51]Donatien de Bruyne, ed., *Les fragments de Freising (épîtres de S. Paul et épîtres catholiques)* (Collectanea biblica latina 5; Rome, 1921).

25

Romans only 14:10–15:13, and the doxology is not present after 14:23. These verses appear at the end of fol. 17v and 1 Corinthians begins on fol. 20r. Thus Rom 15:14 to the end of the letter covered two leaves or four pages. Calculation shows that this space would have been sufficient for Rom 15:14–16:24 with the subscription to Romans and the superscription to 1 Corinthians. There would not have been room for the doxology at the end of the letter unless the subscription and superscription were omitted. Since such an omission is not likely it is safe to suppose that the doxology had no place at all in the MS.[52]

That the complete omission of the doxology was characteristic of the Old Latin text is clearly shown by the great family of Pauline bilingual MSS composed of codices Claromontanus (D; BVL: 75), Boernerianus (G; BVL: 77) and Augiensis (F; BVL: 78).[53] The special character and interrelationships of these MSS have been much discussed by textual critics. A proper understanding of the familial connections was fundamentally worked out by Peter Corssen,[54] but more recently H. J. Frede has revised Corssen's results and has furnished what is certainly the correct solution for the old problem of the relationships obtaining among these witnesses.[55] According to Frede's analysis, G and F derive from a revised common ancestor, designated X, which was a sister MS of D, both having been indirectly drawn from the original bilingual edition, designated Z. A schematic representation appears thus:

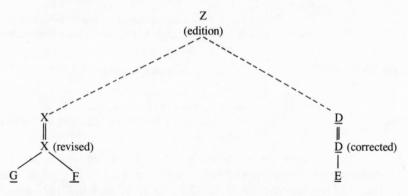

(In this diagram, limited to the major Greek-Latin MSS, underlined sigla represent extant MSS, broken lines indicate indirect dependence, solid lines show direct dependence, and double solid lines show identity of MS.)

---

[52]There is, however, a partial analogy in the MS for the omission of the subscriptive and superscriptive elements. Between 1 and 2 Corinthians there is a subscription to 1 Corinthians, but no superscription to 2 Corinthians. This is quite possibly due merely to scribal oversight, for 2 Corinthians begins a new leaf. Thus we cannot be absolutely certain that the doxology was absent at the end of Romans, even though it appears highly probable.

[53]The fourth member of the family, Codex Sangermanensis (E; BVL: 76), was copied from D after the latter had been corrected and thus has independent value only where D is defective.

[54]P. Corssen, *Epistularum Paulinarum codices Graece et Latine scriptos Augiensem, Boernerianum, Claromontanum examinavit inter se comparavit ad communem originum revocavit* (Programmae gymnasii Ieverensis; 2 vols.; Kiel, 1887–89). Corssen's major conclusions and their significance for the textual history of Romans are summarized in his article "Überlieferungsgeschichte," 1–11. For a brief review of research see W. H. P. Hatch, "On the Relationship of Codex Augiensis and Codex Boernerianus of the Pauline Epistles," *Harvard Studies in Classical Philology* 60 (1951), 187–199.

[55]Frede, *Altlateinische Paulus-Handschriften*, 15–101 *et passim*.

Of these bilingual MSS, only G (with g) lacks the doxology, but a comparative examination leads to the conclusion that here as often elsewhere G alone preserves the reading of the archetype of the whole family.

Codex Claromontanus (D) contains the doxology at the end of the letter, following 16:24 (a benediction). It is evident, nevertheless, that such was not the place of the doxology in the exemplar of D. Whereas D is transcribed throughout *per cola et commata,* that is, in sense lines, the doxology stands apart by its stichometric transcription, that is, according to syllabic enumeration. The greater line lengths and the breaking off of lines in the middle of words in the doxology contrast with the transcription of the rest of the MS. This abrupt change in method is very difficult to understand on the assumption that the doxology was drawn from the same exemplar as the rest of the letter, but is easily comprehended if the doxology was absent in the exemplar and in order to supply it the scribe of D resorted to another MS. The use of a second exemplar is also evident in two other features. The subscription to Romans reads simply

ΠΡΟC ΡΩΜΑΙΟΥC   AD ROMANOS

on one line, whereas the subscriptions to the other letters follow a fuller form consisting of three widely spaced lines, the first giving the title of the letter just concluded (as above), the second having the words

ΕΠΛΗΡΩΘΗ ΑΡΧΕΤΑΙ   EXPLICIT INCIPIT

and the third providing the title of the following letter. Thus the form of the subscription to Romans also suggests the use of another exemplar.[56] This is confirmed, finally, by the Latin of the doxology in d, which, in addition to being inferior to the general usage of the MS,[57] includes two translation equivalents which are peculiar among the usual renderings of d. These are *apocalypsem* for ἀποκάλυψιν, whereas in every other case d renders ἀποκάλυψις with *revelatio,* and *profetarum* for προφητικῶν, the usual form in d being *propheta.*[58]

Thus we must conclude that the exemplar of D did not contain the doxology at the end of Romans. At 16:24 D provides the full benediction, a sufficient conclusion without the doxology following.[59] It is equally certain from a comparison of D

[56]For these phenomena and this conclusion see Corssen, "Überlieferungsgeschichte," 5–8. Another explanation of the peculiarities was advanced by Riggenbach ("Textgeschichte," 574–580) and Zahn (*Introduction,* I, 403–404) and has been approved by J. Dupont ("Pour l'histoire de la doxologie finale de l'épître aux Romains," *RBen* 58 [1948] 3–22, 20 [hereinafter "L'histoire de la doxologie"]). On their view the scribe of D, observing his diminishing space, began to compress the text. The space-consuming colometric method was abandoned, allowing for more words per line. The ten lines of the doxology (11 with the Amen) brought the scribe almost to the end of the page, on which remained only enough space for the title of the preceding letter, and the subscription form was abridged accordingly. A similar case is noted in Ephesians where again colometry is left off and the subscription is shortened, this time to two lines which give the titles of the preceding and following letters. Corssen ("Überlieferungsgeschichte," 7–8) rightly rejected the explanation from spatial limitation, observing that in Philippians an entire page is occupied by the benediction and subscription alone and the colometry is maintained beforehand even though abbreviation would have saved a leaf. The Pastoral letters are similarly transcribed.

[57]E.g., *secum* for *secundum, fidem* for *fidei, solo* for *soli,* the enigmatic *sacramenti temporis aeterni taciturnitatis,* and the absence of subjects for *innotesceret* and *declarasset.*

[58]Corrector d** altered *apocalypsem* to *revelationem.* In addition to all of this evidence, correctors D**, who supplied numerous grammatical and orthographic revisions, and D***, who provided accents and aspiration marks, both neglected to work through the doxology. This may be taken as a sign of disapproval of the position at the end of ch. 16. Cf. Frede, *Altlateinische Paulus-Handschriften,* 158.

[59] D does not contain the benediction of 16:20b. After 16:20a D** placed a critical mark but indicated nothing more, while after 16:20a d*** added the benediction found here in most MSS. See C.

with G and F that the exemplar of D did not have the doxology after 14:23 either, therefore that the doxology lacked altogether.[60]

Codices Boernerianus (G) and Augiensis (F) are equally informative. In G there is an interlinear Latin translation, while F maintains the Greek and Latin in separate columns. The doxology is completely absent in G. At the conclusion of Romans the subscription immediately follows the benediction of 16:24, leaving no room for the doxology. Between 14:23 and 15:1, however, there was left a large space obviously intended to be sufficient for the insertion of the doxology which occurs just here in many MSS. In F on the other hand the doxology is given at the end of the letter, but in the Latin column (f) only, with parallel space remaining in the Greek column. There are two possible means of accounting for this state of affairs. First, it could be supposed that the common ancestor of F and G contained the doxology after 14:23, and that it was perhaps attended by critical marks which left its position doubtful. Thus the scribe of G refused to copy it but manifested his uncertainty by leaving a space for its addition. The scribe of F was not so equivocal and wrote 14:23–15:1 continuously.[61] Alternatively, the data may be accounted for by supposing the absence of the doxology in the common ancestor (X) of F and G. In this case the scribe of F followed his exemplar faithfully and without reflection, while the scribe of G, being acquainted with the tradition placing the doxology after ch. 14, was reluctant to follow his exemplar in omitting it. Yet he did not insert it, but only left a space.

The second of these explanations is clearly to be preferred. Both F and G confirm that the doxology did not stand at the end of the letter, and neither D nor F hints that it stood after 14:23. Since little may be said for its omission by the scribe of G if it stood in his exemplar, it is almost certain that the ancestor of F and G (X) did not have the doxology at all.[62] This means of course that the scribe of G knew the tradition providing the doxology at the end of ch. 14. This knowledge was in all likelihood not merely reminiscent but was concretely conveyed by a text which he had at hand in addition to the bilingual exemplar. This could not have been a Greek text, for wherever the Greek text of his bilingual exemplar was defective the scribe left spaces to be filled when another Greek text could be found. Thus the doxology was found after ch. 14 in a Latin text. Frede has demonstrated the considerable influence on G of an I-type Old Latin text, a text for which the presence of the doxology after 14:23 is usual, and this must have been the source for knowledge of the doxology at this place.[63] The scribe was prevented from adding the doxology by his interlinear method, which required a Greek text for any Latin, and so he left a space sufficient for the later addition of it.

In this light there can be no doubt that the common ancestor of X and D,

---

von Tischendorf, ed., *Codex Claromontanus sive Epistulae Pauli omnes Graece et Latine ex codice Parisiensi celeberrimo nomine Claromontani plerumque dicto sexti ut videtur post Christum saeculi* (Leipzig, 1852) 550 (Appendix).

[60]Corssen ("Überlieferungsgeschichte," 8–11) left open the possibility that the doxology stood after 14:23 in the exemplar of D. As we shall see, that is not necessary.

[61]Cf. Corssen, "Überlieferungsgeschichte," 8–11.

[62]Thus Dupont, "L'histoire de la doxologie," 22; Frede, *Altlateinische Paulus-Handschriften,* 155; and others.

[63]*Altlateinische Paulus-Handschriften,* 54–64, 155.

which according to established usage is designated Z, lacked the doxology completely and offered the text form 1:1–16:24.[64]

Moreover, this same family of MSS may be regarded as indirectly witnessing the fourteen-chapter form of the letter. Corssen conjectured that Z, which offered the sixteen-chapter form of Romans, was actually transcribed from two exemplars, one providing the text of Rom 1–14, the other the text of Rom 15–16. This judgment was based on the observation that the ''Western'' cast of the text in chs. 1–14 disappears in the final two chapters, and that in the final two chapters alone there are as many singular readings as in chs. 1–14 taken together. Thus Corssen maintained that behind Z there lay a ''pure'' short form of Romans, that is, Rom 1:1–14:23 without the doxology.[65] Corssen was certainly correct in noting the difference in textual character of the final chapters. It is unlikely however, and on the basis of the textual evidence it is not demonstrable, that the pure short form lying behind the available MSS was ever available in a *bilingual* MS. The most appealing assumption is rather that the peculiar textual character of chs. 15–16 has its explanation in the nature of separate Greek and Latin MSS from which the editor of the bilingual edition drew his texts, MSS having the short form of Romans ending at 14:23 which were then supplemented by others offering the full sixteen-chapter text.

Such is the evidence for the currency at one time of a short form of Romans without chs. 15–16. Yet it has become clear that we cannot speak of a single short form of the text except insofar as the last two chapters are missing. The evidence attests three variants of this form:

(a) 1:1–14:23

(b) 1:1–14:23 + 16:25–27

(c) 1:1–14:23 + benediction + 16:25–27.

The Fourteen-Chapter Form and the Variants in 1:7 and 1:15

The omission of chs. 15–16 appears to stand in close connection with a failure to specify the addressees of the letter in 1:7 and 1:15. For the latter there are a number of MS and patristic witnesses.

Codex Boernerianus (G) is the only direct MS witness for the complete omission of the Roman address in the first chapter. At 1:7 it gives the reading τοῖς οὖσιν ἐν ἀγάπῃ θεοῦ/*qui sunt in caritate* (alt.: *dilectione*) *Dei*, instead of the customary τοῖς οὖσιν ἐν ῾Ρώμῃ ἀγαπητοῖς θεοῦ/*qui sunt Romae, dilectis Dei*. Similarly in 1:15 G omits the words τοῖς ἐν ῾Ρώμῃ in the phrase καὶ ὑμῖν τοῖς ἐν

---

[64]There are some *capitula* systems which seem to rest on a sixteen-chapter text without the doxology. The last *capitulum* of the series in Codex Bambergensis (vg[B]; BVL: φ[B]) does not suggest the doxology at the end of ch. 16. The case is similar with the *capitula* in the Vulgate MSS C H Θ T U (BVL: C Θ[H] Θ[M] Σ[T] U).

[65]''Überlieferungsgeschichte,'' 15–17, where the most important readings are listed. The suggestion that a short and long form were combined was originally made by Lightfoot, *Biblical Essays*, 316–17, 367–69. He was prompted by the blank space in G after 14:23 to suppose that in the ancestor of G and F a short form with the doxology had been combined with a long form, with the doxology being deferred for use at the end. Although the grounds for Lightfoot's assumption were wrong, his general idea has been proven correct. See further the remarks of H. J. Frede, *Ein neuer Paulustext und Kommentar*, I: *Untersuchungen* (Vetus Latina. Die Reste der altlateinischen Bibel. Aus der Geschichte der lateinischen Bibel 7; Freiburg, 1973) 115–123.

'Ρώμη εὐαγγελίσασθαι and in the Latin reads *et vobis evangelizare* instead of the usual *et vobis, qui Romae estis, evangelizare*. The sister codex, Augiensis (F), is defective from Rom 1:1 to 3:18, but as the Greek text of F is nearly identical with that of G there is good reason to believe that the same readings were present in F also.[66]

The Greek column of Claromontanus (D) also is lost at this point, but the Latin column (d) reads at 1:7 *qui sunt Romae in caritate Dei*, implying the Greek τοῖς οὖσιν ἐν 'Ρώμη ἐν ἀγάπη θεοῦ. A corrector placed a critical mark before *in*, but it is now uncertain what this meant since the margin which may have contained the suggested correction has been torn off. Codex Sangermanensis (E), copied from D after correction, gives the reading τοῖς οὖσιν ἐν 'Ρώμη/*qui sunt Romae*, thus omitting ἐν ἀγάπη θεοῦ/*in caritate Dei*. Here at least the correction was understood to call for an omission.[67] Whatever the intention of the corrector, the uncorrected text of D does not represent the text of the bilingual edition which is shown by G to have lacked the reference to Rome.[68] The reading of d is shared by a large number of old Vulgate witnesses, including Fuldensis and Amiatinus (v.1., *in dilectione*),[69] and is clearly the result of an attempt to adapt the short reading, as we have it in g, to the usual text by inserting the reference to Rome. Therefore we may conclude that all MSS which in Rom 1:7 read ἐν 'Ρώμη ἐν ἀγάπη θεοῦ/*Romae in caritate (dilectione) Dei* thereby betray the omission of the Roman address at some point in their ancestry.

It is also G alone which presently omits τοῖς ἐν 'Ρώμη/*qui Romae estis* in Rom 1:15. Again, this was probably the text of F as well. In D we find here καὶ ἐν ὑμῖν ἐν 'Ρώμη εὐαγγελίσασθαι/*et vobis, qui Romae estis, evangelizare*.[70] The ἐν ὑμῖν/*in vobis* of D is found also in a number of Vulgate MSS,[71] and can be the consequence only of an earlier omission of reference to Rome.

The text without mention of Rome is attested, however, by the oldest commentators on Romans, Origen and Ambrosiaster. Origen's commentary on this section of the letter is preserved only in the Latin version of Rufinus, who substituted for the Greek text on which Origen relied an Old Latin text current in his own time.[72] At 1:7 the Latin lemma provides the ordinary Vulgate reading *qui sunt*

---

[66]In this connection it is significant that F does not provide a subscription for Romans, as it does for the other letters.

[67]Tischendorf (*Codex Claromontanus*, 537 [Appendix]) supposed that the marginal note gave as the preferred reading *dilectis Dei*. It seems more likely that *Romae* and *in caritate Dei* were indicated as alternatives, only one of which was to be used.

[68]H. J. Vogels ("Der Codex Claromontanus der paulinischen Briefe," *Amicitiae Corolla: A Volume of Essays Presented to J. Rendel Harris on the Occasion of his Eightieth Birthday* [ed. H. G. Wood; London, 1933] 274–299) has used irregularities in the colometry of D as an aid to textual criticism. He observed (p. 283) that this line in d is the longest on the page and concluded that it is an expansion, *Romae* having been inserted. This accords with other evidence. The colometry of D must be used discreetly, however, since it does not always preserve the *cola* and *commata* of the archetype.

[69]In the variation found in Latin MSS between *caritate* and *dilectione*, both given by g as alternative readings, there is no sufficient reason to assume independent translations of the Greek or to postulate a further Greek text beyond that on which the Old Latin was patterned. Most probably we have to do merely with an inner change of Latin vocabulary such as is characteristic of the I-type Old Latin.

[70]As at 1:7, this is the longest line of the page in D. D*** erased ἐν and d*** corrected to *vobis Romanis*. See Tischendorf, *Codex Claromontanus*, 537 (Appendix).

[71]Thus A F H Θ (BVL: A F Θ[H] Θ[M]); cf. also minuscules 216 and 440 (!).

[72]This was recognized first, to our knowledge, by B. F. Westcott, "Origenes," *Dictionary of Christian Biography, Literature, Sects and Doctrines* (ed. W. Smith and H. Wace; 4 vols.; London,

Romae, dilectis Dei,[73] as also at 1:15, *et vobis, qui Romae estis, evangelizare*. But it is clear from the exposition of the greeting that Origen's text omitted the mention of Rome, for the comment runs *Benedictio haec pacis et gratiae quam dat dilectis Dei ad quos scribit apostolus Paulus* ("The blessing of peace and grace is given to those beloved of God, to whom the apostle Paul wrote"),[74] and presupposes the absence of the words ἐν ʽΡώμη. This omission in the Greek text used by Origen is conclusively proved by a scholion in Codex 1739 (Athos Laura 184), a minuscule of the tenth century.[75] In the ancestor from which this important MS derives, the text of Romans, as the superscription to the Pauline letters informs us, was drawn not from the exemplar used for the rest of the *Corpus*, but directly from the lemmata of Origen's commentary on the letter, excepting certain portions where the commentary was defective.[76] With this qualification and with due allowance for limited corruption in the process of transmission, it may be said that Codex 1739 preserves the text of Romans used by Origen for his commentary.[77]

In 1739 the words ἐν ʽΡώμη are found both at 1:7 and 1:15, but a scholion on 1:7 states that they were not present in the text used: τοῦ ἐν ʽΡώμη οὔτε ἐν τῇ ἐξηγήσει οὔτε ἐν τῷ ῥητῷ μνημονεύει. Origen himself is the unnamed subject of this sentence.[78] We can be only a little less certain of the reading which Origen had in 1:15. In his exposition of that text there are references to Rome, but this does not compel the conclusion that mention of Rome was present in the text, for Origen certainly accepted the letter's Roman destination. There is in this section a quotation which does not mention Rome, but reads only *et vobis evangelizare*. While an indisputable conclusion on the reading of Origen's text at 1:15 is not available, a

---

1877–87) IV, 116–17. This judgment was later affirmed by Gustave Bardy ("Le text de l'épître aux Romains dans le commentaire d'Origène-Rufin," *RB* 17 [1920] 229–241), who surmised that Rufinus used a Greek-Latin bilingual MS and that his appeals to the Greek text may be to this rather than to the text of the commentary.

[73]It is curious, but probably irrelevant for our concern, that the Latin lemma of Rufinus containing 1:7 lacks the phrase *vocatis sanctis*.

[74]*PG* IV, 853B.

[75]The MS was first collated by E. von der Goltz, *Eine textkritische Arbeit des zehnten bezw. sechsten Jahrhunderts* (TU 17; Leipzig, 1899). A new collation was made by K. Lake, J. de Zwaan and M. S. Enslin, *Six Collations of New Testament Manuscripts* (ed. K. Lake and Silva New; HTS 17; Cambridge, 1932) 141–219. Further observations with some corrections of the previously mentioned studies are made by G. Zuntz, *The Text of the Epistles; A Disquisition upon the Corpus Paulinum* (The Schweich Lectures of the British Academy 1946; London, 1953) 69–71.

[76]Relevant portions of the superscription read: "... the fourteen epistles of the Apostle were written from a very ancient copy which we have reason to believe was prepared from the extant *tomoi* or homilies of Origen on the Apostle. ... But having copied the epistle to the Romans from the *tomoi* upon it which are preserved, we have not used [sigla referring to Origenic readings elsewhere given in the margins]. ..."

[77]This is convincingly shown by the comparison of the text of Romans in 1739 with other preserved fragments (Catena and Philocalia) and with citations of Romans elsewhere in Origen made by Otto Bauernfeind (*Der Römerbrieftext des Origenes nach dem Codex von der Goltz* [TU 44; Leipzig, 1923] 25–52). The discovery of the Tura papyrus fragments of the commentary has resulted in a confirmation of this general judgment, though revealing corruptions in 1739 at particular points. See J. Scherer, *Le commentaire d'Origène sur Rom. III. 5–V.7 d'après les extraits du papyrus No. 88748 du Musée du Caire et les fragments de la Philocalie et du Vaticanus gr. 762* (Cairo, 1957) 59–66.

[78]See Goltz, *Eine textkritische Arbeit des zehnten bezw. sechsten Jahrhunderts*, 53, and Bauernfeind, *Der Römerbrieftext des Origenes nach dem Codex von der Goltz*, 46, 84–85. The same scholion is found in minuscule 1908, eleventh century, which probably does not deserve independent weight. Cf. Zuntz, *The Text of the Epistles*, 74–76. Bauernfeind supposed that the ἐν ʽΡώμη of 1739 was derived from the exemplar used for the rest of the *Corpus*, while Zuntz has assumed that the common

text omitting reference to Rome seems quite probable, and as much is implied by the certain omission in 1:7.

The absence of the specific Roman address in 1:7 is also to be inferred for Ambrosiaster, who states in his comment on 1:7 that *Quamvis Romanis scribat, illis tamen scribere se significat, qui in caritate Dei sunt* ("Although he writes to the Romans, he nevertheless expresses himself as writing to those who are in the love of God").[79] The concessive cast of this remark must be due to the use of a text without reference to Rome, apparently with the reading of the Old Latin, *qui sunt in caritate Dei*.[80] As in the case of Origen, the MS tradition of Ambrosiaster's commentary strongly supports the usual Vulgate text at 1:7, but the old variant *Romae in caritate Dei*, the reading of d, is also attested and is certainly to be preferred.[81] Yet, as we have seen, even this reading is conflated, so that the original text of Ambrosiaster cannot have referred to Rome. For Ambrosiaster we have no direct evidence for the reading at 1:15, but must suppose that reference to Rome was omitted here also.

The case is similar with Pelagius. Both *Romae dilectis Dei* and *Romae in caritate Dei* are attested at 1:7 in the MS tradition of Pelagius' *Expositio in Romanos,* but the latter is certainly earlier.[82] Yet the commentary itself presupposes neither text, but one without any mention of Rome, for it is said only that *hoc est omnibus credentibus* ("This is to all who believe"). This reading is in accord with Pelagius' reliance on a text of the epistles which had numerous Old Latin readings.[83]

Such is the evidence for the omission of the Roman address in 1:7 and 1:15. It is stronger for the omission in 1:7, but it is shown directly by G and indirectly by the other bilinguals that the double omission was current. These omissions must have originated simultaneously, and the double omission is a clear indication that we have to do with an intentional deletion and not merely a scribal error which has been disseminated. That some witnesses can be said to attest with certainty only the omission at 1:7 does not stand in the way of this assessment, for even if it is conceivable that the single omission resulted from mere oversight, that is highly improbable because of the broad attestation for it and because the double omission and the single omission can appear in the same tradition, as they do in the Old Latin. The only sound explanation is that the two omissions have a single cause. When the

---

reading crept in only later during the process of transmission, and Corssen ("Überlieferungsgeschichte," 18) thought the scribe added it from memory. Curiously, Bauernfeind mistakenly included the words ἐν Ῥώμη in 1:7 in his reconstruction of Origen's text from 1739.

Origen certainly knew the common reading, and cites it in *Comm. in Joh.* xix.5 and *Hom. in Num.* x.

It is not necessary to assume that in 1:7 Origen's text read τοῖς οὖσιν ἀγαπητοῖς and therefore gave an abbreviated text different from what we have in G, τοῖς οὖσιν ἐν ἀγάπῃ. Quite probably he had the same text as G, and when the address was introduced into 1739 the immediate context also was normalized.

[79] *PL* XVII, 53B.

[80] This was first observed by Lightfoot, *Biblical Essays,* 288, 365; cf. Hort's objections, ibid., 345.

[81] See H. J. Vogels, *Das Corpus Paulinum des Ambrosiaster* (BBB 13; Bonn, 1957) 33.

[82] A. Souter, *Pelagius's Expositions of Thirteen Epistles of St. Paul* (Texts and Studies 9; 3 vols.; Cambridge, 1922–31) II, "Text and Apparatus Criticus," 9.

[83] Souter, ibid., I, "Introduction," 119–158, came to the conclusion that Pelagius commented upon an Old Latin text, but this idea is now strongly opposed by H. J. Frede, *Pelagius, der irische Paulustext, Sedulius Scottus* (Vetus Latina. Die Reste der altlateinischen Bibel. Aus der Geschichte der lateinischen Bibel 3; Freiburg, 1961) 11–47. Frede holds that Pelagius in fact commented upon a Vulgate text with an admixture of Old Latin readings.

omission at 1:7 affected the tradition, it must have done so in company with the omission at 1:15.

It may be said further that these omissions belonged initially to the fourteen-chapter form of the text. This is persuasively indicated by the testimony of the Pauline bilinguals, which, properly evaluated, attest the phenomena together. Their external testimony is buttressed by internal considerations. The Roman address of the letter is explicit and readily apparent only at its beginning and end. The omissions in 1:7 and 1:15 have the effect of eliminating this specific address, and we must assume that such was the intent. If this intent was consciously followed at the beginning of the letter, it is reasonable to assume that the equally specific notices at the end of the letter in chs. 15–16 lacked for the same reason. The question of the more specific motivations for such generalizations and of who performed them may be left for later determination.[84] Answers to these questions are not required in order to recognize that the references to Rome in ch. 1 lacked precisely in the fourteen-chapter text. That the absence of the Roman address is witnessed also by MSS or writers having the full sixteen-chapter text is of course no objection to the primary association of the omission of the address and the fourteen-chapter text, but is only a consequence of the subsequent development of the tradition.

We have now canvassed all the evidence for the existence at one time of a form of Romans in fourteen chapters. The evidence is geographically widespread, representing Europe (the Amiatine *capitula,* the *Concordia epistularum,* Irenaeus, the bilingual and other Old Latin witnesses), Africa (Tertullian and Cyprian) and the East (the Byzantine text and Origen), and this form of the letter can be traced back with confidence at least as far as the second century in the testimonies of Tertullian and Origen.

The Fifteen-Chapter Form

A fifteen-chapter form of Romans was conjectured long ago purely on the basis of internal arguments from the content of ch. 16, which for various reasons many have regarded as originally addressed to the Ephesian rather than the Roman church. A discussion of these arguments is reserved for the following chapter. Here we are concerned only with external attestation. The hypothesis gained by such internal arguments, that at one time Romans circulated in the form 1:1–15:33, proved attractive to many even though the MS tradition failed to provide any trace of supportive evidence. Thus the discovery of the Chester Beatty Papyrus of the Pauline letters (P[46]) was a matter of great interest for the question of the textual history of Romans, as it provides the doxology not at the end of ch. 16, which the papyrus does contain, but between 15:33 and 16:1.[85] The intrinsic interest of this unique reading is enhanced by the fact that P[46] is by far our oldest MS of the *Corpus Paulinum,* dating from around the beginning of the third century.[86] Thus it antedates

---

[84]For a detailed discussion of these issues, see below, 96–126.

[85]Ch. 16 begins on the line with the doxology but is set off from what precedes by a small diagonal slash. See F. C. Kenyon, ed., *The Chester Beatty Biblical Papyri. Descriptions and Texts of Twelve Manuscripts on Papyrus of the Greek Bible* III, Supplement, part 2, "Pauline Epistles, Plates" (London, 1937) fol. 20v.

[86]Kenyon (ibid., III, Supplement, part 1, "Pauline Epistles, Text" [London, 1936] xiv) suggested a date in the first half of the third century; a date sometime in the third century was favored by

our oldest codices, B and ℵ, by a century and a half. In it we have a form of the Pauline text which was current prior to the great normalizing recensions.

Although the value of the MS is great in these and other respects, it has not worked a revolution in our understanding of the history of the Pauline text, either in general or in respect of particular readings. In textual complexion the affinities of P[46] lie mainly with B and 1739.[87] But the papyrus also exhibits numerous agreements with Western witnesses over against the Alexandrians, and so indicates that many variants previously termed "Western" are by no means either strictly Western or late, and in some cases may very well represent the correct text.[88] Thus Zuntz has denominated the type of text seen in P[46] as "proto-Alexandrian."

It cannot generally be said that the papyrus uniquely preserves important readings with claims to originality. Of course many special readings are to be found in it, but the vast majority of these must be set down to scribal error and alleviative conjectural emendation.[89] Yet the placement of the doxology at the end of Rom 15 clearly cannot be accounted for in these ways.

On the basis of the assumption stated earlier, that the position of the doxology is indicative that at some stage in the history of the witness Romans ended at that point, P[46] may be regarded as representing a tradition in which Romans was brought to a close with ch. 15.[90] We have evidence, then, in the textual tradition of a second short form of Romans, comprising 1:1–15:33+16:25–27. Whether this form like the fourteen-chapter form omitted the reference to Rome in ch. 1 is beyond determination from the text, for folios 1–7, containing Rom 1:1–5:16, are lost.[91]

Far from solving the problem of the textual history of Romans, as some have too readily assumed, P[46] has only complicated the evidence. The textual critic wonders what specific weight to give to a reading which is unique in the entire tradition but enjoys the authority of our most ancient witness to the Pauline text. Whether the placement of the doxology after 15:33 has any claim to originality is an open question, one which cannot be decided on the basis of the textual evidence alone. It is nevertheless important that the evidence afforded by P[46] be considered within the larger context of the whole textual tradition. Only so will its significance be rightly estimated.

H. A. Sanders, ed., *A Third-Century Papyrus Codex of the Epistles of Paul* (University of Michigan Studies, Humanistic Series 38; Ann Arbor, 1935) 13. U. Wilcken ("The Chester Beatty Biblical Papyri," *Archiv für Papyrusforschung* 11 [1935] 12–14) thought an earlier date, even in the second century, was quite possible. The generally accepted date is *ca.* 200.

[87]Zuntz, *The Text of the Epistles*, 61–84; his discussion of the MS is the fullest and most accurate, and for the most part confirms earlier assessments while going beyond them. Cf. H. Lietzmann, "Zur Würdigung des Chester-Beatty-Papyrus der Paulusbriefe," *Kleine Schriften*, II *Studien zum Neuen Testament* (ed. K. Aland; TU 68; Berlin, 1958) 170–79; and H. Seesemann, "Die Bedeutung des Chester-Beatty-Papyrus für die Textkritik der Paulusbriefe," *Theologische Blätter* 16 (1937) 92–97.

[88]Zuntz, *The Text of the Epistles*, 84–150, esp. 142–150; cf. Lietzmann, "Zur Würdigung des Chester-Beatty-Papyrus," 179, and Seesemann, "Die Bedeutung des Chester-Beatty-Papyrus," 95.

[89]Zuntz, *The Text of the Epistles*, 18–23, and Kenyon, *The Chester Beatty Biblical Papyri*, III, Supplement, part 1, xix–xxi.

[90]This inference is confirmed in this case by the character of the text itself, for in ch. 16 P[46] is found to agree much more strongly with Alexandrian witnesses and less with Western witnesses than is the case in chs. 1–15. But the difference is one of degree, not of kind. See C. S. C. Williams, "P[46] and the Textual Tradition of Romans," *ExpT* 61 (1949–50) 125–26. This observation had already been made in passing by T. W. Manson, "St. Paul's Letter to the Romans—and Others," *Studies in the Gospels and Epistles* (ed. Matthew Black; Manchester, 1962) 225–241, 237.

[91]On this question, however, see below, pp. 124–26.

The Sixteen-Chapter Form

Modern printed editions of the Greek NT offer the full sixteen-chapter form of the text with the doxology at the conclusion. There is no need here to detail the evidence for this form of the letter; it is explicit and substantial. Every extant MS contains the final two chapters. The placement of the doxology at the end of ch. 16 is justified, however, not by the quantity of witnesses, which weighs heavily in favor of placing the doxology after 14:23, but by the quality and diversity of some witnesses. By the common canons of textual criticism the position after ch. 16 is preferred. Yet this is a judgment of the tradition of the text and not a certain guarantee of the original character of the text lying behind the tradition.

Strictly speaking, the sixteen-chapter form of the text is not uniform. There is a complex variation in the presence and positions of the benedictions found at the end of ch. 16, a phenomenon usually neglected in discussions of the larger problem. Modern editions read after 16:20a (as 16:20b) the benediction ἡ χάρις τοῦ κυρίου ἡμῶν Ἰησοῦ μεθ' ὑμῶν. This benediction is widely attested in this place, and by witnesses for each of the four placements of the doxology. Superficially this appears to suggest that the position of this grace-benediction is independent of the variation in the position of the doxology. Apart from the benediction at 16:20b, another benediction of slightly different wording, ἡ χάρις τοῦ κυρίου ἡμῶν Ἰησοῦ Χριστοῦ μετὰ πάντων ὑμῶν. ἀμήν, is found in many witnesses after 16:23 (as 16:24), and in fewer witnesses after the doxology as 16:28. A survey of the MSS gives the strong impression that there is an integral relationship between the variations in the use of this benediction and the position of the doxology. Any effort to disentangle the textual history of Romans must reckon with this peculiarity. It comprises one important key to the solution of the problem, and as such will be taken up again below.[92]

At this point we conclude our survey of the textual evidence and formulate briefly the questions which emerge from the data just rehearsed. Given the attested forms of the letter, the most urgent issue is that of the integrity of Romans: which if any of these forms of the text represents the letter of Paul to the Roman church? This problem will occupy us in the following two chapters. Beyond this it must be asked how the other forms of the letter came into existence. Closely tied to these questions is that of the authenticity and original position of the doxology, and of the vacillation in form and position of the benedictions at the end of ch. 16. Finally, some attempt must be made to furnish a coherent explanation of the textual tradition as a whole. These problems will be taken up in Chapters IV and V.

[92]129–132.

35

CHAPTER II

THE PROBLEM OF INTEGRITY:
THE EPHESIAN HYPOTHESIS

Foremost among the questions posed by the facts of the textual tradition is that of the integrity of the letter: given the existence at an early time of three basic forms of the letter, which if any of these may be said to represent the letter of Paul to the Roman church? At one time or another the claim has been made for each of the three forms.

That the fourteen-chapter text was the letter sent to Rome has been urged on occasion, but this view has never secured a firm footing in the internal evidence or any scholarly approbation.[1] This view cannot explain why the exposition concerning the strong and the weak in faith, beginning with 14:1, comes to its natural conclusion only with 15:13. It can hardly be thought to have broken off originally after 14:23. The assumption of an original conclusion with 14:23 creates more problems than it solves, since such a letter, as the textual evidence shows, would have lacked both a specific address and concluding formulae, and since it requires some explanations of the origin and attachment of the final two chapters. But the unquestionable authenticity of ch. 15 and the clear and close relationship between it and ch. 14, as well as between 15:14–32 and 1:8–13, seem to speak decisively against separating ch. 15 from the rest of the letter on internal grounds. It is now generally acknowledged that the fourteen-chapter form of the text cannot be satisfactorily explained as Paul's original letter to Rome. The origin of this form must be accounted for in some other manner.[2] We will return to that question, but for the moment confine our attention to the problem of the letter sent to Rome.

The only viable option on the question of integrity is between the fifteen- and sixteen-chapter forms, the fundamental problem being whether ch. 16, either in whole or in part, can have belonged with Paul's letter to Rome.[3] This question is mainly contingent not on the textual evidence surveyed above but on internal considerations, so that the question of the letter's integrity could be and was disputed before there emerged any textual evidence for the form 1:1–15:33. That this was the Roman form of the letter, and that ch. 16 (or some part of it) was originally a separate piece addressed to some other community, usually thought to be Ephesus,

---

[1]The authenticity of chs. 15–16, and therefore the integrity of the letter, was disputed by F. C. Baur, *Paulus, der Apostel Jesu Christi* (2 vols., 2nd ed.; Leipzig, 1866–67) II, 393–402. He regarded these chapters as a second-century interpolation made to mitigate the antijudaistic thrust of the letter. The authenticity of chs. 15–16 was more recently denied by W. H. Ryder, "The Authorship of Romans XV. XVI," *JBL* 17 (1898) 184–198, and W. B. Smith, "Unto Romans XV and XVI," *JBL* 20 (1901) 129–157.

[2]See below, 96–123.

[3]The integrity of the letter is also placed in doubt, albeit on a smaller scale, with respect to the doxology (16:25–27), which we do not include in speaking of ch. 16. The problems relating to 16:1–23 (24) on the one hand and to 16:25–27 on the other are sufficiently independent to allow separate treatment. On the doxology see below, 122–23.

is a hypothesis which makes a strong appeal to internal considerations and presently commands broad scholarly support.

Following customary usage, we refer to this view as the "Ephesian hypothesis," though the designation is an oversimplification. A common designation is justified to the extent that each statement of the hypothesis distinguishes the addressees of ch. 16 from those of chs. 1–15 and appeals to the same evidence in support of this judgment. Our purpose here is to review and assess both the evidence which is claimed for the non-Roman and probably Ephesian address of ch. 16, and the various formulations of the Ephesian hypothesis, so to gain a critical estimate of its plausibility.

Evidence for a Non-Roman Address of Romans 16

The general argument against the integrity of Romans has two sides. First, there are features of the content of ch. 16 which suggest its incongruity with the Roman address and, conversely, its suitability to an Ephesian address. But there are also observations concerning the form of ch. 16 and certain aspects of the textual tradition which are taken to demonstrate the separability of ch. 16 from the remainder of the letter.

The content of Rom 16 was felt to be troublesome for a Roman destination already in the eighteenth century by J. S. Semler[4] and, somewhat later, by J. G. Eichhorn.[5] Their observations were taken up, expanded, and systematically set out for the first time by David Schulz.[6] Schulz enumerated three arguments from the content of Rom 16 against the Roman address and concluded that Rom 16:1–20 was in fact a letter of Paul to the Ephesian church. These arguments have remained basically the same, despite some refinements, and are found in all contemporary treatments of the question. These arguments must now be detailed.[7]

The major internal argument against the Roman address is derived from the greetings of 16:3–16 and relates (a) generally to the extent of the greetings, and (b) more particularly to the persons greeted and the ways in which they are characterized.

It is clear from Paul's own statements that at the time of writing he had not visited the city or the Christian community of Rome. He only foresees the possibility "now at length to come to you" (1:10–11), a journey which he has long desired to make but from which he has been deterred (1:13). Finally, however, he feels "ready to preach the gospel also to you who are in Rome" (1:15). Again toward the end of the letter he reiterates his wish to come and the fact that he has previously been hindered from doing so by the demands of his labors in the East (15:19b–23). Now he is able to turn to the West with a view to a mission in Spain, and he sees in this westward movement his first real opportunity to visit the Roman community (15:24, 28–29). Yet before embarking to the West it remains for him to bring his work in the East to completion by delivering to Jerusalem the offering of the Gentile

---

[4]*Paraphrasis epistolae ad Romanos* (Halle, 1769) 277–311.

[5]*Einleitung in das Neue Testament* (5 vols.; Leipzig, 1810–27) III, 243.

[6]Review of Eichhorn's *Einleitung in das Neue Testament* and de Wette's *Lehrbuch der historisch-kritischen Einleitung in die kanonischen Bücher des Neuen Testaments,* in *Theologische Studien und Kritiken* 2 (1829) 563–636, esp. 609–612.

[7]Our statement of this evidence is composite for the most part since basically the same evidence is always cited. Individual scholars will be noted for particular contributions or variations.

churches. The impression given by these statements is unmistakable: Paul is anticipating his first visit with the Christian community in Rome. It is entirely in accord with this situation that the body of the letter is devoted to an exposition of the gospel which seems to betray few if any local or personal allusions and to presuppose no prior relationship between the Roman community and Paul himself. In these respects the Roman letter stands apart from the other undisputed letters, which are consistently informed by and refer to the concrete circumstances of the churches addressed and assume a conditioned relationship between those churches and the Apostle. Given Paul's explicit statements and the general nature of the exposition in the letter body, it can only appear as a striking anomaly that in ch. 16 he should proceed to communicate greetings to twenty-six persons, twenty-four of whom are mentioned by name, and five apparently well-defined groups. That Paul, who had never visited Rome, could have known so many Roman Christians must appear highly unlikely, if not altogether impossible, and requires some explanation. It would be much more natural to locate so many acquaintances in a community well known to Paul.

This argument gains force from a scrutiny of the greetings themselves, for no less surprising than the number of persons greeted are the identities and descriptions of some among them. To be sure, most of the names found in ch. 16 are known to us only here in the NT. Notable exceptions are Prisca and Aquila (16:3–4). According to Acts 18:2ff. this couple first encountered Paul in Corinth, to which they had come under the compulsion of the edict of Claudius requiring Jews to leave the city of Rome.[8] Acts further relates that in Corinth Prisca and Aquila worked closely with Paul for a time and then moved with him from Corinth to Ephesus (Acts 18:18–19, 24–26). They were still in Ephesus at the writing of 1 Corinthians, for Paul conveys their greetings to the Corinthians (1 Cor 16:19). It is to be noted that here also he refers to a "church in their house" (τῇ κατ' οἶκον αὐτῶν ἐκκλησίᾳ), which seems to indicate a relatively permanent Ephesian residence. Finally, in 2 Timothy, ostensibly directed to Ephesus, greetings are sent *to* Prisca and Aquila (4:19). Even if the authenticity of the Pastorals is much to be doubted, this reference at least presupposes a tradition of the couple's Ephesian location, and at a time after Romans was written.[9] Thus although Prisca and Aquila had an early association with Rome, the latest information available, and indeed all the evidence apart from Rom 16, places them in Ephesus. If they were in Ephesus as late as the writing of 1 Corinthians, they are hardly expected to be in Rome, with a house church there also (Rom 16:5a), so soon afterward.

Of the remaining individuals named we have no information from other sources which favors their non-Roman location. Inferences are possible, however, on the basis of the descriptions of those greeted. Most significant in this connection

<hr/>

[8]Among many discussions of the edict, its nature, time and consequences, see E. Schürer, *Geschichte des jüdischen Volkes im Zeitalter Jesu Christi* (3 vols.; 4th ed.; Leipzig 1901–09) III, 61–63; V. M. Scramuzza, "The Policy of the Early Roman Emperors towards Judaism," *The Beginnings of Christianity* (ed. F. J. Foakes Jackson and K. Lake; 5 vols.; London, 1920–33) V, 277–297; H. J. Leon, *The Jews of Ancient Rome* (Philadelphia, 1960) 23–27; and W. Wiefel, "Die jüdische Gemeinschaft im antiken Rom und die Anfänge des römischen Christentums," *Jud* 26 (1970) 65–88.

[9]The importance of the reference in 2 Timothy will vary according to one's estimate of the literary character of the Pastorals. P. N. Harrison, who supposed that these letters, while not in their present form deriving from Paul, nevertheless contain authentic Pauline fragments, regarded 2 Tim 4:19 as part of such a fragment. See his *The Problem of the Pastoral Epistles* (London, 1921) 115–126.

is the greeting to Epaenetus, described as "the first convert (ἀπαρχή) in Asia for Christ" (16:5b).[10] Probably Epaenetus was a native of Asia, but at least he was once found there and it is reasonable to assume his continuing presence there, quite possibly in Ephesus itself. No similar geographical notices are attached to the other names,[11] but the characterizations provided for some contain personalized nuances and details which seem to suggest that Paul is personally acquainted with those greeted. Thus with Epaenetus, Stachys is called "my beloved" (16:5b, 9), Mary is said to have "bestowed much love on us" (16:6), Andronicus and Junias are spoken of as "my fellow prisoners" (16:7), and Rufus' mother is affectionately referred to as Paul's own mother (16:13). In all of this the first person possessive pronoun and the apparent closeness of the ties are startling. Beyond these personal descriptions, Paul shows an awareness of several familial and house-church groups (16:5, 10–11, 13–15). From such observations it is not a great step to the conclusion that Paul personally knows the individuals named here. But since he himself has not been to Rome it must be assumed either that many of his former acquaintances have migrated to Rome, or that the greetings are not really directed to Rome at all but to some community which Paul knows well. The former possibility is not entirely satisfactory, and on the basis of what is known of Prisca and Aquila, and to a lesser extent of Epaenetus, as well as of Paul's long ministry in Ephesus, Ephesus is quite likely as the destination of Rom 16.

The second major internal argument against a Roman address of ch. 16 is drawn from the admonition against schismatics in 16:17–20, thought to be unsuitable for Rome in terms of its tone and content. Throughout Rom 1–15 Paul maintains an irenic and solicitous posture, not stressing the apostolic authority which he invokes against problems of false teaching in letters to churches of his own founding. By comparison with the rest of the letter the tone of 16:17–20 appears to be unduly sharp and authoritarian, and to rest on the assertion and acceptance of the writer's prerogative, neither of which we have reason to assume in the case of Paul's relation to Roman Christianity. Further, an attack on false teaching is conspicuous in Rom 1–15 only by its absence. It is strange that at the conclusion of such a letter there is a warning which seems to assume the activity of schismatics in Rome and Paul's knowledge of it. Even the exposition concerning the strong and the weak in faith in chs. 14–15, which may perhaps relate to the Roman situation, is framed differently and more reticently than the admonition of ch. 16, which in any case it is difficult to refer to that issue.[12]

Conversely, both the tone and content of 16:17–20 can be regarded as

[10]The reading τῆς Ἀχαΐας in 16:5b attested by some witnesses is clearly incorrect since it contradicts 1 Cor 16:15, where the members of the household of Stephanus are designated "the firstfruits of Achaia."

[11]It was argued by P. Feine (*Die Abfassung des Philipperbriefs in Ephesus, mit einer Anlage über Röm 16:3–20 als Epheserbrief* [Beiträge zur Förderung christlicher Theologie; Gütersloh, 1916] 122) that ch. 16 could not be addressed to Rome since of the persons greeted, apart from Prisca, Aquila and Junias, only five bear Latin names (Ampliatus, Urbanus, Narcissus, Rufus and Julia), whereas in the Roman church a predominance of Latin names would be expected. This argument has rightly been given up in the knowledge that Roman Christianity was Greek-speaking well into the second century, and in view of inscriptional evidence showing many Greek and Jewish names in Rome at an early time.

[12]The weak and strong in faith of 14:1–15:13 are both accorded a place in the community, and Paul emphasizes the necessity for mutual acceptance and respect (14:1, 3–5; 15:7). The problem, whether actual or paradigmatic, did not have the dimensions of false teaching or schism. The admonition of 16:17–20 must have a different reference, since here Paul counsels avoidance and rejection.

appropriate to Ephesus. The existence there of false teaching is sometimes inferred from 1 and 2 Timothy, which mount a sustained defense against a schismatic tendency with affinities to that characterized in Rom 16, and also from the speech to the Ephesian elders in Miletus which Acts attributes to Paul (20:18–35).[13] The lines of connection between the opponents of Rom 16 and the opponents in Paul's other letters might at least suggest that the problem envisioned in Rom 16 should be localized somewhere in the mission field where Paul has previously worked. This may be construed as a further argument against the Roman address of ch. 16 even if it gives no positive help in determining the community actually in view.[14]

Such are the major internal arguments against the Roman and for the Ephesian destination of ch. 16. Beyond these, there are other considerations which of themselves indicate nothing about the addressees of the chapter but are claimed to justify the hypothesis as such by showing the separability and relative independence of ch. 16 from the rest of the letter.

Reluctance to adopt the view that Rom 16 is a letter (-fragment) to another community, probably Ephesian, was for a long time prompted primarily by the total absence of any textual evidence in its favor. This was not felt to be an obstacle by advocates of the hypothesis, since the Ephesian material could have been joined to Romans at or before the formation of the *Corpus,* from which extant texts supposedly derive.[15] Still, the hypothesis was inevitably bolstered by the discovery in 1935 of the Chester Beatty Papyrus, P[46]; by placing the doxology after ch. 15 it provided the first textual attestation for a fifteen-chapter form of Romans, and thus also for the independence of ch. 16 from the rest of the letter. Although the testimony of P[46] is unique at this point, the age of the MS compensates for the absence of corroborative external testimony. Thus hesitancy to accept the Ephesian hypothesis on text-critical grounds alone is no longer regarded as justified.

Substantiation of the independence of ch. 16 has been sought also in matters of epistolary form. It is claimed that the benediction of Rom 15:33 functions as a proper epistolary conclusion after which nothing more is to be expected, certainly nothing of the extent of ch. 16.[16] Thus the Roman letter can be seen to come to a natural conclusion at the end of ch. 15. The independence of ch. 16 is strongly suggested, furthermore, by its close formal correspondence with the ancient letter of recommendation (ἐπιστολὴ συστατική) as known from the documentary remains of the Hellenistic period.[17] The similarity is to be noted especially in 16:1–2, where we have the three basic elements of the commendatory note, namely (a) the phrase introducing the person in question, (b) the statement of

[13]Thus T. W. Manson, "St. Paul's Letter to the Romans—and Others," 238; and F. J. Leenhardt, *The Epistle to the Romans* (Cleveland, 1961) 27.

[14]This argument is developed by Walter Schmithals, "The False Teachers of Romans 16:17–20," *Paul and the Gnostics* (Nashville, 1972) 219–238.

[15]See further below, 45–47, 118–121, 139–142.

[16]P. Feine and J. Behm, *Einleitung in das Neue Testament* (9th ed.; Heidelberg, 1950) 175; and W. Michaelis, *Einleitung in das Neue Testament* (3rd ed.; Bern, 1961) 160.

[17]Adolf Deissmann, *Light from the Ancient East; the New Testament Illustrated by Recently Discovered Texts of the Graeco-Roman World* (2nd ed.; London, 1927) 171, 235; E. J. Goodspeed, "Phoebe's Letter of Introduction," *HTR* 44 (1951) 55–57; Joseph Fitzmyer, "The Letter to the Romans," *The Jerome Biblical Commentary* (ed. R. E. Brown, J. A. Fitzmyer and R. E. Murphy; 2 vols. in 1; Englewood Cliffs, N. J., 1968) II, 292; J. I. H. McDonald, "Was Romans XVI a Separate Letter?" *NTS* 16 (1970) 369–372.

the bearer's identity, and (c) the request that the recipient accord the bearer some favor.[18] The long list of greetings is not thought superfluous in this case since a woman traveler such as Phoebe would have need of a document assuring her of the hospitality which could be afforded her by the individuals and family groups named.[19] Thus both textual and formal observations are used to justify a separation of ch. 16 from the Roman letter. When these are taken together with the arguments from the content of ch. 16, the evidence for the Ephesian hypothesis is by no means negligible.

Formulations of the Ephesian Hypothesis

We can speak of *the* Ephesian hypothesis only in the most general terms, for there are substantial variations in actual formulations of it. A differentiation among these is provided by their respective positions on two issues which the hypothesis necessarily poses: (a) whether the supposed Ephesian material constitutes a letter completely or almost completely preserved in Rom 16, or only a fragmentary remnant of a larger Ephesian letter; (b) whether the association of the allegedly Ephesian material with Romans is a consequence of Pauline composition and circulation, or is a result of later redactional work, and thus completely extraneous to the circumstances of composition and initial circulation. On the basis of these issues the formulations of the hypothesis tend to be resolved into two groups.

The first type of formulation, which we shall call "compositional," holds that the Ephesian correspondence is preserved in its entirety in Rom 16, that it includes the whole chapter (16:1–23) and that its attachment to Romans was Paul's own work. This point of view was given cogent presentation by T. W. Manson in an essay of wide influence.[20] In this essay Manson briefly reiterated the textual evidence and the traditional arguments for an Ephesian address of Rom 16. Building on these, with the additional evidence of P[46], which he thought "set the whole matter in a new light,"[21] Manson proposed that the letter sent to Rome comprised Rom 1–15, but at the same time a copy of this letter was made to be sent to the Ephesian community. This copy contained the whole of the Roman letter, to which Paul added ch. 16 as a letter of introduction for Phoebe, the carrier of the copy to Ephesus, and in the addition Paul found occasion to greet his many friends in Asia and to include the warning against false teaching.[22] Thus the letter was composed and put into circulation in two "editions," one for Rome and one for Ephesus, and

---

[18]On the resemblance to the Hellenistic letter of recommendation, see below, 84–87.

[19]Thus Goodspeed, "Phoebe's Letter of Introduction," 56–57. Otherwise, comparably lengthy greetings in brief papyrus letters are taken to show that the greetings of Rom 16 are not unusual; so McDonald, "Was Romans XVI a Separate Letter?" 370–71. See below, p. 87 n. 137.

[20]"St. Paul's Letter to the Romans—and Others"; Manson's explanation has been approved by J. Munck, *Paul and the Salvation of Mankind* (Richmond, 1959) 190–203, G. Zuntz, *The Text of the Epistles* 226–27, C. S. C. Williams, "P[46] and the Textual Tradition of Romans," 125–26, P. N. Harrison, *Paulines and Pastorals* (London, 1964) 86–89. A similar general explanation, granting differences on particular points, seems to be assumed by John Knox ("A Note on the Text of Romans," *NTS* 2 [1955–56] 191–93) and M. Jack Suggs (" 'The Word is Near You': Romans 10:6–10 within the Purpose of the Letter," *Christian History and Interpretation: Studies Presented to John Knox* [ed. W. R. Farmer, C. F. D. Moule and R. R. Niebuhr; Cambridge, 1967] 289–312, esp. 292–96).

[21]"St. Paul's Letter to the Romans—and Others," 238, cf. 234.

[22]Ibid., 238–39.

in the latter ch. 16 formed a unity with the rest of the letter.[23] In this way Manson accounted for two of the textually attested forms of Romans. The fourteen-chapter form he attributed to Marcion, who along with the excision of ch. 15 for dogmatic reasons also eliminated all specific references to Rome in response to his rebuff at the hands of the Roman church.[24]

This reconstruction prompted Manson to a new consideration of Paul's motives in writing the letter. Romans was composed at the conclusion of the Apostle's long and arduous struggle in the Corinthian and Galatian and perhaps also the Philippian churches over the relationship of Christianity and Judaism. The problems which initially emerged in this controversy are taken up and discussed more methodically and thoroughly in Romans than anywhere else. From this Manson concluded that we have in Romans a reflective summation of Paul's definitive views on the issues which had long held his attention.[25] Having worked out this theological statement, he wished to have it widely known. In uncertain anticipation of a western mission he sent a copy to Rome with an indication of his future plans. A copy was made for the benefit of the Asian churches and sent to their center in Ephesus, with the supplementary ch. 16. To the Corinthian church and others of the East Paul intended to communicate his views personally during his forthcoming journey to Jerusalem, and so did not dispatch written copies to that area. What we know as Romans is therefore to be understood not merely as an occasional letter of self-introduction to the Roman church, but as "a manifesto setting forth Paul's deepest convictions on central issues, a manifesto calling for the widest publicity, which the Apostle did his best—not without success—to give it."[26]

Despite an element of circularity, the simplicity of Manson's explanation is attractive. Yet, there are several aspects of the argument which diminish its plausibility. First, there are some unfortunate ambiguities of expression which confuse the train of thought. At one moment Manson could speak of a "document" or "statement" summing up positions reached by Paul.[27] There is no suggestion that this "document" was in letter form, and the drift of language implies that it was not. At another point Manson spoke of Paul writing and sending to Rome a letter consisting of Rom 1–15, and of his making a copy of this for Ephesus, with the addition of ch. 16.[28] Yet again he could say that, when Paul had fully worked out his "statement," he decided to send a copy of it to Ephesus, and at the same time had the idea of sending a copy to Rome with a statement of his future plans.[29] Thus it remains obscure whether there was some written statement prior to and embodied in the Roman letter, and likewise unclear is the precise relation between the Roman and Ephesian forms, each of which is seen at different points as something of an afterthought. The argument demands, however, that the Roman form be primary,

[23]Ibid., 239.

[24]Ibid., 230, 235–36. On Manson's view Marcion removed, in addition to the Roman address in 1:7 and 1:15, only ch. 15, since ch. 16 is not supposed to have belonged to the Roman form of the letter to which Marcion had access.

[25]Ibid., 239–241. A similar view of Romans is developed by G. Bornkamm ("The Letter to the Romans as Paul's Last Will and Testament," *AusBR* 11 [1963] 2–14; and *Paul* [New York, 1971] 88–96), though he wishes to consider the impending Jerusalem visit as part of the letter's occasion.

[26]"St. Paul's Letter to the Romans—and Others," 241.

[27]Ibid., 240–41.

[28]Ibid., 238.

[29]Ibid., 241.

42

since it is given in its entirety in the Ephesian form. But if that were so, it must be asked whether Romans was in fact originally conceived as a "manifesto," the primary value and interest of which would be for Pauline churches. Would such a document be addressed first to the Roman community to which Paul was a stranger?[30] And the further question must also be asked: if the Ephesian form were nothing else than the Roman form expanded by ch. 16, which is apparently Manson's view, would not Paul have explained why he was sending the Ephesians the Roman letter? Some such information would seem to be demanded by the presence of 15:14–33, not to mention 1:8–15.[31] Again, if the Ephesian form were substantially a copy of the Roman form (with ch. 16), surely the address would have been altered; but why, then, a wholly generalized address instead of the specifically Ephesian address? Yet the textual tradition preserves no trace of an Ephesian address for Romans.

It is certainly appropriate, in the light of the textual uncertainty of the address of the letter, to consider the possibility that there may have been a general letter, of which our Romans is but a version which has been particularized. Yet a document conceived as a general or circular letter would necessarily be of general interest, and Manson finds this by regarding Romans as a reflective and definitive discussion of issues central to controversies of the past in various churches, controversies about the relationship of Gospel and Law, Christianity and Judaism. In so doing, Manson works with the idea of a united and uniform opposition to Paul, one of an essentially Judaizing nature. But this notion is hardly tenable in view of recent studies suggesting a complex and variegated pluralism among Paul's opponents rather than a homogeneous front.[32] Thus if in Romans a primary concern is the relation between Christianity and Judaism, it is doubtful that the same concern was uppermost in the other controversies, which stood quite as much or more under the influence of syncretistic and/or gnostic tendencies. From this perspective it is less plausible that Romans can be described as a summation of issues and answers from past disputes, or thought to be of such general pertinence and interest as Manson would have us suppose. To that extent, the proposed motive for a Pauline addition of ch. 16 in a copy of the letter to Ephesus also fails to commend itself.[33]

A second formulation of the Ephesian hypothesis, both older and more widely held than Manson's, regards the Ephesian matter of Rom 16 as a larger or smaller fragment of some piece of Paul's Ephesian correspondence, now lost, and

---

[30]It is rightly asked by Suggs, "... why should such a letter be addressed to the church in Rome? What makes it a proper piece of correspondence to send to an unknown church?" (" 'The Word is Near You,' " 291).

[31]Cf. M. Goguel, *Introduction au Nouveau Testament* (4 vols.; Paris, 1922–26) IV/2, 267.

[32]The question remains moot to some extent. The conception of a united homogeneous anti-Pauline front still has an ardent advocate in Walter Schmithals (*Gnosticism in Corinth: An Investigation of the Letters to the Corinthians* [Nashville, 1971]; *Paul and the Gnostics*). Schmithals regards the opposition as everywhere having a Jewish gnostic character. On the general problem see James M. Robinson, "Basic Shifts in German Theology," *Int* 16 (1962) 76–97; Helmut Köster, "Häretiker im Urchristentum," *RGG* (3rd ed.) III, 17–21.

[33]Some scholars who are basically sympathetic to Manson's hypothesis (e.g. Knox, Bornkamm, Suggs) regard the occasion and motive of the assumed general letter in a different and relatively more satisfactory way, and so escape some of the difficulties in Manson's explanation. Their views will be treated below (pp. 96–100) in connection with the origin of the shorter forms of the letter, since they take the validity of the Ephesian hypothesis for granted.

posits no original connection of this fragment with Romans but assumes that it was secondarily joined to the Roman letter by a later redactor.[34] This raises the question of precisely what parts of Rom 16 are to be reckoned to the Ephesian fragment. There is unanimity among the exponents of this explanation that at least 16:3–20 must be Ephesian material since the evidence for an Ephesian address lies in this section. Beyond this, however, there is little agreement on what more can be added. Some have been able to regard 16:1–2, the commendation of Phoebe, as integral to the Roman letter, having been added as a postscript to introduce the letter bearer.[35] On this view the evidence of P[46], which sets off ch. 16 as a whole by placing the doxology after 15:33, is counted for little. Others consider 16:1–2 to belong with the Ephesian matter and think that the Ephesian letter is preserved entirely in ch. 16, excepting only the prescript. This allows Rom 16 to be understood as nothing more than a letter of recommendation for Phoebe and/or a note of farewell to the Ephesian community.[36] Uncertainty prevails also with regard to 16:21–23, containing the greetings from Paul's associates. It is said, on the one hand, that these verses must belong to the Ephesian fragment because Paul's fellow workers would not have been known to the Roman community, and because in other letters Paul appears to name only those associates who are known to his readers.[37] On the other hand, some think it unnatural that greetings are resumed after the admonition of 16:17–20 and the benediction of 16:20b, and so find reason to regard 16:21–23 as originally part of Romans.[38] Generally, a judgment whether 16:21–23 belonged to the Roman or to the Ephesian letter goes hand in hand with the manner in which the redactional work is thought to have been carried out, that is, whether the Ephesian material was merely affixed somewhat mechanically to the conclusion of Romans, or was subtly

[34]Recent advocates of this view include P. Feine and J. Behm, *Einleitung in das Neue Testament*, 174–76; W. Michaelis, *Einleitung in das Neue Testament*, 160–66; E. J. Goodspeed, *Introduction to the New Testament* (Chicago, 1937) 85–86; J. A. Fitzmyer, "The Letter to the Romans," 293; G. Friedrich, "Römerbrief," *RGG* (3rd ed.) V, 1138; Ernst Käsemann, *An die Römer* (HNT 8a; 3rd ed.; Tübingen, 1974) 393–405; W. Schmithals, "The False Teachers of Romans 16:17–20," 236–38; *idem*, "On the Composition and Earliest Collection of the Major Epistles of Paul," *Paul and the Gnostics*, 246–47; H.-M. Schenke, "Aporien im Römerbrief," *TLZ* 92 (1967) 881–84; G. Bornkamm, "The Letter to the Romans as Paul's Last Will and Testament," 8; *idem, Paul*, 79–80, 247; F. J. Leenhardt, *The Epistle to the Romans*, 28; H. W. Bartsch, "The Concept of Faith in Paul's Letter to the Romans," *BR* 13 (1968) 42 n. 1; *idem*, "Die historische Situation des Römerbriefes," *Studia Evangelica* IV (ed. F. L. Cross; TU 102; Berlin, 1968) 282 n. 1; D. Georgi, *Die Geschichte der Kollekte des Paulus für Jerusalem* (Theologische Forschung; wissenschaftliche Beiträge zur kirchlich-evangelischen Lehre 38; Hamburg, 1965) 79–80. Earlier advocates are cited by Rudolf Schumacher, *Die beiden letzten Kapitel des Römerbriefes. Ein Beitrag zu ihrer Geschichte und Erklärung* (NTAbh 14/4; Münster, 1929) 69–72 (hereinafter *Letzten Kapitel*).
[35]Thus, e.g., Feine and Behm, *Einleitung in das Neue Testament*, 175–76; Michaelis, *Einleitung in das Neue Testament*, 162; Schenke, "Aporien im Römerbrief," 883; Leenhardt, *The Epistle to the Romans*, 28. One reason for this view is the phrase συνίστημι δέ, which appears to be a continuation. It might as easily be a continuation of whatever part of the Ephesian letter is supposed to have been lost.
[36]Thus, e.g., Goodspeed, *Introduction to the New Testament*, 76, 85, and "Phoebe's Letter of Introduction"; Fitzmyer, "The Letter to the Romans," 293; Käsemann, *An die Römer*, 394–96.
[37]Michaelis, *Einleitung in das Neue Testament*, 163.
[38]Thus Schenke ("Aporien im Römerbrief," 883) and Schmithals ("The False Teachers of Romans 16:17–20," 237 n. 86). Schmithals reconstructs the original conclusion of the Roman letter as 15:32 + 16:21–23 + 15:33. Other factors taken to suggest that 16:21–23 did not belong to the Ephesian letter are: that within 16:3–20 there are greetings conveyed *from* others, and this is not expected to be repeated in a separate section; that Paul would not have mentioned to the Ephesians that Timothy was his fellow worker (16:21); and that the greeting from Tertius the scribe (16:22) is appropriate only after a letter of considerable length, such as Romans.

worked into the conclusion of Romans.[39] If the former, 16:21–23 is taken as part of the Ephesian letter,[40] but if the latter, these verses can be salvaged for Romans.[41]

Although disagreeing about the exact extent of the Ephesian fragment, advocates of this form of the hypothesis are at one in their conception of the occasion for the addition of the Ephesian material to the Roman letter, namely the collection, redaction and publication of the *Corpus Paulinum*. Yet even with this common ground there is no consensus on the motive for the addition. Many who support the Ephesian hypothesis suppose that the *Corpus* was published in Ephesus, and go on to surmise that the Ephesian fragment may have been preserved in the archives of the Ephesian church and would have been easily accessible to the collector-editor. A certain local esteem would have pertained to this letter (-fragment) of the Apostle, and the desire to include it in the *Corpus* would have been quite natural. Being so brief, however, it could not stand as an independent letter; it was therefore attached to Romans, thus being assured of a firm place in the collected letters of Paul.[42] That the collection of Paul's letters originated in Corinth is maintained by others, and is compatible with the supposed Ephesian address of (part of) Rom 16, though in this case there can be no appeal to the interests of the Ephesian church as the motive for the fragment's inclusion. Possibly the fact that both Romans and the Ephesian fragment were written from Corinth, perhaps about the same time, led to the attachment.[43] If the inclusion of the fragment in the *Corpus* must be justified on grounds other than an attempt to provide all of Paul's extant writings, then it is possible to conjecture dogmatic motives on the part of the redactor.[44]

To speak of an Ephesian letter-*fragment* in Rom 16, whatever its suggested extent, necessarily raises the question of the fate of the rest of the conjectured Ephesian letter. For those who suppose that the Ephesian letter was in itself no more than a brief letter of introduction, only the prescript of the original letter is not found in the preserved fragment, and this because of redactional necessity.[45] Those who

---

[39]The distinction in method is well expressed by the German verbs "anhängen" and "einfügen."

[40]Thus Feine and Behm, *Einleitung in das Neue Testament,* 175; Michaelis, *Einleitung in das Neue Testament,* 163–64.

[41]Thus Schmithals, "The False Teachers of Romans 16:17–20," 237 n. 86; Schenke, "Aporien im Römerbrief," 882–83.

[42]Goodspeed, *Introduction to the New Testament,* 85–86; Feine and Behm, *Einleitung in das Neue Testament,* 176; Michaelis, *Einleitung in das Neue Testament,* 163; Leenhardt, *The Epistle to the Romans,* 28. The theory of Deissmann (*Light from the Ancient East,* 235–36) explaining the attachment of the Ephesian and Roman letters as a result of their being found together in Paul's "copy book" is only a romantic speculation with very little likelihood.

[43]Fitzmyer, "The Letter to the Romans," 293.

[44]Schmithals ("On the Composition and Earliest Collection") provides both a specific and a general motive for the attachment of the Ephesian to the Roman letter. Specifically, the addition of Rom 16:1–20 served, through the presence of vss. 17–20, to give Romans an anti-gnostic polemical character which it otherwise lacked. This was necessary since in Schmithals' view the collection and redaction of Paul's letters were undertaken to provide a weapon against the gnostic threat. More generally, in order to demonstrate the catholic pertinence of Paul's letters, a collection of exactly seven letters was required, and the combination of more than one letter into a unit was necessary for this reason. See his essay, 262–63.

[45]This is apparently assumed by Goodspeed ("Phoebe's Letter of Introduction," 55–57) and Fitzmyer ("The Letter to the Romans," 292–93). Alternatively, James Moffatt (*Introduction to the Literature of the New Testament* [3rd ed. rev.; Edinburgh, 1918] 137) supposed that the note was unaddressed so as to allow Phoebe to use it in several places.

suppose that Rom 16 offers only a small part of a larger letter to Ephesus ordinarily admit that the rest of this letter is unknown to us and was probably already lost when the *Corpus* was formed.[46] A further question to be considered concerns the time and place of composition of the partially preserved Ephesian letter, but in dealing with such a small amount of material it is natural that judgments on this point are diverse and purely speculative.[47] There is, of course, no firm basis for a conclusion on this matter, which has no real importance unless it can be demonstrated that there is an Ephesian letter (-fragment) in Rom 16.

The redactional formulation of the Ephesian hypothesis is obviously far more complex than the compositional formulation of Manson, but this constitutes no objection to the theory as such. Neither does the lack of unanimity on particular points, however much it illustrates the difficulty of framing a generally acceptable explanation. Still, the redactional hypothesis is not without difficulties. In general, the effort to account for the addition of Ephesian material to Romans by reference to the formation of the *Corpus Paulinum* is less than satisfying, for the origin of the *Corpus* is itself an obscure phenomenon about which we can say little with any confidence. In effect, one problem is employed to solve another.[48]

The sub-forms of the redactional explanation, which differ as to how much of the Ephesian matter is preserved, how it was attached to Romans and why, are susceptible to more specific objections. If the Ephesian letter is supposed to be almost completely preserved, lacking only address and salutation, its inclusion on the basis of Ephesian pride is hardly adequate; such a motive would require the inclusion of the letter under its own title or with some indication of its Ephesian destination, but just this is eliminated with the omission of the prescript.[49] If, however, Rom 16 is supposed to contain but a small fragment of a larger letter to Ephesus, of which nothing is known, this entails the positing of a further hypothesis, namely, that there was such a letter and that it is lost.[50] Even if that is conceded as a possibility it remains a matter of note that only *this part* of the Ephesian letter, which must have been a rather insignificant part of the whole, was

---

[46]A recent exception is Schenke ("Aporien im Römerbrief," 883–84), who has revived the improbable view of some older commentators that other parts of the alleged Ephesian letter are embedded elsewhere in Romans. Schenke thinks that 14:1–15:13 belonged to the Ephesian letter on the grounds that this section seems to be self-contained and to be the only part of Romans in which Paul speaks concretely and knowledgeably of the community situation of the addressees. He thus presupposes not only that ch. 16 had an Ephesian destination, but also that Romans must have been an entirely general letter. The latter, however, cannot be decided a priori. For earlier efforts to find Ephesian matter beyond Rom 16 in the letter see Schumacher, *Letzten Kapitel,* 64–65.

[47]Among the suggestions are: that it was written about the same time and at the same place as Romans (so Fitzmyer, "The Letter to the Romans," 293; Georgi, *Geschichte der Kollekte,* 80); that it was written near the time of 2 Corinthians, shortly after Paul had left Ephesus (Feine and Behm, *Einleitung in das Neue Testament,* 176); that it was written after Romans, either during the journey to Jerusalem, perhaps at Philippi (Michaelis, *Einleitung in das Neue Testament,* 164–66), or even during the Roman imprisonment (Schenke, "Aporien im Römerbrief," 884, with the peculiar idea that the Ephesian letter either never reached Ephesus or a copy was preserved in Rome, thus finding further motive for its combination with Romans). For older positions on the question of the time and place of composition of the Ephesian matter see Schumacher, *Letzten Kapitel,* 65–66.

[48]On redactional hypotheses in relation to the formation of the *Corpus,* see below, pp. 139–142.

[49]Cf. John Knox, "The Epistle to the Romans; Introduction and Exegesis," *The Interpreter's Bible* (ed. George A. Buttrick; New York, 1954) IX, 366–67.

[50]Against this cf. the strictures of Hans Lietzmann, *An die Römer* (HNT 8; 4th ed.; Tübingen, 1933) 129–130.

46

preserved. This objection can be neutralized by admitting this peculiarity as a completely fortuitous result or by seeking out other preserved fragments of the larger Ephesian letter, but neither of these options seems adequate. On the whole, however, the redactional formulation of the hypothesis is, in the nature of the argument, resistant to criticism, for it appeals for the occasion, motive and agent of redaction to a process about which we know all too little, the formation of the *Corpus*. For this reason it is as incapable of demonstration as it is immune to specific criticisms.

When all is considered it cannot be gainsaid that on their own terms both the compositional and redactional expositions of the Ephesian hypothesis possess a certain coherence. Most criticisms of them are very weak.[51] But these explanations presume and are required by a positive estimate of the evidence for an Ephesian address of (part of) ch. 16. The Ephesian hypothesis can and should be tested not first at the level of formulation but at the level of the evidence itself.

The Evidence Re-examined

It is admittedly striking that at the conclusion of the Roman letter, in which explicit concrete references to the community situation defer so largely to theological exposition *in abstracto,* and which is addressed to a community not previously visited, Paul should proceed to convey greetings to a large number of individuals by name. Yet several considerations combine to reduce the force of the argument from the extent of the greetings against the Roman address.

First, the fact that Paul at the time of writing had not visited the Roman community in no way excludes the possibility that he had acquaintances who were counted among its membership. The general mobility of individuals and groups about the *Imperium Romanum* and the forceful westward thrust of the early Christian missionary enterprise only underline the possibility that some of Paul's prior acquaintances had penetrated to Rome.[52] While the question is not so much whether this was possible but whether it was in fact the case, it is necessary to keep in mind the possibility rather than to rule it out at the beginning. Second, it is a purely gratuitous assumption that Paul was personally acquainted with all whom he greeted.[53] Yet personal acquaintance must be presumed in some instances, above all with Prisca and Aquila, and probably also with Epaenetus, Andronicus, Junias,

---

[51]This applies especially to the often quoted dictum of Lietzmann that "ein fast aus Grüssen bestehender Brief, wie es Kap. 16:1–23 als selbständiges Schreiben sein würde, mag im Zeitalter der Ansichtspostkarte verständlich sein, für jeder frühere Zeit ist es ein Monstrum," a comment found only in the first edition of *An die Römer* (1907). Later editions lack the rhetoric and refer to such a letter only as "ein Unding." But this is not fairly applied to any statements of the hypothesis since even those who hold the Ephesian letter to consist almost entirely of ch. 16 are able in some way to rationalize the greetings. Goodspeed ("Phoebe's Letter of Introduction," 55–57) not only rationalizes the greetings as essential to the purpose of recommendation, but feels that the absence of substantial remarks is natural since Paul had only lately left Ephesus. Georgi (*Geschichte der Kollekte,* 80) finds that "durch die lange Grussliste gewinnt aber das Schreiben nach Ephesus den Charakter eines Abschiedsbriefes"; similarly, Bornkamm (*Paul,* 247). McDonald, citing several examples, maintains that "even shorter letters in the Greco-Roman world contain greetings in practically the same proportions" ("Was Romans XVI a Separate Letter?," 370–71). But on such observations see below, pp. 87 n. 137 and 91–93.

[52]Cf. the lengthy essay of G. La Piana, "Foreign Groups at Rome," *HTR* 20 (1927) 183–403.

[53]Against Michaelis, *Einleitung in das Neue Testament,* 160, and J. Knox, "The Epistle to the Romans," 365. For the view stated here cf. Zahn, *Introduction,* I, 417; Goguel, *Introduction au*

Ampliatus, Stachys, Rufus, and the mother of Rufus.[54] This conclusion is virtually inescapable given the familiar descriptive characterizations of these persons.[55] For others who are greeted either by name only or by name and some more general description there is no necessity to posit firsthand acquaintance; hearsay knowledge would be adequate grounds for this. That Paul did possess some measure of hearsay knowledge of the Roman community is difficult to dispute in view of his own statements in Romans and of his relations with Prisca and Aquila.[56] We cannot reliably estimate the extent of that knowledge, but it would be strange if along with whatever general notices he received he gained no information naming individual persons. In this way the remaining names can perhaps be accounted for. Third, the argument from the extent of the greetings can with some plausibility be used to yield the opposite result. In none of Paul's other letters do we find anything remotely approximating the greetings which we encounter in Rom 16, either in extent or in character. All of these letters are addressed to churches of Paul's own founding and under his apostolic auspices, churches which he knew well, and yet in none of them do we find particularized individual greetings. The most we have is a brief collective greeting.[57] Is it to be assumed in this light that the greetings of Rom 16 were directed to a community which Paul knew personally and well as a community? Or are these greetings not rather the exception which proves the rule: Individuals are not greeted in letters to churches with which Paul is personally acquainted.[58] Moreover, it is easy enough to discover a purpose for such greetings in the Roman letter. Assuming that it was at least one of Paul's purposes in writing to Rome to prepare the way for his coming and to enlist the support of Roman Christianity for his

---

Nouveau Testament, IV/2, 265; and J. Huby, *Epître aux Romains* (ed. S. Lyonnet; Verbum Salutis 10; Paris, 1957) 493–94.

[54]Rightly Otto Michel, *Der Brief an die Römer* (Meyer; 4th ed.; Göttingen, 1966) 376 n. 3 referring to vss. 2, 4, 7, 8, 10, 13; and Lietzmann, *An die Römer*, 129.

[55]This judgment is compelled by the phrase ἀγαπητός μου, which would be natural and expected only in referring to one personally known. This need not apply to the simple unqualified adjective ἀγαπητός. Goguel, *Introduction au Nouveau Testament*, IV/2, 264, wished to deny personal acquaintance with Andronicus and Junias, supposing that συναιχμάλωτοι (16:7) means only that they had been prisoners like Paul, not necessarily with Paul.

[56]Especially Rom 1:8–13, 15:14–16, and of course 14:1–15:13, if this section is understood to have the Roman situation in view. That Prisca and Aquila were Christians before meeting Paul, and thus already in Rome, there is no reason to doubt. See below.

[57]Cf. 1 Cor 16:19–20; 2 Cor 13:12–13; Phil 4:21–22; 1 Thess 5:26; 2 Thess 3:17; Phlm 23–24. Galatians has no greetings at all. In Col 4:10–18, although several individuals are named, only one is singled out to receive greeting; otherwise those named are the senders of greetings.

[58]This argument appears to have originated with Zahn, *Introduction*, I, 387–88, but is widely found. Cf. also Lietzmann, *An die Römer*, 129; Goguel, *Introduction au Nouveau Testament*, IV/2, 265–66; Huby, *Epître aux Romains*, 495; Michel, *Der Brief an die Römer*, 375; C. H. Dodd, *The Epistle of Paul to the Romans* (Moffatt New Testament Commentary; London, 1932) xix; etc. Efforts to rationalize the greetings in Rom 16, conceived as an almost wholly preserved piece of Ephesian correspondence (above, p. 47 n. 51), are either presumptive or ill-founded. Goodspeed, e.g., thinks the greetings are to be understood as contributing to the effectiveness of the recommendation, while McDonald adduces comparably lengthy greetings in other ancient letters; but, in fact, in ancient letters of *recommendation* any greetings at all are rare, and extensive greetings non-existent. That in Rom 16 the greetings serve the function of a final farewell is only an *a posteriori* assumption which seeks to render them intelligible. Actually, when all the evidence is considered, such greetings are, at least in terms of their form and extent, just as difficult to rationalize on the Ephesian hypothesis as they are for the Roman destination. On the Pauline greetings generally, see below, pp. 73–75, and for the greetings of Rom 16, pp. 91–93.

western missionary work, one means of achieving this was to single out those whom he knew or was known by, thus claiming them as his personal references.[59]

Precisely those descriptive characterizations of individuals which advocates of the Ephesian hypothesis have taken to show the non-Roman destination of (part of) ch. 16 can also be turned to the opposite effect. If these persons had their homes in Ephesus and so were well known to each other and to Paul, then the Apostle's rather elaborate descriptions appear superfluous and pointless. Would not the Ephesians already know very well that Prisca and Aquila had been his fellow workers, that Epaenetus was the first convert of their own province, that Andronicus and Junias were esteemed among the apostles? Would they not also know that Timothy was Paul's fellow worker, and be acquainted with the other co-workers mentioned in 16:21–23? Even the more general greeting of 16:16, "All the churches of Christ greet you," seems not quite appropriate for Ephesus, nor for that matter does the encomium for Prisca and Aquila, stating that for them "all the churches of the Gentiles give thanks" (16:4). Such broadly conceived expressions seem to rest on the idea of a large and self-contained group of churches in distinction from a church lying outside their perimeter.[60] In short, the content of the greetings is in some ways more appropriate to Rome than to Ephesus.

More specific observations are demanded by the names themselves, mainly those of Prisca and Aquila, on whose mention here rests a forceful argument for the Ephesian destination of this chapter. The available evidence, though slight, calls for careful scrutiny. There is no doubt that Prisca and Aquila had a connection, apparently close, with Ephesian Christianity. Rom 16 aside, it still may not be overlooked that Acts posits an earlier association with Rome. Luke has characterized Aquila as a Jew (Acts 18:2). Perhaps this identification is made so as to have it understood why Aquila left Rome, namely, because of the edict of Claudius against the Jews. It is quite unlikely that Aquila was, strictly speaking, a Jew, for Luke does not follow his propensity and narrate a conversion and baptism of Aquila; in fact, it would not be in keeping with Luke's conception of the history of the Christian mission if he allowed that there were Christians in Corinth before Paul's arrival.[61] Probably, then, Aquila was a Christian at the time of his encounter with Paul, and therefore a Roman Christian.[62] Nothing certain is known of the final issue of the edict of Claudius. Clearly its effects were not lasting and probably it was either formally rescinded or tacitly permitted to lapse upon Claudius' death in 54. If Prisca and Aquila left Rome as a result of the edict, which need not be doubted, it is entirely possible that they returned when the edict was no longer in force and thus were there when Paul wrote to the Roman church.[63]

[59]Cf., e.g., Zahn, *Introduction*, I, 390–91; Dodd, *The Epistle of Paul to the Romans*, xx; L.-G. Lönnermark, "Till frågan om Romarbrevets integritet," *SEA* 33 (1968) 147; and below, pp. 91–93.

[60]Thus, e.g., Zahn, *Introduction*, I, 390–91; Knox, "The Epistle to the Romans," 366; Schumacher, *Letzten Kapitel*, 82, 96.

[61]Ernst Haenchen, *The Acts of the Apostles* (Philadelphia, 1971) 533 n. 4; Hans Conzelmann, *Die Apostelgeschichte* (HNT 7; Tübingen, 1963) 105.

[62]In any case, that Paul converted him and Prisca is excluded by 1 Cor 1:14ff. Of course, for Luke "Christian" and "Jew" are not mutually exclusive terms.

[63]See W. Marxsen, *Introduction to the New Testament* (Philadelphia, 1968) 98–100; Karl P. Donfried, "A Short Note on Romans 16," *JBL* 89 (1970) 441–49. Some have sought to alleviate the

Of the remaining greetings in Rom 16 there is no evidence which permits a determination of their geographical location. This holds true even for Epaenetus, whose conversion in Asia imposes no necessity that he should have remained there, and even less that he be placed specifically in Ephesus.[64]

Proponents of the integrity of Romans, thus of the Roman address of ch. 16, have sought to support their opinion by correlating a number of the names in this chapter with various bits of literary evidence gleaned from other sources and with inscriptional evidence. The suggestion has often been made that the Rufus mentioned in Rom 16:13 is to be identified with the Rufus of Mark 15:21, one of the sons of Simon of Cyrene, on the assumption that, since Mark is a Roman Gospel, Rufus must have been known to Mark's Roman readers, and therefore was a Roman Christian.[65] But the identification and the assumptions on which it is based are dubious.[66] Considerably more important is an argument first advanced by J. B. Lightfoot on the basis of the mention in 16:10–11 of οἱ ἐκ τῶν Ἀριστοβούλου and οἱ ἐκ τῶν Ναρκίσσου.[67] Lightfoot supposed that these designations referred to persons among the households of Aristobulus, grandson of Herod the Great and brother of Agrippa and Herod, who apparently lived out his life in Rome, and of Narcissus, the powerful Roman freedman who exercised influence with Claudius. The persons greeted under these terms were understood by Lightfoot to be now members of the imperial household by inheritance from their former heads, whose names were retained for the groups, as appears to have been customary. Thus a Roman location is indicated for these. The argument is not conclusive, of course,

---

problem by assuming that Prisca and Aquila were well-to-do, and on departing Rome left their business (home) under the temporary supervision of another. This is meant to explain both how they could easily have returned to Rome and how they could have had a house church in Ephesus and Rome. Thus Lietzmann (*An die Römer*, 128) and Dodd (*The Epistle of Paul to the Romans*, xxi). If the couple did not return merely out of natural inclination, it has been suggested that, since their movements usually accord with Paul's missionary plans, Paul may have sent them ahead to Rome in connection with his plans to go there himself. So Zahn (*Introduction*, I, 390), followed by Michel (*Der Brief an die Römer*, 378). Zahn (*Der Brief des Paulus an die Römer*, 605 n. 52) attempted to account for a later return to Ephesus, suggested by 2 Tim 4:19, as a consequence of the Neronian persecution. It is an open question how much weight should be allotted to 2 Tim 4:19. Given the early uncertain textual history of the Roman letter, it is possible that the author of the Pastorals did not know Rom 16.

[64]Lietzmann (*An die Römer*, 134), using inscriptional evidence, pointed to the case of a wealthy matron of the East who transferred her entire household to Rome, and F. R. M. Hitchcock ("A Study of Romans XVI," *CQR* 121 [1935–36] 187–209, esp. 189) referred to a parallel in Cicero (*Ad fam.* xiii. 78), who, in writing to Allienus, proconsul of Sicily, commended to him one Democritus, himself in Sicily, who *hospes meus est, eum tu paene Achaiae principem cognosces*. Michel (*Der Brief an die Römer*, 345) explains Paul's acquaintance with some Roman Christians besides Aquila and Prisca on the basis of Claudius' edict: they could have met Paul while in exile from Rome, but by the time Romans was written could have returned to their homes.

[65]Thus Zahn, *Der Brief des Paulus an die Römer*, 610–11; idem, *Introduction*, I, 392; Otto Bardenhewer, *Der Römerbrief des heiligen Paulus* (Freiburg, 1926) 215; Dodd, *The Epistle to the Romans*, xxii; Michel, *Der Brief an die Römer*, 381; among others.

[66]This applies also to the occasional suggestion that the name Nereus (16:15) points to Rome, since one of this name figures in the legendary "Acts of Nereus and Achilleus," which portrays the two as eunuchs to Domitilla, the cousin of Domitian punished for atheism (Christianity?).

[67]*Saint Paul's Epistle to the Philippians* (2nd ed.; London, 1869) 172–73. Lightfoot was led to his discussion of Rom 16 by Phil 4:22, which conveys greetings from "those of Caesar's household" (οἱ ἐκ τῆς Καίσαρος οἰκίας).

but it does retain a certain force, not least because it explains the designation οἱ ἐκ τῶν . . . , which Paul did not use for house-church configurations.[68]

In the same study Lightfoot formulated a general inscriptional argument in favor of the Roman address of ch. 16.[69] Making full use of the growing body of Roman inscriptions, he showed that most of the names in Rom 16 could be paralleled in Rome at an early date, many in connection with the imperial household. Lightfoot was not so bold as to suggest that the inscriptions referred to the very individuals named in Rom 16, but concluded only that "the names and allusions at the close of the Roman Epistle are in keeping with the circumstances of the metropolis in St. Paul's day."[70]

Although more specific archaeological and inscriptional evidence has been sought, such arguments are not and cannot be decisive.[71] Even though many of the names in Rom 16 can be found among old Roman inscriptions, there is no likelihood whatever that these can be referred to the individuals named by Paul. The most such arguments can show is that the given configuration of names was *possible* in Rome. But the fortuitous preservation of inscriptional evidence must always qualify the attempt to regard any group of names as indicative of a specific locale, and the force of inscriptional arguments is diminished with the further discovery of inscriptions from extra-Roman sites, especially in Asia Minor.

Summarily, arguments based on the greetings of Rom 16, whether they

[68]The usual Pauline designation of a house church is ἡ κατ' οἶκον ἐκκλησία (1 Cor 16:19; Phlm 2; Rom 16:5; cf. Col 4:15). οἱ ἐκ τῶν . . . is approximated in Paul outside of Romans only in Phil 4:22.

[69]*Saint Paul's Epistle to the Philippians*, 169–176. In the same connection cf. also E. Ronneke, *Das letzte Kapitel des Römerbriefes im Lichte der christlichen Archäologie* (Leipzig, 1927), and A. Rouffiac, "Remarques sur les noms propres de Rom. xvi," *Recherches sur les caracteres du grec Nouveau Testament d'après les inscriptions de Priene* (Paris, 1911) 87ff. Lightfoot's accumulation of archaeological materials was enlarged by Zahn, *Introduction*, I, 419–420, and W. Sanday and A. C. Headlam, *A Critical and Exegetical Commentary on the Epistle to the Romans* (ICC; 2nd ed.; New York, 1926) 418–428.

[70]*Saint Paul's Epistle to the Philippians*, 175. In only a few instances did Lightfoot consider a "faint probability" for identifying persons mentioned in inscriptions with those of Rom 16. Sanday and Headlam (*The Epistle to the Romans*, xciv) not only thought that this combination of names was possible in Rome, but went further to suggest that outside of Rome these names were "very rare" and indeed that "such a combination of names—Greek, Jewish and Latin—could as a matter of fact be found only in the mixed population which formed the lower and middle classes of Rome." Only slightly more judicious was Lietzmann (*An die Römer*, 125), who held that the evidence "illustriert doch nur die Tatsache dass in Rom alles zusammenströmt. Aber wahrscheinlicher wird dadurch doch die römische Adresse von c. 16: ob in Korinth oder Ephesus aller diese z.T. seltenen Namen ebenso leicht sich zusammenfinden könnte, ist sehr fraglich."

[71]Specific arguments based on inscriptional and archaeological materials have been introduced in the cases of Prisca and Ampliatus in an effort to show that these had a direct and continuing connection with early Roman Christianity. As regards Prisca, appeals have been made both to an ancient church of St. Prisca in Rome and to the cemetery (catacomb) of Priscilla in Rome. It was supposed that the church of St. Prisca was built on the site of the home of Prisca and Aquila. This suggestion derives ultimately from the researches of J. B. de Rossi on the Roman catacombs as published in the *Bullettino di Archaeologia Cristiana*, ser. 4 (1888–89) 129ff. See the summary of his findings in Sanday and Headlam, *The Epistle to the Romans*, 418–19. In the cemetery of Domitilla, an early Christian catacomb, there are two inscriptions bearing the name Ampliatus, which some have taken to show that one by this name was prominent in the early history of the Roman church. This argument also goes back to de Rossi, *Bullettino di Archaeologia Cristiana*, ser. 3 (1881) 57ff., again summarized by Sanday and Headlam, 424. Such identifications cannot be made probable, and de Rossi characteristically dated the catacombs too early.

concern the individuals named or simply the extent and character of the greetings, are not decisive for either the Roman or Ephesian destination of this chapter.

The appropriateness of the admonition of 16:17–20 to the Roman church has been questioned in terms of its tone and content. Advocates of the integrity of the letter have traditionally accepted the premises of the argument while rejecting the conclusion as unwarranted. It is supposed instead that Paul received fresh news which altered his previously reticent posture,[72] or that the warning is only general and proleptic, not an ad hominem rebuke,[73] or that here Paul himself took pen in hand, which is supposed to explain the alleged change of tone.[74] If such conjectures are inadequate, it can be argued on purely formal grounds that there is no change of "tone" in this passage, and hence little to be accounted for by such reasons. By a thorough examination of the παρακαλῶ periods in the Pauline letters and parallel materials Carl Bjerkelund has shown that the formula παρακαλῶ δὲ ὑμᾶς ἀδελφοί, which introduces Rom 16:17–20 among many other passages, is not an expression of authoritative demand or admonition, but a fixed epistolary element which functions as a polite, "urbane" expression of request.[75] It carries no polemical import, and appears to be used by Paul when his authority is not in question. Thus it is a mistake to see in this passage a significant departure from the mood of the letter as a whole.

With regard to the alleged inappropriateness of the content of this passage to Rome, several things may be said. It has to be acknowledged that in chs. 1–15 we find no suggestion of the actual and present existence of false teaching or resultant schism within the Roman community. The statements of 16:17–20 are bound to appear anomalous if they are regarded as speaking to a developed state of conflict. But this understanding seems to be prohibited by 16:19, which lends to the preceding remarks a preparatory and prophylactic character, and at the same time admits the soundness of the community's present life in an obedience known to all, about which Paul rejoices. Thus there is no reason to insist that the danger in view is present and already having effect. Further, the content of the request is framed in such general terms that it must remain uncertain whether Paul here addresses a situation intimately and personally known to him, i.e., Ephesus. His sketch of the potential danger, regardless of the intent, provides no sure basis for determining the specific opponents in view, and the inferences of commentators are diverse.[76] If the description of the opponents were intentionally general, that would coincide with the potentiality of the problem. But if it is insisted that Paul had in mind a particular type of false teaching, even this would not stand in the way of retaining ch. 16 for

[72]Considered a possibility by C. K. Barrett, *A Commentary on the Epistle to the Romans* (Harper's New Testament Commentaries; New York, 1957) 274–75.

[73]So most commentators, including Sanday and Headlam, *The Epistle to the Romans*, xciv; Dodd, *The Epistle of Paul to the Romans*, xxiv, 242; W. G. Kümmel, *Introduction to the New Testament* (rev. ed.; Nashville, 1975) 319.

[74]Lietzmann, *An die Römer*, 127, comparing Gal 6:11–16; Bardenhewer (*Der Römerbrief des heiligen Paulus*, 11) refers to interruptions in writing or dictation.

[75]Carl J. Bjerkelund, *Parakalô. Form, Funktion und Sinn der parakalô-Sätze in den paulinischen Briefen* (Bibliotheca Theologica Norvegica 1; Oslo, 1967) 110, 188 and *passim*, but esp. 159–161. But contrast Käsemann, *An die Römer*, 401.

[76]Judaizers are in view according to Lietzmann (*An die Römer*, 127); Sanday and Headlam (*The Epistle to the Romans*, 429); Huby (*Epître aux Romains*, 505); Schenke ("Aporien im Römerbrief," 882 n. 1); and H. W. Schmidt (*Der Brief des Paulus an die Römer* [Theologischer Handkommentar zum Neuen Testament 6; 2nd ed.; Berlin, 1966] 257). Schmithals ("The False Teachers of Romans 16:17–

Romans, provided the danger is only possible rather than already effective in the Roman community.[77] Either case suffices to explain why the body of the letter betrays no similar concern.[78]

The only textual evidence to which the Ephesian hypothesis may appeal is that of P[46], with its placement of the doxology between chs. 15 and 16. While no more prestigious witness could be desired, it remains a single witness and cannot carry the case for the originality of the fifteen-chapter text form by itself unless compelling internal arguments substantiate the reading.[79] It is natural that the testimony of this MS is brought in by advocates of the Ephesian hypothesis as affording a clear external confirmation of the deduction from internal observations. But this has been done rather uncritically, and the real import of this evidence has not been carefully weighed.

Actually, the form of the text attested by P[46] is not wholly congenial to either the compositional or redactional formulations of the hypothesis. Manson, for example, was forced to regard P[46] as representing a conflation of the Roman and Ephesian forms, since the doxology could not have stood after 15:33 in the Ephesian form and since ch. 16 could not have followed the doxology in the Roman form.[80]

20'') thinks of Jewish-Christian gnostics, while Michel (*Der Brief an die Römer,* 376 n. 2, 383), Friedrich ("Römerbrief," 1138), Knox ("The Epistle to the Romans," 662) and Dodd (*The Epistle of Paul to the Romans,* 243) find some sort of gnostic threat implied.

[77]Schmithals ("The False Teachers of Romans 16:17–20") contends with a number of small arguments that the warning is directed against definite opponents already encountered in Paul's fields of mission. If this is correct it still does not necessitate either that Paul knew of their activity in Rome, which Schmithals considers unlikely, or that the passage must be addressed to some other community, for Paul could have anticipated that previously encountered opponents might seek to exert their influence in Rome also. Georgi (*Geschichte der Kollekte,* 80), although favoring an Ephesian address of the chapter, speaks of the "testamentarischer Charakter" of 16:17–20 and thinks that concrete persons are not meant and that the warning presupposes only the possibility, not the actuality, of their activity.

In fact—and this is too often unconsidered—there is as little evidence supportive of the existence of false teaching in Ephesus as in Rome. The Pastorals, which do occupy themselves with this issue, are too late to illuminate the Ephesian situation of Paul's time, and their pseudonymity casts doubt on their Ephesian address anyway. Likewise the speech of Paul to the Ephesian elders given in Acts 20:18–35 is hardly to be accepted as an authentic and accurate portrayal either of Paul or of the Ephesian situation of his time. Cf. Haenchen, *The Acts of the Apostles,* 602–605.

[78]The mention in 16:17 of "the teaching which you learned" (τὴν διδαχὴν ἣν ὑμεῖς ἐμάθετε) has occasionally been regarded as a further indication that the community addressed was founded by Paul. Not only is such an inference unjustified, but the phrase may be interpreted to favor the integrity of the letter. To churches of his own founding Paul expresses himself differently, and ordinarily with specific references to himself (cf. 1 Thess 4:1–2; 1 Cor 1–2; 15:1ff.; Phil 4:9). The similarity in phraseology and import, striking but too little noticed, of this phrase and that of Rom 6:17b, "the pattern of teaching to which you were committed" (εἰς ὃν παρεδόθητε τύπον διδαχῆς) is significant. In each case the term διδαχή is coupled closely with obedience on the part of the addressees (6:17a, 16:19). To be sure, 6:17b was judged an interpolation by R. Bultmann ("Glossen im Römerbrief," *Exegetica: Aufsätze zur Erforschung des Neuen Testaments* [ed. Erich Dinkler; Tübingen, 1967] 278–284, esp. 283). The grounds for this are insufficient. The precise meaning of 6:17 is of course problematic, and recent inquiries have not made it transparent. But it is possible to understand 6:17 more easily by bringing it into connection with 16:17–20. The difficulty posed by the terminology of these verses, unusual in Paul, is reduced somewhat if in both places Paul addresses a community not founded by himself, and probably not by anyone known to him. This fact he acknowledges by speaking obliquely of the community's founding, through the impersonal use of μανθάνω and παραδίδωμι. In this case διδαχή or τύπος τῆς διδαχῆς belongs to the veiled allusion, and should not be over-interpreted.

[79]The age and general value of the MS do not *ipso facto* bestow any probability on the correctness of individual readings, which must be tested according to established principles of criticism. Cf. the remarks of Kenyon, *The Chester Beatty Biblical Papyri,* III, Supplement, part 1, "Pauline Epistles, Text," xxii.

[80]"St. Paul's Letter to the Romans—and Others," 239.

Thus it is not a direct witness to either of the text forms postulated by Manson. The text of P[46] can be explained from Manson's perspective only as the consequence of a complicated process in the tradition whereby the Roman form interacted with the Marcionite form, thus gaining the doxology, and then interacted with the Ephesian form, thus gaining ch. 16. That is possible, to be sure, but it ought to be made clear what is involved in claiming P[46] as evidence for the original Roman form of the text. The witness of P[46] is perhaps even more problematic for the redactional explanation, which attributes the attachment of the Ephesian material to the editor of the *Corpus*. Practically, this ruled out the expectation of textual evidence for the independence of ch. 16, extant texts being traced to the *editio princeps* of the *Corpus*. But it also ruled out the desirability of such textual evidence as P[46] offers, since this can only cast doubt on the appeal to the formation of the *Corpus* as the occasion of the addition. Even those who take P[46] to favor the Ephesian hypothesis cannot easily regard its form of the text as representing that of the original *Corpus;* if it did, surely more traces of this form would have been preserved in the tradition, even if we allow for a natural tendency to move the doxology to the end of ch. 16. If, on the other hand, P[46] is thought to represent a pre-*Corpus* form of the text, it could still be claimed for the hypothesis, though the formation of the *Corpus* could no longer be seen as the occasion for the addition. But then the *motive* for the addition would become even more difficult to determine, none of the previously mentioned motives being applicable.

It is of chief importance, however, that as a result of the witness of P[46] the Ephesian hypothesis now stands not only within the domain of internal literary criticism but also under the aegis of textual criticism. If P[46] cannot be said to strengthen materially the Ephesian hypothesis in its traditional forms, at least it serves to broaden the base of general evidence. It also underlines the necessity for a more rigorous inquiry into the relationships between literary-critical theories and the data of textual criticism. In these ways the accession of this evidence helps toward a solution of the larger problem of the textual history of Romans.

Apart from the witness of P[46], several formal features of chs. 15 and 16 have also been taken to suggest the separability and independence of ch. 16 from the remainder of the letter. These matters will be discussed in detail below. In passing, however, we note that 15:33, often regarded as the concluding formula of the ostensibly original Roman letter, is completely unparalleled in the rest of the Pauline correspondence as an epistolary conclusion. By the standards of epistolary style, the Roman letter cannot have ended here. It is possible, of course, that a more usual conclusion was removed or displaced in the process of redaction (or even by Paul, on the compositional explanation), and if this is assumed 15:33 poses no problem for the Ephesian hypothesis. The additional observation that 16:1–2 has the character of the ancient letter of recommendation is certainly correct, but more evidence must be examined before the implications of this fact become clear. At any rate, we cannot immediately deduce from the similarity that ch. 16 ever had independent existence.

Before concluding this review of arguments and hypotheses which dispute the integrity of Romans, we may note briefly another view of the matter suggested by John Knox.[81] Dissatisfied with the alternative, Rome or Ephesus, for the destina-

---

[81] "The Epistle to the Romans," 367–68. Knox stresses the tentativeness of his suggestion.

tion of ch. 16, Knox disputes the authenticity of the chapter, choosing to regard it as a later addition to the Roman letter which originally concluded with 15:33. He finds the occasion and motive of such an addition in the struggle against heretical movements during the middle of the second century, a struggle in which the Roman church assumed a dominant role. To provide a strong defense against these movements the Pauline *Corpus* was expanded by the inclusion of the Pastoral letters; simultaneously, and for the same reason, Paul's Roman letter was supplemented with ch. 16. The specific aim in this was to appropriate Pauline authority to the Roman church by showing that Paul was indeed acquainted with its members (thus the greetings) and to allow Paul to speak explicitly to the present divisive threats (thus the admonition of 16:17–20). This proposal obviously mitigates some of the problems for both the Roman and Ephesian addresses and is dependent on some historically probable tendencies, yet it raises its own set of difficulties, which diminish its attractiveness.[82] It would emerge for serious discussion only in the event that both the Roman and Ephesian destinations of ch. 16 could be ruled out of consideration, but this has not been shown.[83]

Our overview of the types of evidence and particular problems which have cast doubt on the integrity of Romans and of the explanations advanced to account for these difficulties leads to no obvious conclusion. Indeed, on balance there seem to be no decisive and compelling arguments either way, and the question remains moot.[84] The task now is to seek other evidence which can relieve the repetition of standard observations and carry the discussion along more productive paths, and perhaps to a solution.

[82]It is difficult to make a case for inauthenticity, since the chapter is composed largely of formulaic items. Knox's arguments rest mainly on the admonition of 16:17–20, in which he discovers several expressions unusual in Paul. It is curious, incidentally, that the pseudonymous author is supposed to have attempted to link Paul more closely with the Roman church by using names which are suggestive, at least to many today, of the Ephesian church. But most telling against Knox's theory is the textual history which must be assumed. On his view, the omission of the Roman address in ch. 1 resulted when Romans held first place in some edition of the *Corpus,* while the addition of the doxology and ch. 16 occurred in an edition of the *Corpus* which placed Romans last. He does not, in this discussion, correlate the omission of the address with the omission of chs. 15–16, though the textual evidence requires this. Moreover, his theory requires that the doxology stood first after ch. 16, but, as we shall see, this is shown to be most unlikely by the textual evidence. Also, if the form of Romans belonging to the first edition of the *Corpus* did not contain ch. 16, which was supposedly added perhaps half a century later, we would expect far more evidence for the fifteen-chapter form of the letter. Knox's understanding of the textual history of the letter has not remained unchanged; his later views are discussed below, 97–98.

[83]Brief note may be taken of another theory which has failed to attract support, namely that ch. 16 was not originally part of the Roman letter, but was nevertheless addressed to Rome. This view was proposed in somewhat different ways by F. R. M. Hitchcock ("A Study of Romans XVI") and K. Erbes ("Die Bestimmung der von Paulus aufgetragenen Grüsse, Röm. 16,3–15," *Zeitschrift für Kirchengeschichte* 22 [1901] 224–231, and "Zeit und Ziel der Grüsse Röm. 16,3–15 und der Mittheilungen II Tim. 4,9–21," *ZNW* 10 [1909] 128–147, 195–218). Though the content of ch. 16 is not thought to indicate an Ephesian address, it is seen to presuppose a later situation, but still a Roman situation. Thus some time elapsed between the two letters, during which Paul could have gained closer acquaintance with the Roman community and the problem of false teaching could have emerged. Possibly the occasion of the second letter was to commend Phoebe (Hitchcock), or to prepare for Paul's arrival in Rome as a prisoner (Erbes). Although these conjectures clearly stand under the influence of some of the evidence for the Ephesian hypothesis, they do not escape other evidence against the Roman address, and it is hard to see what is gained by maintaining a Roman address for ch. 16 in this way. The only virtue of this view is in offering some reason for the continuous association of two allegedly independent pieces.

[84]The balance of the arguments is not tipped merely by appealing to the textual tradition which knows Rom 16 only as part of the Roman letter (Dodd, *The Epistle to the Romans*, xxiv), for it is just this tradition which stands in question.

CHAPTER III

THE PROBLEM OF INTEGRITY:
THE PAULINE EPISTOLARY CONCLUSIONS

The problem of the integrity of Romans cannot, it seems, be solved through text-critical or internal analysis, or even a combination of these approaches. Yet as long as the original extent of the letter remains in doubt we are without a fixed point of reference by which to assess accurately its subsequent textual history. Efforts to decide the question of integrity have been vitiated, however, by a consistent neglect of one type of evidence which can go far toward solving the problem, namely, the style of the Pauline letter, particularly the style of the Pauline epistolary conclusion.[1]

The form- and style-criticism of the epistolary materials of the New Testament has in recent decades made substantial if still somewhat fragmentary gains.[2] Among the numerous studies devoted to this task very few have been specifically concerned with the epistolary conclusions, which have nowhere been thoroughly and methodically treated.[3] Whatever the reasons for this neglect, a comprehensive delineation of the form and style of the Pauline letters requires that their conclusions be closely studied. Thus the discussion to follow, though having special application in this study, will perhaps help toward understanding the form of the Pauline letter.

Our purpose here is to identify and describe the constituent elements of the epistolary conclusions and to determine whether and to what extent these elements are structured in a definable pattern.[4] If these tasks can be accomplished we will gain an additional and more reliable vantage point from which to evaluate the conclusion of Romans and make a judgment on the letter's integrity.

[1]In the literature on Romans scattered allusions to the style of the conclusion are found, but these have nowhere been rendered effective for the problem of integrity. See de Bruyne, "La finale marcionite," 136–37; Lightfoot, *Biblical Essays,* 307–308, 317–18; Dodd, *The Epistle of Paul to the Romans,* 241–42; Corssen, "Überlieferungsgeschichte," 11–13; Zahn, *Introduction,* I, 382–83; and most recently and effectively Lönnermark, "Till frågan om Romarbrevets integritet," 141–48.

[2]Concise and valuable surveys of such efforts may be found in Robert W. Funk, *Language, Hermeneutic and Word of God; the Problem of Language in the New Testament and Contemporary Theology* (New York, 1966) 250–274 ("The Letter: Form and Style"); Béda Rigaux, *The Letters of St. Paul: Modern Studies* (Chicago, 1968) 115–146 ("Form Criticism and the Letters"); and W. G. Doty, *Letters in Primitive Christianity* (Philadelphia, 1973).

[3]Recent studies directly relevant to the conclusions are: Gordon J. Bahr, "The Subscriptions in the Pauline Letters," *JBL* 87 (1968) 27–41, and Terence Y. Mullins, "Greeting as a New Testament Form," *JBL* 87 (1968) 418–426. Floyd V. Filson has attempted to confirm the integrity of Hebrews in part by means of examining formal and stylistic features of the epistolary conclusions of the NT in *Yesterday: A Study of Hebrews in the Light of Chapter 13* (SBT, 2nd series, 4; London, 1967) 13–25, but his treatment is too general to be very useful. Limited attention is given to the style of the Pauline conclusions by Schmithals in "The Historical Situation of the Thessalonian Epistles" (*Paul and the Gnostics,* 123–218) esp. 129–132. But his analysis stands so completely under the influence of his own literary theories that it has little independent value.

[4]The definition of style criticism given by Funk, *Language, Hermeneutic and Word of God,* 259–260, is apt and adequate to our design: "Style analysis in the first instance is concerned to identify

Concluding Elements in Hellenistic Letters

We must begin by looking to the epistolary theory and practice of the ancient world to which Paul as letter writer is clearly indebted.[5] The materials for this are furnished in part by the vast number of papyrus letters which have come to light since the turn of the century. Their value for understanding the language and form of the New Testament letters is generally and properly recognized, and it is as great with respect to the epistolary conclusions as to other sections of the letters. But beyond the papyrus letters, which are usually described as "non-literary" because they were not intended for "publication," it is equally necessary to pay attention to the "literary" letters of antiquity, by which we may refer either to letters transmitted through literary tradition or to letters composed in rather sophisticated and artful style. The differences between these two types of letters, the "non-literary" and the "literary," is a difference only of degree; the boundary between them is quite fluid, and so we are well advised to be sensitive to the whole range of Hellenistic epistolography.[6]

A letter may be understood as a written conversation, or at least half of one, though lacking the exchange of actual verbal intercourse, and takes the place of personal presence. As a surrogate for personal presence, the basic form of a letter reflects the progress of encounter in three stages: salutation, body, and conclusion, corresponding to personal greeting, information exchanged, and farewell.[7] In a letter the particular matter is largely confined to the letter body, while the opening and closing are made up primarily of more general and formalized elements—phrases and formulae widely current which by nature and custom find their appropriate places at the beginning and end of a letter. Our first task is to describe briefly the conclusions of Hellenistic letters.

A review of the Hellenistic epistolary tradition reveals the availability of several more or less formulaic elements and leading ideas regularly employed to

---

characteristic words and phrases, individual literary and rhetorical devices, and eccentricities of expression which betray an author's affinity with a certain tradition or traditions, or reveal his own distinctive use of language. . . . In the second place style analysis attempts to discern sentence and period structure. . . . And finally, style analysis may be taken in the broad sense to mean the investigation of the form and function of constituent elements within the whole, or of the form and function of the literary form *as a whole*."

[5]In addition to the various collections of papyrus and literary letters, the most important studies of the Hellenistic letter are: F. X. J. Exler, *The Form of the Ancient Greek Letter* (Washington, 1923); Heikki Koskenniemi, *Studien zur Idee und Phraseologie des griechischen Briefes bis 400 n. Chr.* (Annales Academiae Scientiarum Fennicae, series B, CII, 4; Helsinki, 1956); Otto Roller, *Das Formular der paulinischen Briefe; ein Beitrag zur Lehre vom antiken Briefe* (BWANT 4/6 [58]; Stuttgart, 1933); F. Ziemann, *De epistularum Graecarum formulis sollemnibus: quaestiones selectae* (Dissertationes philologicae Halenses 18; Halle, 1911); Klaus Thraede, *Grundzüge griechisch-römischer Brieftopik* (Zetemata: Monographien zur klassischen Altertumswissenschaft 47; Munich, 1970). Further reference to these studies is made under the name of the author only.

[6]It is especially necessary to stress the importance of "literary" letters in this sense, for in the form- and style-critical work which has so far been done on the Pauline letters they have been unduly neglected. This neglect must be due in part to the work of Adolf Deissmann, who saw in the papyri "real letters," which, to him, stood in clear contrast to letters of a literary type. Since Deissmann, the contrast expressed in his distinction between "Brief" and "Epistel" has assumed too normative a role, and the papyrus letter has often been seen as the only appropriate comparative material for the early Christian letter. For form-critical work such a distinction and preference cannot be justified. See especially the remarks of Thraede, 1–4.

[7]For the letter as a substitute for personal presence and the structure of the letter as corresponding to personal encounter, see Koskenniemi, 34–47 and Thraede, *passim*.

construct the close of a letter. Some of these appear with great frequency and little variation, while others are less widespread and lacking strict consistency of phrasing. General usage furnished a stock of formal and stylistic elements suitable to the epistolary conclusion, and from these a selection was made in accordance with the custom of the writer, that is, his own "style," and the requirements of the epistolary situation itself.[8] Here we shall review these elements in terms of their form and function.[9]

A. The Final Wish

Among Hellenistic letters only one element is so ubiquitous as to appear essential for the construction of the letter conclusion, the final wish.[10] Functionally, the final wish marks the definitive conclusion of a letter, much in the manner of the concluding asseveration ("sincerely," etc.) and signature in modern usage. It was probably present from the beginning in the development of the Greek letter.

The final wish is found in two principal forms, ordinarily only the single words ἔρρωσο ("Farewell") or εὐτύχει ("May you prosper"), the former predominant by far.[11] Toward the end of the first Christian century the more expansive phrase ἐρρῶσθαί σε εὔχομαι (or βούλομαι) ("I pray for your health") is often met in place of the older forms, and eventually superseded them.[12] Though characteristically brief and stereotyped, the final wish frequently admits of some elaboration, and this in three respects. Since it is implicitly intended for the addressee, the final wish requires no specification of its object; yet in many letters the recipient is explicitly mentioned, not by name, but by some term of endearment or respect (e.g., ἄδελφε, πάτερ, κύριέ μου, τιμιώτατε, φίλτατε, etc.). Further, the scope of the wish is often extended to include others together with the recipient by means of such collective additions as μετὰ τῶν σῶν πάντων, σὺν τοῖς σοῖς πᾶσι, πανοικησία. Lastly, the final wish is sometimes introduced by adverbial phrases which enlarge its temporal scope, and so enhance it (διὰ ὅλου βίου, πολλοῖς χρόνοις, διὰ παντός, etc.). Such elaborations become increasingly frequent from about the second century B.C. on. Since they are not essential to the purely "mechanical" function of the wish, their use must be set down to a desire to provide a letter with a familiar, friendly tone and to avoid mere formalism.[13]

[8]This inference is readily available on the basis of extant letters, but it is also explicitly laid down in the ancient letter-writing handbook of Demetrius that various formal and stylistic items are incorporated in letters, and that the situation determines which shall be used: τῶν ἐπιστολικῶν τύπων... ἐχόντων τὴν θεωρίαν τοῦ συνεστάναι μὲν ἀπὸ πλειόνων εἰδῶν ἀναβάλλεσθαι δὲ ἐκ τῶν ἀεὶ πρὸς τὸ παρὸν ἁρμοζόντων, καὶ καθηκόντων μὲν ὡς τεχνικώτατα γράφεσθαι, γραφομένων δ' ὡς ἔτυχεν ὑπὸ τῶν τὰς τοιαύτας τοῖς ἐπὶ πραγμάτων ταττομένοις ὑπουργίας ἀναδεχομένων. (Cited from V. Weichert, ed., *Demetrii et Libanii qui ferunter ΤΥΠΟΙ ΕΠΙΣΤΟΛΙΚΟΙ et ΕΠΙΣΤΟΛΙΜΑΙΟΙ ΧΑΡΑΚΤΗΡΕΣ* [Leipzig, 1910] 13.)

[9]Since these elements are so largely stereotyped we will provide only representative examples. Most concluding elements are extensively cataloged by Exler.

[10]On the final wish, see especially the discussions of Ziemann, 334–365 and Koskenniemi, 151–54.

[11] The distinction often drawn in the use of these two forms, ἔρρωσο in letters to peers or inferiors and εὐτύχει in letters to superiors (thus, e.g., Roller, 481–82) seems to have no firm basis. At least the distinction cannot be made so sharply, as Ziemann, 350–56, has shown.

[12]See below, 61.

[13]For the "philophronetic" aspect of the Hellenistic letter, that is, the fundamental assumption of friendly sentiment between the correspondents and its expression and cultivation by means of the letter, see the discussion of Koskenniemi, 35–37 and *passim*.

Since the final wish is meant to provide a definitive conclusion, nothing should follow it, strictly speaking, save possibly the date. There are not a few letters in which the final wish is nevertheless duplicated. In most instances this is occasioned by the addition of postscriptive remarks after the final wish, which call into question the end of the letter and so prompt a second "definitive" conclusion.[14] But in a few cases the final wish is repeated even without intervening material.[15] The second wish is usually in a hand different from the first, indicating that dictation carried through the final wish, which is then repeated by the sender. We will consider the motive for this when we speak of the concluding autograph. In a few other instances in which the final wish is duplicated, the first is in a second hand and the second in yet a third hand. In these letters it would appear that someone associated with the sender adds a wish for the addressee, who is a mutual acquaintance.[16]

B. Greetings

Among letters dated prior to the first Christian century, concluding greetings are only infrequently present and cannot be called an integral feature of the epistolary conclusion.[17] This situation changed markedly in the first Christian century, for letters from this and later periods usually contain personal greetings and show that expressions of greeting had gained a fixed form and a firm position at the close of a letter.[18] Since the appropriate greeting of the writer to the addressee was located at the beginning of the letter, either in the prescript (A to B, χαίρειν) or immediately following it,[19] the concluding greetings are as a rule directed to others somehow affiliated with the addressee, either family or friends. The basic form of the concluding greetings consists of the verb of greeting and the object, with each of these components being liable to various modifications.[20]

The verb commonly employed for concluding greetings is ἀσπάσεσθαι, though προσαγορεύειν is sometimes encountered.[21] When final greetings began to play a role they were presented imperativally (ἀσπάζου, ἄσπασαι), the writer calling upon the addressee to convey greetings to others. Thus, for example, ἀσπάζου Ἥρωνα καὶ Ὀρσενοῦφιν καὶ τοὺς ἐν οἴκῳ πάντας (P.Fay. 112). The first person form ἀσπάζομαι is very poorly attested in final greetings, and only began to be used in this position in the second century A.D.[22] Characteristic, on the

---

[14]For example: P.Lond. 413, 897; BGU 249, 665, 815, 1874; P.Oxy. 298; P.Fay. 115, 119; Ign Smyrn 13:2; Ign Pol 8:3; Cicero ad Fam. xiv.3; xvi.4, 9, 15; Fronto ad Marc. i.8; v.27; etc.

[15]Thus P.Oxy. 931; P.Giess. 16; P.Princ. 67; P.Brem. 5, 9, 21, 22, 50, 54.

[16]See U. Wilcken, Die Bremer Papyri (Abhandlungen der preussischen Akademie der Wissenschaften, phil.-hist. Klasse, Jahrgang 1936, 2; Berlin, 1936) 27–28.

[17]Ziemann, 325–26, Exler, 111–12. Some of the oldest examples of letters with final greetings are P.Oxy. 745 (ca. 25 B.C.) and Cicero ad Fam. xvi.4 and 5 (ca. 50 B.C.).

[18]Koskenniemi, 148; cf. Roller, 67–68, whose opinion that it was Paul himself who first invested epistolary greetings with significance and popularized their use is certainly wrong.

[19]During the second century A.D. the writer's greeting to the addressee came to be given fuller expression, but still in immediate connection with the prescript, usually in the form ἀσπάζομαί σε.

[20]On the possible forms of final greetings, see the discussion of Mullins, "Greeting as a New Testament Form," 418–423, which is descriptively useful, though we disagree with his interpretation of the NT parallels at several points.

[21]ἐπισκοπεῖν is sometimes used in the same formula, but has a nuance different from actual greeting.

[22]It is found in P.Oxy. 1767, 1494, 1067, BGU 276, P.Tebt. 415, among other places. The scarce use of this form in final greetings is due—apart from the presence of the writer's greeting to the

other hand, is the third person form ἀσπάζεται (ἀσπάζονται), whereby the greetings of a third party or parties (necessarily named) are conveyed through the writer to the addressee (e.g., P.Oxy. 300, ἀσπάζεται ὑμᾶς Λογγεῖνος) or even through the writer and addressee to yet a fourth party (e.g., P.Oxy. 114, ἀσπάζεται Αἶαν Ξάνθιλλα καὶ πάντας τοὺς αὐτῆς). Thus the greeting phrase can become rather extensive in scope.

The verb of greeting is subject to elaboration. Chief among these additions is πολλά (ἀσπάζεσθαι πολλά, "to greet warmly").[23] Sometimes the entire clause is introduced with πρὸ πάντων or πρὸ τῶν ὅλων ("above all," "by all means").[24] Though originally such elaborations were doubtless meant to avert mere conventionality and impart a more cordial tone, in time their wide use made them conventional also.

The objects of the greeting are variously designated. They may be specified by proper names alone, but often along with the name there appears a brief personal description, either simply a statement of relationship (e.g., P.Oxy. 533, ἀσπάσασθε Στατίαν τὴν θυγατέρα μου καὶ Ἡρακλείδην καὶ Ἀπίωνα τοὺς υἱούς μου) or a term of approbation or affection (e.g., P.Oxy. 1757, ἄσπασαι Κλαυδίαν τὴν ἀγαθοτάτην).[25] But just as often the objects of the greetings are not named but are merely taken up in a general collective designation. Thus we meet these phrases: πάντας τοὺς ἐν οἴκῳ (ἐνοίκους) ("all among your household," "your whole family"); τοὺς φιλοῦντάς σε ("those who love you," or "your friends").[26] The impersonality of such phrases is often mitigated, at least by intent, by the supplement κατ᾽ ὄνομα ("by name" or "personally"). The extremity of such generalization is well illustrated in P.Mich. 206, ἀσπάζου τοὺς σοὺς πάντας κατ᾽ ὄνομα. ἀσπάζονταί σε καὶ τοὺς σοὺς πάντας οἱ ἐμοὶ πάντας κατ᾽ ὄνομα. Collective greetings of this type are obviously generated more by epistolary form than by the actual relationship which may obtain between the correspondents; they function to give the letter a familiar tone even though close acquaintance with the addressee may be lacking.[27]

C. The Health Wish

A third element frequently found in the epistolary conclusions from the Ptolemaic period on is the *formula valetudinis,* a wish for the well-being of the addressee.[28] The original and preferred position of such a wish is at the beginning of

---

addressee in the prescript—to the limited readership intended for private letters. Parties other than the immediate addressee were greeted mediately through him.

[23]Occasionally we find even a doubling of the adverb, e.g., P.Mich. (III) 201: ἀσπάζεται ὑμᾶς θερμουθᾶ πολλὰ πολλά. . . .

[24]This is not frequent in final greetings, but is often used in greeting connected with the prescript, or to introduce the proscynesis at the beginning of the letter. Its use in these greetings is probably due to transference from the proscynesis when a separate clause of greeting was brought to the beginning of the letter.

[25]Occasionally there is no name, and the identification is made by a statement of relationship only (e.g., P.Oxy. 1676; P.Tebt. 412, 415; BGU 48).

[26]On the philophronetic nature of these phrases see Koskenniemi, 150–52 (with examples).

[27]We cannot assume, however, on the basis of a generalized or collective greeting, that a close familiarity with the addressee is lacking, but only that the use of these phrases does not require such familiarity.

[28]Extensive discussions of this element are given by Ziemann, 302–325, and Koskenniemi, 130–39; cf. Roller, 62–65.

the letter, where it is variously expressed. Most simply, it is joined directly to the salutation, resulting in the combinations χαίρειν καὶ ὑγιαίνειν and χαίρειν καὶ ἐρρῶσθαι. The opening health wish may also maintain syntactical independence and follow the prescript as a separate clause, in which case its usual form is εἰ ἔρρωσαι (ὑγιαίνεις). εὖ ἂν ἔχοι. καὶ αὐτὸς δ' ὑγίαινον, often abbreviated, εἰ ἔρρωσαι, αὐτὸς δ' ὑγίαινον. Independently stated, the scope of variation is greater, allowing the use of elaborative phrases.[29]

Though originally a health wish stood at the beginning of the letter, hardly less frequently is a health wish found in its conclusion, just before the final wish.[30] There are letters which exhibit only the introductory formula, or only the concluding formula, but a large number of letters contain both. When the wish is found in the conclusion, however, it assumes a special form which admits of little variation. It is consistently constructed with ἐπιμέλεσθαι, usually in the imperative, and takes the basic form, ἐπιμέλου σεαυτοῦ ἵν' ὑγιαίνῃς.[31] The primary variations are ὅπως for ἵνα, σώματος for σεαυτοῦ, and occasionally we find the participle ἐπιμελόμενος, which then depends on another verb.[32] The formal and terminological fixity of this wish reveals it as a pure convention by means of which the writer intimates his concern for the condition of the addressee.[33]

This concluding *formula valetudinis* passed out of extensive usage in the late first and early second centuries A.D. One reason for this may have been the increased use of the expanded final wish, ἐρρῶσθαί σε εὔχομαι, which modified the earlier ἔρρωσο into an explicit health wish and thus rendered the ἐπιμέλεσθαι formula superfluous.

D. Dating

The matter of dating is relatively unimportant for our concern with the style of the Pauline epistolary conclusions and may be dismissed with some brief general comments. Not all ancient letters were dated, and it appears that there was no definite or generally accepted practice for the dating of correspondence.[34] Letters seem to have been dated only when it was considered important, for whatever reason, that the recipient know the time of writing.[35] Generally, we may suppose

---

[29]Although in this formula ὑγιαίνειν often replaces ἐρρῶσθαι, the ὑγιαίνειν wish usually takes another form altogether: πρὸ μὲν πάντων εὔχομαί σε ὑγιαίνειν. This wish is frequently connected with the proscynesis: πρὸ μὲν πάντων εὔχομαί σε ὑγιαίνειν καὶ τὸ προσκύνημά σου ποιῶ παρὰ τῷ κυρίῳ, giving the wish a dimension of prayerful petition. The independent formulation of the ὑγιαίνειν wish seems to be a later development, belonging to the second century A.D. (Koskenniemi, 134–35). The only earlier independent conception of this formula occurs in P.Oxy. 292 (*ca.* A.D. 25), where it is found at the end of the letter instead of after the prescript.

[30]On this development, see Ziemann, 313–17, and Koskenniemi, 133–34 (his "Type B").

[31]For example: P.Oxy. 294, 743, 1154; P.Tebt. 19, 284; P.Amh. 39. The Latin equivalent: *cura, ut valeus.*

[32]For variations, see the listing in Exler, 113–14.

[33]Koskenniemi, 134, noting that in sense and style this concluding formula is a true counterpart to the *formula valetudinis* of the letter opening and that both belong to the same period (third century B.C. to first century A.D.), appearing and disappearing about the same time.

[34]On the problem see the concise and valuable discussion of B. Olsson, *Papyrusbriefe aus der frühesten Römerzeit* (Uppsala, 1925) 18–20, refuting earlier attempts to adduce firm rules for dating. On a rough estimate, perhaps less than half the extant ancient letters carry dates.

[35]Ibid., 20. But even this did not always require a written date, since the letter carrier could in some cases indicate the time of writing. Some interesting notes about the dating of letters are found in Cicero's correspondence. He customarily dated his own letters, and clearly wished that his corre-

that letters dispatched over longer distances by means of uncertain post were more likely to be dated than others. When a date is provided its normal position is just after the final wish, and it takes the basic form of year, month and day.[36]

E. The Concluding Autograph

In many ancient letters a portion of the conclusion was written in a different hand from the body. Having dictated the substance of the letter, the sender would finish it in his own writing. The change of script lies open to our view in the extant papyrus letters, just as it did to their original readers, so there was little need for an explicit avowal that at a given point the sender himself took pen in hand.[37] In those ancient letters preserved through literary tradition the evidence is less obvious, but even here we can recognize autographic conclusions in dictated letters. Among the correspondence of Cicero and of Fronto, though each strongly preferred to write his letters autographically throughout,[38] we find numerous dictated letters. But we must suppose that these dictated letters were at least concluded with an autograph, and indeed there are often indications to this effect. For example, the last few lines of one of Cicero's letters to Atticus (xiii.28) follow the statement *hoc manu mea,* "the rest is in my own hand." Similarly, in *ad Att.* xii.32 a rather lengthy autographic conclusion (following a brief note and greetings) is introduced with the notice *haec ad te mea manu,* "I write this to you in my own hand." *Ad Att.* xiv.21 concludes with words which are very likely autographic, *haec scripsi seu dictavi . . . ,* "this I have written, or rather dictated . . . ," and in the same way we should consider the final lines of *ad Att.* viii.15, *plura scriberem, si ipse possem. Sed, ut mihi videor, potero biduo,* "my letter would be longer if I myself could write. But I think I will be able in a couple of days."[39] Fronto is on one occasion quite apologetic when compelled to dictate a letter, and he concludes it autographically with the remark:

---

spondents did the same. In *ad Fam.* iii.2, referring to two letters received simultaneously from the same party, he says, "In one of them the date given was April 5, but the other, which I surmised to be later, was not dated," and in *ad Att.* iii.23 he speaks of "another letter which, contrary to your custom, is not dated." In *ad Fam.* iii.19 he says, "I received a letter you had sent me . . . but it gave no indication of the place or date of its dispatch, and the carrier who delivered it was not the one to whom you gave it, who might have said where and when it was dispatched."

[36]A large collection of dating formulae is given by Exler, 78–98. Abbreviated forms have only the month and day, while expanded forms apply the imperial title to the year. There are a few exceptions to the normal positioning of the date after the final wish (e.g., P.Petr. 32; P.Oxy. 891) and these are perhaps influenced by the documentary form, which called for the date at the beginning.

[37]Some examples: *BGU* 37, 106, 544, 615, 844, 1031; P.Oxy. 62, 66, 1025; P.Petr. (II) 4, 11, 13; P.Eleph. 13, 16, 22. The name signature naturally had no place in the Hellenistic letter, since the name of the sender is given in the prescript. Instances of the name signature are quite rare (e.g., P.Lond. 413 and P.Petr. 2, 44). On the question see especially the detailed remarks of Roller, 493–98. The case is quite different for documents (deeds, receipts, etc.), in which the name signature is the rule.

[38]Cf. Cicero *ad Att.* iv.16: "The mere fact that my letter is in the hand of an amanuensis will indicate how busy I am" (*occupationum mearum vel hoc signum erit, quod epistula librarii manu est*), and ii.3: "I do not think you ever before read a letter of mine which I had not written in my own hand. From that you may infer how much business hinders me . . ." (*numquam ante arbitror te epistulam meam legisse nisi mea manu scriptam. Ex eo colligere poteris, quanta occupatione distinear*). See also *ad Att.* v.14; vii.2, 3; viii.13; xvi.15; etc. Fronto, *ad Marc.* iv.9, remarks that because of a shoulder pain "I could not write the letter. . . , but, contrary to my usual custom, had to employ another hand" (*sed uterer contra morem nostrum aliena manu*).

[39]In *ad Att.* viii.1, Cicero refers to a letter from Pompey, and quotes from it a statement said to be "written autographically in conclusion" (*in extremo ipsius manu*).

Neque mihi succenseas, quod non mea manu tibi rescripserim. . . . Digitis admodum invalidis nunc utor et detractantibus. Tum haec epistula multorum verborum indigebat, mea autem dextera manus hac tempestate paucarum litterarum.
Do not be offended at me that I did not respond to you in my own hand. . . . My fingers are now quite weak and unmanageable. This letter required many words, but my right hand is capable of only a few characters at the moment (*De bello Parth., ad Anton.*).

In another final autograph he explains, *mea manu non scripsi, quia vesperi loto tremebat etiam manus. Vale.*, "I have not written (the letter) in my own hand because after my bath my hand was shaky. Farewell" (*de nepote amisso* i), and again, *quod librari manu epistula scripta est, a labore gravi digitis consolui . . . ,* "In having this letter written by my secretary I have saved my fingers a difficult task" (*de eloq.* ii). In these letter collections there are doubtless many other dictated letters which in their originals manifested the concluding autograph, even if this can no longer be specified with the aid of clear verbal indications.

The extent of the concluding matter which is found in the sender's own hand varies widely, but as a rule it is quite limited, often comprising no more than the final wish. In other letters the date and postscriptive remarks also are given in the second hand.[40] On occasion, however, the autograph may carry a final paragraph or two of substantive matter.[41]

It has been a common assumption that the function of a conclusion in the sender's hand, regardless of its extent, is to attest a letter's authenticity.[42] Such a motive, or at least such an effect, was certainly operative in some instances, particularly in letters of official or specially urgent import.[43] But this is a less than adequate explanation for concluding autographs in informal, private letters to family or friends, where the intent of formal authentication would seem neither necessary nor quite appropriate. In such cases the autographic closing must have served simply to invest the letter with a more intimate personal aspect.[44] But the presence of autographic conclusions in letters of such various types suggests a general conclusion: in letters which were dictated it was a widely acknowledged matter of epistolary

---

[40]E.g., P.Oxy. 1063; *BGU* 844; P.Giess. 97. On postscripts, see further below.

[41]E.g., Cicero *ad Att.* xii.32; xi.24; xiii.28.

[42]Thus Ziemann, 362–65; Roller, 70–78; Deissmann, *Light from the Ancient East,* 166–67. Bahr ("The Subscriptions in the Pauline Letters") seems also to accord the greatest weight to this motive of certification.

[43]While such a motive remains only implicit in the papyrus letters, it is supported by some remarks in literary letters which show that the autographic manner of writing was a strong inducement to credibility. Plancus, in a letter to Cicero (*ad Fam.* x.21), says, "I put my trust in his autographic letters" (*credidi chirographis eius*), and "Laterensis, a man of the greatest integrity, sends me a letter in his own handwriting" (*Laterensis, vir sanctissimus, suo chirographo mittit mihi litteras*). In this letter, whether a letter is written autographically is apparently taken as a factor in determining genuineness. Conversely, when on one occasion Cicero does not want his letters to be traced to himself he says, "I will not use my own handwriting or my seal if the letters are the type I would not want to come into a stranger's possession" (*cum neque utar meo chirographo neque signo, si modo erunt eius modi litterae, quas in alienum incidere nolim* [*ad Att.* ii.20]).

[44]Koskenniemi, 168–69. Cf. Cicero *ad Att.* vii.2, "Your letters are each more delightful than the last—I mean those in your own handwriting . . ." and vii.3, "I was pleased at first glance to see that your letter was in your own hand, and was delighted with the care and attention it showed." Also Fronto *ad Marc.* iii.3: "Indeed, I dote on the very characters of your writing; so whenever you write, do so in your own hand." Thus the autographic mode itself performs a philophronetic function.

etiquette that the conclusion should be in the hand of the sender.[45] This conclusion does not rule out other motives; rather, a fixed stylistic custom was sometimes drawn into the service of particular motives, depending on the nature and purpose of a given letter.[46]

F. Postscripts

A postscript, that is, remarks made subsequent to the final wish, is hardly to be considered a normative stylistic element, but insofar as we are concerned to describe what is found in the conclusions of ancient letters the postscript cannot be ignored. The postscript is frequently encountered, not merely among the common papyrus letters of ordinary men, but also in the letters of more sophisticated writers.[47] For the most part, postscripts are very brief, and are often linked syntactically with the final wish. They commonly consist of a concluding convention, most often a greeting or health wish.[48] But there are many letters which exhibit more extensive postscripts, which contain a wide variety of notices, some of which are resumptive of concerns discussed in the letter body, but most of which introduce new topics.[49] The use of the postscript is entirely contingent on the immediate situation of writing, and serves to supplement the letter with items which might have been included within the formal boundaries but through oversight or the arrival of new information were not.[50]

G. Miscellaneous Matters

We have reviewed the most common aspects of the conclusions of ancient letters. Other features may be more briefly mentioned.

A further formulaic item which frequently belongs to the epistolary conclusion is the request for a letter in reply, a request natural to those familiar letters belonging to situations where continuing correspondence is possible and desirable.

[45]Thus Roller, 78: "Ob der ganze Brief eigenhändig war oder nicht, unter allen Umständen verlange es der Briefstil dass der Schlussgruss persönlich von dem Aussteller unterschrieben wurde."

[46]One particular motive, for example, was confidentiality. Cicero, *ad Att.* xi.24, says: "Here I take the pen myself, for I have to deal with confidential matters" (*sed ad meam manum redeo; erunt enim haec occultius agenda*); cf. iv.17: "our letters are so full of secrets that we cannot even trust an amanuensis."

[47]The postscripts are ordinarily written in the lower margin, but among the papyrus letters they are also found in the side margin (*BGU* 1097; P.Oxy. 298), or even at the head of the letter, above the prescript (P.Lond. 893), and thus apparently wherever there was available space. The a priori assumption that a postscript, as a violation of a letter's formal boundaries, would be uncommon in letters of more sophisticated men does not hold, since postscripts are very frequent in the letters of Cicero, Fronto, and others.

[48]For postscripts containing only formal conventions, see among the papyrus letters *BGU* 601, 824, 1079; P.Fay. 112; P.Lond. 897; P.Ryl. 231 (all greetings); P.Oxy. 300, 805; P.Amh. 133 (requests for replies). Such conventional postscripts are also common in the literary letters: Cicero *ad Fam.* xv.19; xiv.3; xvi.4; Fronto *ad Marc.* iii.3, 9, 12, etc. Such formal conventions are often linked syntactically to the final wish.

[49]More extensive postscripts of some substance are found in P.Giess. 97; *BGU* 665; P.Fay. 119, for example, and, among literary letters, Cicero *ad Fam.* x.21; xi.1; xiv.1; xvi.15, 19; *ad Att.* iii.22; xi.4A; Fronto *ad Marc.* iii.8; iv.2; *ad Anton.* i.1; among many others.

[50]Cicero's postscripts are often motivated by the reception of news or of a letter after completing his own letter. See *ad Fam.* xii.12; xvi.15; *ad Att.* viii.12C; xii.11: xv.6, 29; xvi.15. For recollection of an overlooked matter, see Fronto *ad Marc.* iii.4.

The leading idea is the writer's concern about the circumstances and activities of the addressee and the desire for information through a letter. The common form of the request is γράφε περὶ τῆς σωτηρίας, with additional phrases supplying motivations.[51] We may also mention that the epistolary conclusions frequently contain admonitory remarks, exhorting the addressee to carry out the instructions or abide by the requests laid down in the letter body. The content of these remarks is too varied to be characterized more precisely, but among them we often meet the stereotyped phrase, μὴ οὖν ἄλλως ποιήσῃς ("do not do otherwise"), which is often found alone, but sometimes accompanied by a specification of what is to be observed, or by a motivation.[52]

H. Summary

We may summarize this overview by saying that available materials show that a large number of formal and stylistic elements belonged properly within the epistolary conclusion. The use of these elements was selective—it is rare that a letter contains almost all the possible components—and selection was made in accordance with the exigencies of the particular situation and the style of the writer. There is, however, a generally consistent order in which the selected elements are ranged: greeting, health wish, final wish and date. Admonitions and requests for letters usually precede all of these formulaic items. This progression of elements tends to be maintained no matter what particular formulae are omitted—except, of course, when a greeting or health wish is appended as a postscript.

Conclusions of the Pauline Letters

As in the ancient letters generally, so also in Paul's letters the greatest stylization, the most concentrated use of formalized phrases, appears at the beginning and in conclusion. While Paul's use of current epistolary conventions is quite obvious at the beginnings of his letters, it is less so in their conclusions, since here we lack, for the most part, a readily evident identity or similarity of terminology and form with the comparative materials. Apart from the greeting formulae, the disparity between the Pauline and the common epistolary conclusions seems large. But, as we shall see, this disparity is more apparent than real. Our procedure will be to discuss individually the various features of the Pauline conclusions, and then to seek whatever structure may govern the conclusions.

A. The Grace-Benediction

The most obvious, frequent and formally consistent element of the Pauline epistolary conclusions is the χάρις benediction. Its uniformity of phraseology,

---

[51]On this request, see Koskenniemi, 68–75. Generally it is aimed at promoting continued correspondence by assuring the reader that a reply will be well received.

[52]See, e.g., *BGU* 824, 884; P.Fay. 109, 110, 111, 112, 115, 116, 118; P.Ryl. 230; P.Oxy. 745; P.Lond. 356; P.Tebt. 408, 411. Compare the admonition, similar in intent, μὴ ἀμελήσῃς, also found in conclusions, as in P.Oxy. 742, 1665. The specification of what is to be observed can be very general, referring to the whole letter (*BGU* 844: ὑπὲρ ὧν σοι γράφοι). For motivations cf. P.Oxy. 745 (οἶδα δὲ ὅτι πάντα καλῶς ποιήσεις); P.Lond. 356 (ἐὰν γὰρ ἄλλως ποιήσεις . . . γίνωσκε σαυτὸν ἕξοντα πρὸς ἐμέ); and P.Ryl. 230 (μὴ ἵνα δόξωμέν σε εὐθέως ἠλλάχθαι τὰ πρὸς ἡμᾶς).

65

structure and position is clear from the following listing:

1 Cor 16:23	ἡ χάρις τοῦ κυρίου Ἰησοῦ μεθ' ὑμῶν.
2 Cor 13:13	ἡ χάρις τοῦ κυρίου Ἰησοῦ Χριστοῦ καὶ ἡ ἀγάπη τοῦ θεοῦ καὶ ἡ κοινωνία τοῦ ἁγίου πνεύματος μετὰ πάντων ὑμῶν.
Gal 6:18	ἡ χάρις τοῦ κυρίου ἡμῶν Ἰησοῦ Χριστοῦ μετὰ τοῦ πνεύματος ὑμῶν, ἀδελφοί· ἀμήν.
Phil 4:23	ἡ χάρις τοῦ κυρίου Ἰησοῦ Χριστοῦ μετὰ τοῦ πνεύματος ὑμῶν.
1 Thes 5:28	ἡ χάρις τοῦ κυρίου ἡμῶν Ἰησοῦ Χριστοῦ μεθ' ὑμῶν.
2 Thes 3:18	ἡ χάρις τοῦ κυρίου ἡμῶν Ἰησοῦ Χριστοῦ μετὰ πάντων ὑμῶν.
Phlm 25	ἡ χάρις τοῦ κυρίου Ἰησοῦ Χριστοῦ μετὰ τοῦ πνεύματος ὑμῶν.
Rom 16:20b	ἡ χάρις τοῦ κυρίου ἡμῶν Ἰησοῦ μεθ' ὑμῶν.
Rom 16:24	ἡ χάρις τοῦ κυρίου ἡμῶν Ἰησοῦ Χριστοῦ μετὰ πάντων ὑμῶν. ἀμήν.
Eph 6:24	ἡ χάρις μετὰ πάντων τῶν ἀγαπώντων τὸν κύριον ἡμῶν Ἰησοῦν Χριστὸν ἐν ἀφθαρσίᾳ.
Col 4:18b	ἡ χάρις μεθ' ὑμῶν.
1 Tim 6:21b	ἡ χάρις μεθ' ὑμῶν.
2 Tim 4:22b	ἡ χάρις μεθ' ὑμῶν.
Tit 3:15b	ἡ χάρις μετὰ πάντων ὑμῶν.
Heb 13:25	ἡ χάρις μετὰ πάντων ὑμῶν.
Rev 22:21	ἡ χάρις τοῦ κυρίου Ἰησοῦ μετὰ πάντων.

Although there are close similarities among these benedictions, certain distinctions are not to be overlooked. The use of the modifier τοῦ κυρίου (ἡμῶν) Ἰησοῦ (Χριστοῦ) is confined to the undisputed letters, but including 2 Thessalonians, whereas the deutero-Paulines use ἡ χάρις absolutely.[53] While the object of the benediction is always introduced with μετά, the object is variously expressed, but a second-person reference to the addressees is never absent.[54]

Since the verb is constantly elided, it is a question whether the force of the clause is indicative (ἔστιν) or optative (εἴη). Previous discussions of this issue have gone wrong from the outset by setting up the alternatives "pious wish" or "declarative statement," and attempting to make the benediction fit one of these categories.[55] But the grace-benediction is neither wish nor statement; it is a blessing,

[53]The genitive denotes source; although Paul ordinarily speaks of God as the source of grace, he does on occasion refer to Christ in this way (2 Cor 8:9, Gal 1:6, 2 Thes 1:12). But the latter usage seems to be especially characteristic of the epistolary introductions and conclusions.

[54]Among the Paulines and deutero-Paulines the personal reference lacks only in Eph 6:24 with its expansive designation of the objects of the benediction. Cf. among the papyrus letters P.Fay. 118, ἀσπάζου τοὺς φιλοῦντές σε πάντες πρὸς ἀληθίαν; BGU 984 substitutes ἀγαπᾶν for φιλεῖν in this formula; cf. also Tit 3:15b. Personal reference is present in Heb 13:25, but probably absent in Rev 22:21, which is textually uncertain.

[55]On this basis most have favored the declarative (indicative) sense. Thus W. C. van Unnik, "Dominus Vobiscum; the Background of a Liturgical Formula," New Testament Essays in Memory of T. W. Manson (ed. A. J. B. Higgins; Manchester, 1959) 270–305, esp. 291; C. F. D. Moule, Worship in the New Testament (London, 1961) 78; Gerhard Delling, Worship in the New Testament (Philadelphia, 1962) 75. Van Unnik argues that to understand the benediction as a wish would not accord with "the certitude of Paul's faith" while Delling starts from 1 Cor 16:24, where Paul communicates his love to the

and as such it incorporates aspects of both. Its wish character remains intact, even though qualified by confidence of its effectiveness. That it is not simply a statement of fact is supported by epistolary considerations. In every letter the grace-benediction stands in the final position.[56] Functionally, then, it serves to bring the letter to a definitive conclusion and corresponds in this respect to the ἔρρωσο of the secular letter, which is a wish.[57]

The question of the origin of this formula admits no easy answer. A concluding grace-benediction is not unique to the Pauline and deutero-Pauline letters, but is found also in Revelation (22:21), Hebrews (13:25) and 1 Clement (65:2). The prevalence and similarities of these benedictions, and the widespread view that Paul's letters were intended to be read in the gathered (liturgical) assembly, have led to the assumption that Paul did not create the grace-benediction formula but appropriated it from the liturgy of the primitive church.[58] We will not enter here a discussion of this possibility, but will be content for the moment simply to regard the epistolary use of the benediction as a Christian innovation.[59]

Though grace-benedictions are used in letters other than Paul's, the undisputed Pauline occurrences stand apart by reason of their consistent three-member pattern, which includes the genitive qualification and the personal reference to the addressees. Within this pattern, Paul exercises freedom in varying the christological phrase, in naming the objects of the blessing and in expanding the benediction.[60] Thus, whatever its origin, the expression of the wish was not rigidly fixed.

B. The Wish of Peace

Hardly less characteristic of the Pauline conclusions than the grace-benediction is what may be termed the wish of peace. Among the undisputed letters this is absent only in 1 Corinthians and Philemon.

Corinthians, reasoning that this statement must have indicative force and so, by analogy, must the grace-benediction which precedes it. But 1 Cor 16:24 is very likely itself a wish. It is likewise tenuous to argue for a declarative sense on the basis of the presumed character of "Paul's faith." On the ellipsis of the copula in these and related passages see F. Blass and A. Debrunner, *A Greek Grammar of the New Testament and Other Early Christian Literature* (trans. and rev. by Robert W. Funk; Chicago, 1961) 70–71.

[56]1 Cor 16:24 is an exception but does not alter the case. On the proper positions of the grace-benedictions at the end of Romans (16:20b, 16:24) see below, 129–132.

[57]There is every reason to believe that the prescriptive greeting of the Pauline letters, χάρις ὑμῖν καὶ εἰρήνη, also should be understood as a blessing, not simply as a declaration. Though the verb is always absent in Paul, elsewhere optative forms are found in similar formulae; cf. 1 Pet 1:2, 2 Pet 1:2, Jude 2, Dan 4:1 (LXX).

[58]Thus, among numerous commentators, L. G. Champion, *Benedictions and Doxologies in the Epistles of Paul* (Oxford, 1934) 29; Delling, *Worship in the New Testament*, 74–75; Werner Kramer, *Christ, Lord, Son of God* (SBT 50; Naperville, Ill., 1966) 90–91; P. E. Langevin, *Jésus seigneur et l'eschatologie: exégèse de textes prépauliniens* (Paris, 1967) 191–92.

[59]See below, pp. 143–44.

[60]The additions are: Gal 6:18, adding ἀδελφοί; 1 Cor 16:24, supplementing the grace-benediction with ἡ ἀγάπη μου μετὰ πάντων ὑμῶν ἐν Χριστῷ Ἰησοῦ, and 2 Cor 13:13, where the grace-benediction is expanded by two further members, resulting in the tripartite formula. The first two of these are stylistically in accord with common epistolary usage (see above, 58). The third is more difficult, since here the formula as such is elaborated. But even those who favor liturgical derivation here have difficulty excluding the likelihood of Pauline expansion, especially in the third member by reason of the shift from the subjective to the objective genitive. See, e.g., Kramer, *Christ, Lord, Son of God*, 91–92. Even the parallel use of the genitives in the first two members is no sure sign that the second member also is not an addition.

In general it should be observed that the term εἰρήνη does not appear with great frequency in the Pauline letters, at least by comparison with the primary vocabulary of Pauline preaching. Within this restricted usage more than half of the occurrences are found in the epistolary framework, that is, in the opening salutations and the concluding peace-wishes.[61] Thus, it is not a matter merely of the occurrence of the term, but of its presence in obviously formulaic expressions. The texts of the peace-wishes are as follows:

Rom 15:33	ὁ δὲ θεὸς τῆς εἰρήνης μετὰ πάντων ὑμῶν· ἀμήν.
Rom 16:20a	ὁ δὲ θεὸς τῆς εἰρήνης συντρίψει τὸν Σατανᾶν ὑπὸ τοὺς πόδας ὑμῶν ἐν τάχει.
2 Cor 13:11	καὶ ὁ θεὸς τῆς ἀγάπης καὶ εἰρήνης ἔσται μεθ' ὑμῶν.
Phil 4:9b	καὶ ὁ θεὸς τῆς εἰρήνης ἔσται μεθ' ὑμῶν.
1 Thes 5:23	αὐτὸς δὲ ὁ θεὸς τῆς εἰρήνης ἁγιάσαι ὑμᾶς ὁλοτελεῖς, καὶ ὁλόκληρον ὑμῶν τὸ πνεῦμα καὶ ἡ ψυχὴ καὶ τὸ σῶμα ἀμέμπτως ἐν τῇ παρουσίᾳ τοῦ κυρίου ἡμῶν Ἰησοῦ τηρηθείη.
2 Thes 3:16	αὐτὸς δὲ ὁ κύριος τῆς εἰρήνης δῴη ὑμῖν τὴν εἰρήνην διὰ παντὸς ἐν παντὶ τρόπῳ.
Gal 6:16	καὶ ὅσοι τῷ κανόνι τούτῳ στοιχήσουσιν, εἰρήνη ἐπ' αὐτοὺς καὶ ἔλεος, καὶ ἐπὶ τὸν Ἰσραὴλ τοῦ θεοῦ.
Cf. Eph 6:23	εἰρήνη τοῖς ἀδελφοῖς καὶ ἀγάπη μετὰ πίστεως ἀπὸ θεοῦ πατρὸς καὶ κυρίου Ἰησοῦ Χριστοῦ.

From a comparison of these texts and their contexts several features of the peace-wish stand out. None of these wishes is final, but each stands within the epistolary conclusion, shortly before the final grace-benediction. With only one exception (Gal 6:16), εἰρήνη is brought into immediate connection with θεός (once κύριος) by means of a genitive construction, giving the constant designation ὁ θεὸς/κύριος τῆς εἰρήνης. On the other hand, the predicates of the peace-wishes are diverse. In three cases we have the simple μεθ' ὑμῶν, as in the grace-benedictions (Phil 4:9, 2 Cor 13:11, Rom 15:33). Among these the verb suffers ellipsis only once, while the other two employ the future indicative. The verb is absent also in the deviant form of Gal 6:16. For the rest we have more explicit and extensive predicates with transitive verbs, all in the optative. This verbal usage shows that in the peace-wishes, as in the grace-benedictions, we have to do with actual wishes (or blessings), not with indicative pronouncements. This holds true even where indicative forms are used, for these are always in the future tense.[62]

If now we enlarge our purview to include other Pauline and non-Pauline prayer-wishes, regardless of their particular content, it becomes evident that they share a number of features suggestive of a definite form. The additional texts are:

[61]Omitting Ephesians (8), Colossians (2) and the Pastorals (4), the term appears 29 times. Of these, 8 appear in the opening salutations and 8 belong properly to the conclusions. In 2 Corinthians εἰρήνη is found only in the framework, and in Galatians, Philippians, and 1 and 2 Thessalonians there is only one instance each outside the framework.

[62]It should be noted that in Rom 16:20a and in the wish of similar form in Phil 4:19 there is textual variation between the future indicative and the optative, which shows how closely related in meaning these verbal forms could be. In Rom 16:20a the future is read by most witnesses, but the optative by A, some Old Latin MSS and vg^c1; the optative is read in Phil 4:19 by D F G 1739 et al. On the other hand, the optative of 1 Thes 5:23 is read as future indicative by F G.

1 Thes 3:11–13 αὐτὸς δὲ ὁ θεὸς καὶ πατὴρ ἡμῶν καὶ ὁ κύριος ἡμῶν
       Ἰησοῦς κατευθύναι τὴν ὁδὸν ἡμῶν πρὸς ὑμᾶς· ὑμᾶς
       δὲ ὁ κύριος πλεονάσαι καὶ περισσεύσαι τῇ ἀγάπῃ εἰς
       ἀλλήλους καὶ εἰς πάντας, καθάπερ καὶ ἡμεῖς εἰς ὑμᾶς,
       εἰς τὸ στηρίξαι ὑμῶν τὰς καρδίας ἀμέμπτους ἐν
       ἁγιωσύνῃ ἔμπροσθεν τοῦ θεοῦ καὶ πατρὸς ἡμῶν ἐν τῇ
       παρουσίᾳ τοῦ κυρίου ἡμῶν Ἰησοῦ μετὰ πάντων ἁγίων
       αὐτοῦ.

2 Thes 2:16–17 αὐτὸς δὲ ὁ κύριος ἡμῶν Ἰησοῦς Χριστὸς καὶ ὁ θεὸς ὁ
       πατὴρ ἡμῶν, ὁ ἀγαπήσας ἡμᾶς καὶ δοὺς παράκλησιν
       αἰωνίαν καὶ ἐλπίδα ἀγαθὴν ἐν χάριτι, παρακαλέσαι
       ὑμῶν τὰς καρδίας καὶ στηρίξαι ἐν παντὶ ἔργῳ καὶ
       λόγῳ ἀγαθῷ.

2 Thes 3:5   ὁ δὲ κύριος κατευθύναι ὑμῶν τὰς καρδίας εἰς τὴν
       ἀγάπην τοῦ θεοῦ καὶ εἰς τὴν ὑπομονὴν τοῦ Χριστοῦ.

Rom 15:5–6   ὁ δὲ θεὸς τῆς ὑπομονῆς καὶ τῆς παρακλήσεως δώῃ
       ὑμῖν τὸ αὐτὸ φρονεῖν ἐν ἀλλήλοις κατὰ Χριστὸν
       Ἰησοῦν, ἵνα ὁμοθυμαδὸν ἐν ἑνὶ στόματι δοξάζητε τὸν
       θεὸν καὶ πατέρα τοῦ κυρίου ἡμῶν Ἰησοῦ Χριστοῦ.

Rom 15:13   ὁ δὲ θεὸς τῆς ἐλπίδος πληρώσαι ὑμᾶς πάσης χαρᾶς καὶ
       εἰρήνης ἐν τῷ πιστεύειν, εἰς τὸ περισσεύειν ὑμᾶς ἐν τῇ
       ἐλπίδι ἐν δυνάμει πνεύματος ἁγίου.

Phil 4:19   ὁ δὲ θεός μου πληρώσει πᾶσαν χρείαν ὑμῶν κατὰ τὸ
       πλοῦτος αὐτοῦ ἐν δόξῃ ἐν Χριστῷ Ἰησοῦ.

(Cf. also 1 Pet 5:10; Heb 13:20–21; Barn 21:5.)

We note first the almost invariable use of post-positive δέ in these wishes, for which καί is substituted in two instances (2 Cor 13:11; Phil 4:9). The consistency of this usage speaks against its being a stylistic proclivity of any one author; it must belong to the form.[63] Its moderately disjunctive force serves to set the wish off from the context and adds a note of solemnity.[64]

Quite noticeable is the marked tendency of these wishes to elaborate on the divine name, especially by means of the genitive attribute but also by means of the participial clause.[65] Paul's clear preference is for the genitival phrase, the content of

[63]The post-positive δέ also functions as an introductory particle in doxologies of the frequent type τῷ δὲ.... Cf. Phil 4:20; Eph 3:20–21; Rom 16:25–27; Jude 24–25; Mart Pol 20:2. Although Robert Jewett ("The Form and Function of the Homiletic Benediction," *ATR* 51 [1969] 18–34) supposes that in these prayer-wishes δέ has a connective function, it seems from its consistent presence to have no real syntactical function, but to be intrinsic to the form.

[64]The occasional addition of αὐτός, which among the Pauline wishes is present only in the Thessalonian letters, has no obvious basis and is difficult to render satisfactorily. Since it appears elsewhere in similar wishes we may regard it as an optional formal element, functioning, perhaps, to heighten the solemnity of the wish. αὐτός rarely occurs in the NT with θεός. We can only conjecture the reason for its use in wishes of this type. Possibly the expression αὐτὸς δὲ ὁ... is an Aramaism, αὐτός being used proleptically to "anticipate for the sake of emphasis a following noun." Cf. Matthew Black, *An Aramaic Approach to the Gospels and Acts* (Oxford, 1946) 70. G. Harder (*Paulus und das Gebet* [Gütersloh, 1936] 26 n. 4) finds in the phrase a third person equivalent to the second person address of the LXX Psalms, σὺ δέ, and the Greek rendering of אתה הוא; similarly Martin Dibelius (*An die Thessalonicher I II, an die Philipper* [HNT 3; Tübingen, 1911] 14). But a firm decision as to the basis of the use of αὐτός in these wishes is not possible.

[65]The participial clause is present in 1 Pet 5:10 and Heb 13:20, but both times together with the genitive modifier. In Barnabas the participial clause stands alone. It is noticeable that, whereas in the prayer-wish form the genitive attribution is the rule, in doxological formulae the participial clause and appositional title are preferred.

which he varies freely. As in the Pauline peace-wishes, so also in other wishes of the general type the predicates are variously framed. No two are identical throughout, although terms sometimes reappear.[66] Beyond the immediate import of a given wish, sometimes the purpose of the wish is also expressed by a ἵνα or an εἰς clause, but apparently this is not an indispensable element.[67] Taking all the features of these wishes into account, we can delineate a formal pattern, which to a greater or lesser degree holds good for all these prayer-wishes:

Introductory element	Subject	Modifiers	Wish	[Purpose clause]
(ὁ) δὲ or αὐτὸς δὲ (ὁ) or καὶ (ὁ)	θεός and/or κύριος	genitive phrase and/or participial clause	verb in optative or fut. ind.	ἵνα or εἰς

On the whole these wishes exhibit a fulsome manner of expression. In addition to the clear tendency to expand upon the 'divine name, this is seen in the multiplication of specific wishes[68] and in the extension of the scope of the wish.[69] Both the formal regularity and the expansive style of these prayer-wishes create a presumption that they bear a close relationship to liturgical usage.[70] This judgment extends, however, only to their form, not necessarily to their particular content, which varies widely, or to their positions within the letters, which seem to rest on epistolary needs.[71] What we have, then, is a common pattern which is taken up and

[66]Thus κατευθῦναι in 1 Thes 3:11 and 2 Thes 3:5; καταρτίζειν in Heb 13:21 and 1 Pet 5:10; στηρίζειν in 1 Thes 3:13, 2 Thes 2:17 and 1 Pet 5:10.

[67]See Rom 15:6, 13; 1 Thes 3:13; and Heb 13:21. A further optional element could be called a "ratifying supplement" to the prayer-wish. This takes no single form, but appears in Phil 4:20, Heb. 13:21 and 1 Pet 5:11 as a doxology; in 1 Thes 5:24 we have a word of assurance following the wish, and in 2 Thes 3:16 a second benediction follows the first.

[68]Especially 1 Pet 5:10; 1 Thes 3:11–13; Heb 13:20–21. In this respect Paul's wishes are usually simple and brief.

[69]Rom 15:33: μετὰ πάντων ὑμῶν; 1 Thes 3:12: εἰς ἀλλήλους καὶ εἰς πάντας; 1 Thes 5:23: ὁλοτελεῖς... τὸ πνεῦμα καὶ ἡ ψυχὴ καὶ τὸ σῶμα; 2 Thes 2:17: ἐν παντὶ ἔργῳ καὶ λόγῳ ἀγαθῷ; 2 Thes 3:16: διὰ παντὸς ἐν παντὶ τρόπῳ; Phil 4:19: πᾶσαν χρείαν; Heb 13:21: ἐν παντὶ ἀγαθῷ.

[70]Jewett ("The Form and Function of the Homiletic Benediction," 30) supposes, especially on the basis of Hebrews, where the doxology follows the prayer-wish, that the original setting of this type of wish was at the conclusion of the sermon. But the evidence does not suffice to show this.

[71]Nevertheless, it is often difficult to discover specific and firm ties between the prayer-wishes and their immediate contexts. The influence of the preceding contexts upon the specific wish is clearly visible in Phil 4:19; Rom 15:5–6; 2 Thes 3:5; and the general concern of 1 Thessalonians with the parousia is probably reflected in 1 Thes 5:23b. The peace-wishes are difficult to relate to the context especially in terms of their content.

Regarding the positions of these prayer-wishes within the letters, it may be said generally that they function as concluding elements of discrete parts of the letters. Thus, e.g., 1 Thes 3:11–13 is the conclusion of the extended thanksgiving period of 1 Thessalonians, and 2 Thes 2:16–17 ends the small thanksgiving period of 2:13–15. On these passages see Paul Schubert, *Form and Function of the Pauline Thanksgivings* (BZNW 20; Berlin, 1939) 18–22, 29–30; and Jack T. Sanders, "The Transition from Opening Epistolary Thanksgiving to Body in the Letters of the Pauline Corpus," *JBL* 81 (1962) 348–362. The formal request periods analyzed by Bjerkelund (*Parakalô*) are also sometimes concluded with such wishes: Rom 15:33; 16:17–20a. Other parts of the letters which are defined by subject matter rather than by formal structure can also be rounded off by such wishes: Rom 15:13, apparently concluding the whole section 14:1–15:12 (but cf. Rom 15:5–6); 2 Thes 3:5, closing 3:1–4; Phil 4:19, closing 4:10–18.

to some extent adapted to the context. Thus we can recognize that the peace-wishes within the conclusions of the Pauline letters constitute a sub-group of a large number of prayer-wishes manifesting a high degree of stylistic uniformity.

ὁ θεὸς τῆς εἰρήνης is but one among several divine designations constructed with the genitive. This use of the genitive, together with the presence of the term εἰρήνη (שׁלום), suggests dependence on a Semitic model.[72] Still, for this particular designation there are only two non-Pauline parallels, T Dan 5:2, ἔσεσθε ἐν εἰρήνῃ, ἔχοντες τὸν θεὸν τῆς εἰρήνης, and Heb 13:20, where it occurs in a concluding prayer-wish. Thus little can be said of the tradition-history of the designation. From the appearance of this and similar phrases in prayer contexts, a liturgical derivation is possible.[73] But the important question for our purposes, given the fact that prayer-wishes of the same form are found at various points in the letters, is why the peace-wishes are present only in the epistolary conclusions. How is this to be explained?

For this, too, liturgical usage could be a precedent, since there is ample evidence of the liturgical use of peace-wishes (blessings and petitions) in Judaism, and a number of Jewish prayers exhibit the proclivity to place the peace petition at the close.[74] Yet it would be hasty to conclude from this that the Pauline peace-wishes depend even in substance on such liturgical usage, since ready analogies to them are also available in Semitic letters.[75]

[72]Harder (*Paulus und das Gebet,* 44–45, 65–66) has observed that designations formed on this pattern are frequent in Jewish prayer style, and especially in the Psalms of the LXX, e.g., Ps 4:2, ὁ θεὸς τῆς δικαιοσύνης; 17:47, ὁ θεὸς τῆς σωτηρίας; 30:6, ὁ θεὸς τῆς ἀληθείας; 58:6, ὁ θεὸς τῆς δυνάμεων; 61:8, ὁ θεὸς τῆς βοηθείας. On these genitival attributions see the comments and further examples of R. Deichgräber, *Gotteshymnus und Christushymnus in der frühen Christenheit; Untersuchungen zu Form, Sprach und Stil der frühchristlichen Hymnen* (Studien zur Umwelt des Neuen Testaments 5; Göttingen, 1967) 88–96.

[73]In 1 Cor 14:33, instructing the community on the proper order of worship, Paul concludes his remarks on the problem of prophetic utterances with the statement οὐ γάρ ἐστιν ἀκαταστασίας ὁ θεὸς ἀλλὰ εἰρήνης. The contrast between ἀκαταστασία and εἰρήνη is not completely natural; τάξις might perhaps have been expected instead of εἰρήνη. This, together with the liturgical subject matter of the context and what we have been able to discover about the prayer-wish form, suggests that Paul does not here coin an *ad hoc* divine designation but employs one known to the Corinthians from their own worship. Such is the conclusion of Deichgräber (*Gotteshymnus und Christushymnus in der frühen Christenheit,* 94–95), who assumes that this designation had a special connection with paraenesis. The designation could also have an apocalyptic background. This would accord well with its use in T Dan and 1 Cor 14:33 (prophecy), as well as with the presence in some of the peace-wishes of apocalyptic motifs (1 Thes 5:23 but esp. Rom 16:17–20, where "crushing Satan" points toward the conquest of the serpent promised in Gen 3:15; cf. T Levi 18:2; Rev 20:1–10). An apocalyptic derivation is supposed by Wolfgang Schenk, *Der Segen im Neuen Testament* (Theologische Arbeiten 25; Berlin, 1967) 92. The materials are too sparse for any more than conjectures.

[74]Thus the Aaronic benediction (Num 6:24–26), which enjoyed a long history of use in Temple and synagogue, has as its final element the petition for peace; in the *Shemoneh 'Esreh* the concluding benediction is one of peace, and similar petitions for peace, often in conclusion, characterize some of the old rabbinic prayers, e.g. the *Kaddish*. There was, then, a strong tendency in early Judaism to conclude prayers, homilies, lessons, etc. with words of peace. On this see the remarks of D. de Sola Pool (*The Kaddish* [New York, 1929] 70–71), who finds in this tendency the influence of the customary greeting of peace (cf. bBer 64a, bTa'an 9b, bMo'ed Katan 21b). Synagogue inscriptions also point to the use of liturgical peace-wishes; see Hans Lietzmann, "Zwei Notizen zu Paulus," *Kleine Schriften,* II, *Studien zum Neuen Testament* (ed. K. Aland; TU 68; Berlin, 1958) 284–291, esp. 286, and Carl H. Kraeling, *The Synagogue* (The Excavations at Dura Europa VIII, 1; New Haven, 1956) 263 ("Tile A").

[75]We have consulted the following collections: Arthur Cowley, ed., *Aramaic Papyri of the Fifth Century B.C.* (Oxford, 1923); Emil G. Kraeling, ed., *The Brooklyn Museum Aramaic Papyri; New Documents of the Fifth Century B.C. from the Jewish Colony at Elephantine* (New Haven, 1953); G. R. Driver, ed., *Aramaic Documents of the Fifth Century B.C.* (Oxford, 1954); P. Benoit, J. T. Milik and R.

In Near Eastern letters the best attested position of peace-wishes is in the prescript, where they function as the greeting in the formula מן ... ל ... שלום. Often the peace-wish is separated from the prescript and given independent statement in the formulae שלום ושררת שליא הושרת לך and שלום מראן אלה ישאל בכל אדן.[76] More pertinent is the use, less frequent but not seldom, of peace-wishes in the conclusions of such letters. This is attested quite early but among preserved letters is more customary at a later period, and in the letters from Wadi Murabba'at appears to be a rather firmly established epistolary convention which takes the form הוי שלום, once expanded to אהוה שלום לכל בית ישראל.[77] So there was a strictly epistolary precedent for the use of concluding peace-wishes, even though this is peculiar to Semitic letters and Greek letters under Semitic influence (e.g. 3 John 15, 1 Pet 5:14). But the position of peace-wishes in these letters is final, and they are therefore functionally equivalent to the ἔρρωσο of the Greek letter.

If we can only speculate as to the derivation of the Pauline peace-wish, we must be all the more attentive to its epistolary function. We must assume that the peace-wish has a particular function, for although prayer-wishes of the same form appear throughout Paul's letters the peace-wish occurs only in conclusion. That cannot be merely coincidental, especially since there is a general absence of any close ideological or syntactical connections between the peace-wishes and their contexts. This suggests that their presence is prompted by epistolary considerations alone. If we note that the wish of peace is the first formulaic item of the Pauline conclusions, and recognize it as being *mutatis mutandis* a wish for the welfare of the recipients (construing שלום in its broad Semitic sense), then in content and function it is closely analogous to the *formula valetudinis* which belongs to the conclusion of the common Hellenistic letter.[78] Thus we may speak of a non-epistolary form which has been adopted and adapted for epistolary use, being substituted for a common convention.[79]

In any case, it is evident that the peace-wish has become for Paul an

de Vaux, eds., *Discoveries in the Judean Desert,* II, *Les Grottes de Murabba'at, Texte* (Oxford, 1961). These collections are cited by the name of the editor only. For a recent and illuminating survey of Aramaic conventions cf. Joseph A. Fitzmyer, "Some Notes on Aramaic Epistolography," *JBL* 93 (1974) 201–225.

[76]"The peace (health, welfare) of your lordship may God (or: the gods) seek after at all times" (Cowley, nos. 17, 21, 30, 37, 38, 39, 40, 41; Kraeling, no. 13), and "I send you many greetings of peace and prosperity" (Driver, nos. 3 and 5; cf. Benoit *et al.,* no. 48 with the formula . . . דברי שלום מן, "Words of peace from . . ."

[77]Early attestation is seen in Cowley, no. 34 (cf. 41), which concludes: שלום ביתן ובניוי על אלהיא יהוונא בהן,"Peace be to your house and your children until the gods let us see (our desire) upon them." In later letters, for the brief formula see Benoit *et al.,* nos. 44, 46 and 48, and also two letters of a later find discussed by Y. Yadin, "The Expedition to the Judean Desert, 1960; Expedition D," *IEJ* 11 (1961) 36–52, esp. 40–50. The expanded formula is found in Benoit *et al.,* no. 42. These wishes constitute the final element and stand before the signature, if any. Almost every letter containing a final peace-wish exhibits a peace-wish in the prescript also. Final peace-wishes are regularly constructed with imperatival forms of היה.

[78]See above, 60–61.

[79]Thus we could legitimately speak here of a conflation of liturgical and epistolary elements, as has been suggested for the thanksgiving periods by James M. Robinson, "Die Hodajot-Formel in Gebet und Hymnus des Frühchristentums," in *Apophoreta: Festschrift für Ernst Haenchen* (BZNW 30; Berlin, 1964) 194–235, esp. 201–202. On the problem of liturgical elements in the letters, see below, 143–44.

Roller (66–67, 196–197) wished to regard the peace-wishes as marking the formal conclusion of the letter body, and thought this favored the equivalency in function with the *formula valetudinis.* While

epistolary convention which belongs to the style of his letters, properly within the epistolary conclusion. How integral it is may be suggested in that the prescriptive greeting of his letters, χάρις ὑμῖν καὶ εἰρήνη, is clearly echoed in the conclusions by the prayer-wish for peace and the grace-benediction. We might say that the letters are bracketed by a chiastic repetition of corresponding wishes.[80]

We may mention briefly now those letters which deviate from the norm in respect of the peace-wish. A peace-wish is present in Galatians (6:16), but in a variant form. The explicitly conditional formulation of this wish is obviously contingent on the strained epistolary situation, just as the opening elements are.[81] But even here we cannot speak of a completely free phrasing, for the pattern ἐπὶ . . . καὶ ἐπὶ . . . , with the second phrase enlarging upon the recipients of the wish, is characteristically Jewish. It appears frequently in blessings, but also as an epistolary formula.[82]

Among the undisputed letters the wish of peace in conclusion is absent only in Philemon and 1 Corinthians. There seem to be no clear grounds for the omission. On the other hand, it would be erroneous to posit a fixed number of elements which "should" invariably be used by a given writer. Style in letter writing is not so inflexible. We must be content to recognize and define what is possible and what is usual, but always allowing for limited variations.

C. The Greetings

The communication of greetings to the addressees is a regular aspect of the Pauline epistolary conclusion. Among the undisputed letters, Galatians alone lacks greetings of any sort, and in this deviation the effect of the epistolary situation is again to be seen.[83] Generally, the Pauline expressions of greeting stand within the formal possibilities evidenced in Hellenistic letters; indeed it is here that the similarity between the Pauline and the Hellenistic letter conclusions is most immediately

---

we also regard the two as having an identical function, it cannot be said that either serves consistently to close the body of the letter. In fact, in the common letter and in the Pauline letter a firm dividing line between body and conclusion is difficult to draw.

[80]That Paul merely appropriated these formulae singly from another context or that this structural correspondence is only coincidental seems most unlikely; we more probably have to do with the creative forging of a distinctive epistolary framework. The association in the epistolary conclusions of grace with Christ and of peace with God speaks in favor of the suggestion of R. Gyllenberg ("De inledande hälsningsformlerna i de paulinska breven," *SEA* 16 [1951] 21–31) that the terms of the prescriptive greeting, χάρις and εἰρήνη, are to be chiastically related to the sources named, God and Christ. The phrase "God our Father and the Lord Jesus Christ" is not found outside the introductory epistolary greetings. Elsewhere we have "the God and Father of our Lord Jesus Christ" (Rom 15:6; 2 Cor 1:3; 11:31; Eph 1:3, 17; Col 1:3). The simple conjunction of the two is a feature of prayer-wishes (cf. 1 Thes 3:11; 2 Thes 2:16; also Eph 6:23).

[81]See below, 89.

[82]For its (liturgical) use in blessings see above, 71 n. 74; for its epistolary use see above, 72. The phrase "the Israel of God" in this formula must denote the Christian church, as is shown by N. A. Dahl ("'Der Name Israel; Zur Auslegung von Gal. 6,16," *Jud* 6 [1950] 161–170), not Jewish Christians, as is held by G. Schrenk ("Der Segenswunsch nach der Kampfepistel," *Jud* 6 [1950] 170–190), and not the righteous remnant of the Jews, as suggested by E. de Witt Burton (*A Critical and Exegetical Commentary on the Epistle to the Galatians* [ICC; New York, 1920] 358). Peter Richardson (*Israel in the Apostolic Church* [NTSMS 10; Cambridge, 1969] 74–84) prefers to think of "those within Israel to whom God will show mercy" (82). His arguments will not stand, however, against Dahl's interpretation (which, incidentally, Richardson misunderstands).

[83]Greetings are also absent in the deutero-Pauline Ephesians and 1 Timothy.

obvious. Still, within the Pauline greetings there is a considerable diversity of form and scope which requires examination.[84]

Paul shares with the Hellenistic letters the basic formula of greeting composed of ἀσπάζεσθαι with the object. All instances of the verb in Paul are either imperative or third person indicative; Paul never employs the first person form of greeting, ἀσπάζομαι, which is found in the NT only in the greeting of the scribe Tertius in Rom 16:22. This verbal usage accords well with what we find in the common letters.

Equally consistent with Hellenistic practice are Paul's elaborations on the basic elements. These take several forms, and serve the following purposes: (a) to intensify the verb (thus 1 Cor 16:19, ἀσπάζεται . . . πολλά); (b) to specify the verb in some way (thus again 1 Cor 16:19, ἀσπάζεται . . . ἐν κυρίῳ, and Phil 4:21, ἀσπάσασθε . . . ἐν Χριστῷ Ἰησοῦ, the verb being "christianized" by the additions[85]); (c) in the case of third person forms, to identify the ones greeting, either by name only (1 Cor 16:19-20; 2 Cor 13:13) or more frequently by name and some descriptive phrase which makes the identity more exact (thus Phil 4:21, οἱ σὺν ἐμοὶ ἀδελφοί; 4:22, πάντες οἱ ἅγιοι, μάλιστα δὲ οἱ ἐκ τῆς Καίσαρος οἰκίας; Phlm 23-24, Ἐπαφρᾶς ὁ συναιχμάλωτός μου ἐν Χριστῷ Ἰησοῦ; cf. further Rom 16:21-23); and (d) to identify by name and/or personal description those who are greeted, but apart from the single instance of Col 4:15 this occurs only in Rom 16.

In addition to greetings which conform to the basic pattern, we encounter several times a completely different greeting formula, namely ὁ ἀσπασμὸς (γέγραπται) τῇ ἐμῇ χειρὶ Παύλου (1 Cor 16:21; 2 Thes 3:17; Col 4:18). Many have assumed that ὁ ἀσπασμός must refer to something outside this clause, and in particular to the grace-benediction, which is regarded consequently as Paul's personal greeting.[86] But it is not at all necessary to suppose that ὁ ἀσπασμός points forward to the grace-benediction, which is actually no "greeting" at all, but the final wish. The greeting consists simply in the statement that Paul now sends greeting in his own hand. Ὁ ἀσπασμὸς ἐν τῇ ἐμῇ χειρὶ Παύλου is therefore equivalent to "I (hereby) greet you in my own hand."

Several features of Paul's concluding greetings deserve special notice. In terms of verbal usage, the imperative form ἀσπάσασθε appears a total of twenty times, the indicative forms only ten. But this computation is misleading until the greetings are considered letter by letter, for then it appears that outside of Rom 16 imperative forms are found only four times, and three of these belong in the requests for the exchange of the kiss. We are left with only one instance, outside of Romans, of a common epistolary greeting expressed with the imperative (Phil 4:21). Further, all of the indicative forms convey the greetings of others, whether of individuals (1 Cor 16:19; Phlm 23; Rom 16:21-23), of well-defined groups (Phil 4:21-22; 1 Cor 16:19), or of general groups (Phil 4:21; 2 Cor 13:13; 1 Cor 16:19-20; Rom

---

[84]On what follows, cf. the latter half of Mullins' article, "Greeting as a New Testament Form," 423-26.

[85]In the greeting with the holy kiss, the elaboration ἐν φιλήματι ἁγίῳ may be regarded as a specification of the *means* of greeting.

[86]Thus, e.g., Ziemann, 364-65, Roller, 70, 165-66. This misunderstanding rests in large part on a faulty reading of 2 Thes 3:17.

74

16:16). In all of this it is especially striking how small a role is played by Paul's personal greetings. Romans aside, in the other letters we have to reckon only with Phil 4:21 and the different formula found in 1 Cor 16:21; 2 Thes 3:17 and Col 4:18. It is also noteworthy that apart from Romans there is no individualization of the recipients of greetings through naming names or adding descriptive phrases.[87]

In the later letters it can be observed that Paul conveys to the addressees the greetings of his constituency as Apostle to the Gentiles. Paul is the agent of the greetings of "all the saints" (Phil 4:22; 2 Cor 13:13), "all the brethren" (1 Cor 16:20), "the churches of Asia" (1 Cor 16:19), and even "all the churches of Christ" (Rom 16:16). Thus Paul himself sums up and communicates the sentiment of his churches. These comprehensive greetings not only provide an insight into Paul's conception of his apostolic status, but show that he conceived of his letters as serving, among other things, the unity and fellowship of the whole church.

D. The Greeting with the "Holy Kiss"

The request that the addressees exchange the "holy kiss" (φίλημα ἅγιον) is found four times in Paul, always in the epistolary conclusion (1 Thes 5:26; 1 Cor 16:20b; 2 Cor 13:12; Rom 16:16), but elsewhere in the NT only in 1 Pet 5:14, with the designation "kiss of love" (φίλημα ἀγάπης). In every case the request is made with ἀσπάσασθε, and the object of the action is ordinarily expressed with ἀλλήλους, a variant being τοὺς ἀδελφοὺς πάντας in 1 Thes 5:26.[88]

Again, it has often been supposed that the kiss is requested in the letters as preparatory and introductory to the eucharistic celebration, and is therefore to be understood as a specifically cultic action drawn from liturgical usage.[89] But consideration of the request for the kiss should take its starting point in the present epistolary contexts rather than in speculation on its derivation. In every case[90] it stands in immediate connection with the epistolary greetings and is introduced with the verb of greeting.[91] Since concluding greetings are a convention of the Hellenistic letter it is precarious to build too much merely on the position of the request for the kiss at the end of the letters, as though this assured a liturgical function. Although we cannot be certain of the precise significance of the kiss, the verbal parallelism and the constant connection with actual epistolary greetings suggest that in the holy kiss we have to do above all with a real greeting, although in this case it is not

---

[87]Colossians, often mentioned as a parallel to Romans in respect of the greetings, singles out as the object of greeting only one person (Nympha, 4:15). The greetings of Colossians are primarily from others, and these are named.

[88]The question may be raised, in view of Paul's use of this verb for greeting (see above, 74). whether Phil 4:21a might be a request for the exchange of the kiss, even though this is not specified. This is the only place outside the requests for the exchange of the kiss where the imperative verb is used with a general object.

[89]Thus G. Bornkamm, "The Anathema in the Early Christian Lord's Supper Liturgy," *Early Christian Experience* (New York, 1969) 169–176; and J. A. T. Robinson, "The Earliest Christian Liturgical Sequence?," *Twelve New Testament Studies* (SBT 34; Naperville, Ill., 1962) 154–57; cf. also the monograph of K. M. Hofmann, *Philema Hagion* (Beiträge zur Förderung christlicher Theologie 38; Gütersloh, 1938) 23–26.

[90]Except 1 Thes 5:26, where there are no other greetings.

[91]The translation suggested by H. Windisch, ἀσπάζομαι, *TDNT* I, 501, "embrace one another with the holy kiss," may convey the nature of the action, but obscures the verbal continuity.

merely a spoken greeting but a greeting extended in a formal and tangible way as a communal act.[92] Therefore it is possible to think of the exchange of the kiss as a concrete actualization of the greetings given in the letter, as a sign of fellowship within the community, of the community with the Apostle, and indeed of one community with others.[93] Thus, as far as the letters are concerned, there is no need to ascribe a formal liturgical significance to the action of the kiss. We should think only of an act of mutual greeting, a visible sign and seal of fellowship within the congregation on any occasion. On the other hand, because of the consistent designation of the action and the absence of any explanation of what is meant by it, we must assume that the kiss was customary in the communities. But granting that, a formal liturgical usage in any special connection cannot be determined.

E. The Autographic Conclusion

That at least some of Paul's letters originally exhibited the Apostle's own handwriting is shown by remarks in the conclusions of several letters that at a given point it is no longer the amanuensis who writes but Paul himself. Three times in letters attributed to Paul we meet with the formula mentioned earlier, ὁ ἀσπασμὸς τῇ ἐμῇ χειρὶ Παύλου (1 Cor 16:21; 2 Thes 3:17; Col 4:18). To this we may now add Gal 6:11, Ἴδετε πηλίκοις ὑμῖν γράμμασιν ἔγραψα τῇ ἐμῇ χειρί, and Phlm 19, ἐγὼ Παῦλος ἔγραψα τῇ ἐμῇ χειρί. For the remaining letters there are no explicit indications that the concluding remarks were written in Paul's own hand. The presence and absence of these notices raise several related questions: did Paul customarily provide his letters with autographic conclusions; what in the various letters is to be reckoned to the autograph; what were the motives for Paul's use of autographic conclusions?

The question whether Paul habitually concluded his letters with his own hand presupposes that amanuenses were employed for all the letters.[94] This is certain at least for the letters containing explicit references to Paul's hand which distinguish between what is written by Paul and what by the amanuensis.[95] Even in

[92]Kissing as a social custom of greeting in Semitic and Hellenistic antiquity is not to be forgotten here, and may be the immediate origin of the "holy kiss" in Christian communities.

[93]Lyder Brun, *Segen und Fluch im Urchristentum* (Skrifter utgitt av Det Norske Videnskaps-Akademi i Oslo, II, Hist.-Filos. Klasse, 1932, 1; Oslo, 1932) 67–68; cf. also Hofmann, *Philema Hagion,* 20. The close connection between the kiss-greeting and the greetings from other communities is to be noted (Rom 16:16; 1 Cor 16:20; 2 Cor 13:12–13; cf. Phil 4:21–22).

[94]This seems to be generally accepted. For the several modes of dictation used in antiquity see A. Eschliman, "La redaction des épîtres pauliniennes," *RB* 53 (1946) 185–196; Gordon J. Bahr, "Paul and Letter Writing in the First Century," *CBQ* 28 (1966) 465–477; and O. Roller, 16–23, 153–187. All of these wish to allow for a considerable compositional role on the part of the amanuensis. Yet the vigor, individuality, and consistency of style in the undisputed letters, which often bears the marks of oral speech, favor the view that these were dictated in the verbatim mode. Nevertheless, the question of the possible uses of amanuenses and the types of dictation needs a fresh investigation.

[95]Roller (187–191) assumed on the basis of the explicit mention of autographic writing that 2 Thessalonians, Galatians, 1 Corinthians and Philemon were written entirely in Paul's hand, and that most of the latter part of Colossians was in Paul's hand. He reasoned that such explicit notices would be necessary only in letters written wholly or mostly by Paul himself, since otherwise the difference in writing would be obvious. In particular he refers (190) to a letter cited by Ziemann (365) which concludes, ἀσπάζομαί σε πλαγγών. ταῦτά σοι γέγραφα τῇ ἐμῇ χειρί. ἔρρωσο, where the reference seems to be to the letter body. Even if this is correct, Paul's mention of his own hand in the formula ὁ ἀσπασμὸς τῇ ἐμῇ χειρί has a much narrower reference. Where this particular formula lacks (Gal 6:11; Phlm 19) there is more room for question, but even in Gal 6:11 the idea of contrast comes through—

the case of Philemon, which is quite brief by comparison with Paul's other letters, it is probable that an amanuensis was used.[96] Did Paul, then, provide all his letters with autographic conclusions?

The most important single *text* for a decision on this matter is 2 Thes 3:17, where the formula ὁ ἀσπασμὸς (γέγραπται) τῇ ἐμῇ χειρὶ Παύλου is extended by the addition ὅ ἐστιν σημεῖον ἐν πάσῃ ἐπιστολῇ· οὕτως γράφω. The syntax of this statement is not completely transparent and it can be misconstrued. ὅ is not resumptive of ὁ ἀσπασμός, as though the greeting were a "token" in every letter,[97] nor is the grace-benediction to be equated with σημεῖον, as though the benediction were a constant sign.[98] The σημεῖον is rather simply the autographic manner of writing, and this is borne out by the next clause, οὕτως γράφω. Thus we should render: "Greeting in my own hand, Paul's, which [autograph] is a token in every letter. This is how I write." Leaving aside for the moment the question of the authenticity of 2 Thessalonians, the statement ὅ ἐστιν σημεῖον ἐν πάσῃ ἐπιστολῇ suggests that Paul always concluded his letters autographically, and therefore that we should suppose this to be the case also for those letters where there is no explicit acknowledgment of it.

Deissmann properly perceived the relevance of the papyrus letters for this possibility, for among them are letters which exhibit in their conclusions a change of hands, without this change being verbally noted.[99] Thus, that a change of hands is not always mentioned in Paul's letters is in itself no argument against the presence of an autograph in the original. On the other hand, the presence of an explicit acknowledgment, if it requires any explanation at all, can perhaps be accounted for on the basis of the epistolary situation.[100] In any case—and for this the authenticity of 2 Thessalonians is irrelevant—the facts that Paul's letters were dictated, that in antiquity dictated letters were customarily concluded autographically, and that for some of Paul's letters the autograph is clearly noted, are compelling arguments that the autographic conclusion was the rule for Paul.

The further question of how much of each letter was penned by Paul himself admits no simple or general answer but has to be decided with respect to the individual letters. In the cases of 1 Corinthians, 2 Thessalonians and Colossians, the formula ὁ ἀσπασμὸς τῇ ἐμῇ χειρὶ Παύλου, with its implied contrast, indicates that the autographic portion embraces only this formula and what follows it, which in each case is very brief. A more extensive autograph must be assumed for Galatians, where the words Ἴδετε πηλίκοις ὑμῖν γράμμασιν ἔγραψα τῇ ἐμῇ χειρί appear in 6:11. Again, the emphatic (Ἴδετε) contrast suggests that only at this point

Paul's handwriting is noticeably larger. Cf. S. Lyonnet, "De arte litteras exarandi apud antiquos," *VD* 34 (1956) 3–11. Moreover, in letters written entirely in the sender's hand, if there were to be an acknowledgment of the fact, it should be more precise, as in fact it is in P.Gren. II, 89 with the phrase ὁλόγραφον χειρὶ ἐμῇ, as noted by A. Oepke, *Der Brief des Paulus an die Galater* (Theologische Handkommentar zum Neuen Testament 9; 2nd ed.; Berlin, 1957) 157.

[96]On this, see below, 79.

[97]σημεῖον in this verse is perhaps to be taken in a technical sense, analogous to the σύμβολον given to letter carriers as proof of commission, and thus "token" is an appropriate rendering. See A. Deissmann, *Light from the Ancient East*, 166–67, and F. Preisigke, *Wörterbuch der griechischen Papyrusurkunden* (3 vols.; Berlin, 1925–31) III, 509–510, *s.v.*

[98]See above, 65–67. The benediction as such could hardly be a distinctive sign in any authenticating sense.

[99]*Light From the Ancient East*, 172.

[100]See below, 79, for possible specific motives of such verbal acknowledgment.

77

does Paul himself begin to write, so that 6:11–18 are autographic. The aorist is strictly epistolary and does not refer to anything preceding.[101] In Phlm 19 the words ἐγὼ Παῦλος ἔγραψα τῇ ἐμῇ χειρί have occasionally been thought to refer to the entire letter,[102] but this judgment seems to be based as much on the relative brevity of this letter as on the sense of vs. 19. It may be true that Philemon is sufficiently brief not to have required the service of an amanuensis, but that does not mean no amanuensis was used.[103] That a scribe was employed cannot be proved of course, but is probable by analogy with the other letters, especially those with similar acknowledgments of the presence of Paul's own hand.[104]

In those letters which lack explicit reference to the autograph we are without any sure means of discovering the extent of the autographic portion, which we assume to have been present. The brevity of the autographs among the papyrus letters, which is approximated in 1 Cor 16:21–24 (also 2 Thes 3:17–18), is not necessarily to be assumed for all the Pauline letters. The longer autograph of Galatians, paralleled by some of those in Cicero's letters, shows that a conclusion in the sender's own hand could be rather extensive.[105] The effort to determine their scope must rely on internal considerations, with attention also to features of style.

[101]Most patristic commentators took 6:11 to mean that Paul wrote the whole letter himself. Thus also George S. Duncan, *The Epistle of Paul to the Galatians* (New York, 1934) 189. Other modern commentators have supposed that the autograph might have begun at 5:2 instead, but the strong statement of contrast in 6:11 makes that most unlikely. The commencement of a new line of thought and the strong first-person statement of 5:2 are insufficient indices for an autograph.

[102]Thus, e.g., J. B. Lightfoot, *Saint Paul's Epistles to the Colossians and to Philemon* (3rd ed.; London, 1900) 342.

[103]M. Dibelius (*An die Kolosser, Epheser, an Philemon* [HNT 12; 3rd ed. rev. by H. Greeven; Tübingen, 1953] 107) suggested that, in view of the resumptive character of Phil 19b ff., only 19a may have been injected in Paul's hand. Similarly G. Friedrich in H. W. Beyer, *et al.*, *Die kleineren Briefe des Apostels Paulus* (NTD 8; Göttingen, 1965) 193.

[104]For the special motive of this acknowledgment, see below, 79.

[105]It has occasionally been suggested that in some of the Pauline letters lengthy autographic sections may be assumed. This view has recently been advocated anew by Bahr ("The Subscriptions in the Pauline Letters"), who proposes that in Paul's letters we may discover the presence originally not merely of autographic conclusions but of extensive autographic reiterations or "summaries" of the primary points contained in the letter body. He has sought to support this thesis both from ancient epistolary practice and from alleged indications to this effect within the Pauline letters.

Bahr has observed that ancient papyrus records (deeds, contracts, receipts, etc.) usually contain subscriptions in a hand distinct from that of the record body, written by the scribe, and that the subscriptions characteristically recapitulate the essence of the record and provide certification. This custom of adding reiterative subscriptions in records, which in itself is correctly noted, is supposed by Bahr to have been followed for actual *letters* as well, on the assumption that "in antiquity there was no sharp distinction in form between letters and records" and that "there was some confusion of the two formats" (p. 32).

It is perfectly true that we often find autographic conclusions in ancient letters. However, such "subscriptions" are usually brief and perfunctory, and are comprised mostly of formulaic items. If autographic remarks go beyond purely conventional items, the additional matters are usually incidental to the concerns of the letter body. Rarely indeed do they ever approach being "summaries" of the letter body. Moreover, Bahr is much too bold in positing a confusion of letter and record forms. In fact, while some very limited influence of letter form on the composition of records is apparent, no appreciable influence in the other direction is evident in the available materials, and the respective forms remain well defined and differentiated (see Roller, 49–54). Most damaging to his thesis is his neglect of the *function* of autographic subscriptions in records and letters: records, as legal documents, had to show that the terms of the agreement or transaction were recognized and accepted by the parties to it. But such a requirement is totally foreign to ordinary epistolary exchange.

The hypothesis is also inadequate from the point of view of the Pauline letters. Only Galatians exhibits in the autograph what might be termed a reiterative "summary." Bahr further minimizes the attractiveness of his view by suggesting autographic subscriptions of extraordinary scope (Rom 12–16;

For the motive of the Pauline autographic conclusions we need seek no further than the appropriateness of an autograph in dictated letters, which, as we have seen, was a stylistic custom in ancient letter writing. In several letters, however, Paul apparently employs the autograph with special nuances. In 2 Thessalonians there is some likelihood that the autograph is given specially formal prominence in view of the circulation of letters falsely attributed to Paul (cf. 2:2), and so gains a particular overtone of authentication.[106] In Philemon there is a very precise reason why Paul should have begun his autograph just with 19a, and why he should have called attention to it. In vs. 18, in attempting to prepare the way for the return of Onesimus to his master, Paul makes himself accountable to Philemon for whatever restitution may be required. As a (quasi-) legal commitment this required the personal certification of the one to be held liable, and this is what Paul adds in the form of an autographic asseveration (ἀποτίσω).[107] Thus the autograph here takes on a specifically legal aspect. In Galatians, the autographic portion is used for the purpose of adding special emphasis to what is said; this is the sense of the reference to the "large characters."[108] In all of these instances it is a matter of special uses to which a convention is put, and not of the basic motive for autographic conclusions generally. In other letters too we may have to reckon with particular uses of the autograph.[109]

Regarding the motive of authentication, Deissmann was correct in stating that the claim of an autographic conclusion is no disproof of authenticity, as though the author protested too much.[110] But it must also be observed that the claim of an autographic conclusion may not, *ipso facto,* be a guarantee of authenticity. This problem is especially acute in 2 Thessalonians and Colossians, for although each claims an autographic conclusion, serious doubts have been raised about their authenticity. If one or both of these letters is not from Paul, then the *claim* of an autograph presupposes either that the addressees would not be able to recognize Paul's handwriting or, what is perhaps more likely, that Paul's letters were available in copies in which only the claim, and not the autograph itself, would be evident. The second

---

2 Cor 10–13; Gal 5:2–6:18; Col 2:8–4:18; etc.), and even these are hardly to be regarded as "summaries." In these judgments Bahr relies heavily on connections which he perceives with earlier parts of the letters, but these are either debatable or of questionable importance. While Bahr is surely correct in affirming the presence of autographic conclusions, he has misjudged the pertinence of the comparative materials and has failed to give useful criteria for ascertaining the scope of the autographs. As a result, he has overestimated their extent and misconstrued their character.

[106]Cf. Béda Rigaux, *Saint Paul, Les épîtres aux Thessaloniciens* (EBib; Paris, 1956) 718; William Neil, *The Epistle of Paul to the Thessalonians* (Moffatt New Testament Commentary; London, 1950) 199; George Milligan, *St. Paul's Epistles to the Thessalonians; the Greek Text with Introduction and Notes* (London, 1908) 188. See above, n. 43.

[107]The appropriate comparative materials for this type of asseveration are the documentary pieces among the papyri for which autographic certification was necessary as a legal safeguard (see note 105). Eduard Lohse (*Colossians and Philemon* [Hermeneia; Philadelphia, 1971] 204) speaks of "a promissory note which is inserted in a parenthesis." There is an interesting parallel in Cicero *ad Fam.* v.8: "I would be happy for you to consider this document as having the force of a compact and not a mere letter" (*has litteras velim existimes foederis habituras esse vim, non epistulae*).

[108]Heinrich Schlier, *Der Brief an die Galater* (Meyer; 4th ed.; Göttingen, 1965) 280; A. Oepke, *Der Brief des Paulus an die Galater,* 158. Deissmann (*Bible Studies* [Edinburgh, 1901] 348–49) saw in the reference to large characters "a piece of amiable irony... calculated to make an impression on children," but this is discounted by the tone of the whole letter.

[109]See below, 93–94.

[110]*Light From the Ancient East,* 166–67; cf. Roller, 188.

possibility would have important consequences for the early history of the Pauline letters; if Colossians or 2 Thessalonians is not authentic, as many suppose with good reasons, they may have been composed in view of the fact that Paul's letters were already circulating in the form of copies, a situation which could have obtained at a relatively early date, depending on the date assigned to these letters.

F. Miscellaneous Elements

Thus far we have specified and described the most formulaic and frequent components of the Pauline conclusions. The content of the conclusions is not, of course, exhausted thereby, for in addition to the elements already mentioned we occasionally encounter further features which do not bear the impress of a fixed form or characterize the conclusions generally. Several of these may be noted here.

In the conclusions we often find final notices of a hortatory nature, and often these consist simply of a concatenation of imperatives. For the most part these resist precise definition; sometimes it is a matter only of general paraenetic remarks which have no impetus discernible from the concrete epistolary situation,[111] while elsewhere, or even in the same context, a specific connection between the hortatory remarks and the situation of the addressees is clear.[112] Nevertheless, their appearance in the conclusions accords with a similar tendency in the common letter. While these remarks have no set form or content, several groups of them are introduced with παρακαλῶ or an equivalent term, and share in the general form of the παρακαλῶ periods, which have been carefully described by Bjerkelund. He found, however, that several παρακαλῶ periods, namely 1 Thes 5:12–14, Phil 4:2–3, 1 Cor 16:15–18 and Rom 16:17–20, have two peculiarities which distinguish them from related requests: they do not contain the usual prepositional phrase (διά + genitive), and they are strictly concerned with relationships between the community addressed and specific individuals or groups.[113] This variant form seems, then, to be characteristic of *concluding* requests.

Not seldom do we find toward the end of Paul's letters—but not always within the conclusion as such, so far as it can be delimited—notices about Paul's own movements and/or those of his associates, especially as these include visits to the addressees.[114] Insofar as letters are substitutes for personal presence it is natural that in them we should have anticipations of actual personal presence, and that these should often be expressed toward the end of the letter where the epistolary situation, in its basic aspect of the separation of writer from addressee, comes increasingly into view.[115] Robert Funk has dealt at length with these passages under the rubric of "The Apostolic *Parousia*," seeking to characterize them in formal terms, and to

[111] 1 Thes 5:12–22; Phil 4:4–9; 1 Cor 16:13–14; 2 Cor 13:11. There may, of course, be connections with the concrete situations of the addressees which cannot be identified as such. Calvin Roetzel has recently attempted to show that these "imperative clusters" are motivated by and apply concretely to community problems, but his arguments are frequently hypercritical and generally unconvincing. See his study "I Thess. 5:12–28: A Case Study," in *SBL Seminar Papers* (1972) II, 367–383.

[112] 2 Thes 3:6–12; Gal 6:11–15; 2 Cor 13:5–10.

[113] Bjerkelund, *Parakalô*, 128.

[114] Relevant texts for the epistolary conclusions are 1 Cor 16:3–12; 2 Cor 13:1–10; Phlm 22; Rom 15:14–33; cf. also Eph 6:21–22; Col 4:7–9. For statements of the same type appearing elsewhere in the letters, see 1 Cor 4:14–21; 1 Thes 2:17–3:13; Phil 2:19–24; 2 Cor 8:16–23; 9:1–5.

[115] On this feature of the common letter, see Koskenniemi, 169–180, and Thraede, *passim*.

show by means of them that Paul understood his presence with his congregations in three "modes": that of the letter, that of his emissary and that of his personal presence.[116] For our purposes it must be noted that, in several of Paul's statements about third parties whom he expects to visit the addressees, we very likely have to do with statements about the carriers of the letters. In this way we understand 1 Cor 16:17–18 (Stephanus *et al.*), Phil 2:25–30 (Epaphroditus), probably 2 Cor 8:16–23, as well as Col 4:7–9 and Eph 6:21–22 (Tychicus in both cases). Carrier notices, usually of a very similar nature, frequently occur in the common letters, most often within the conclusion.[117]

Another element found in some of the Pauline conclusions is the request for prayer (Rom 15:30–33, 1 Thes 5:25, 2 Thes 3:1; cf. Col 4:3, Eph 6:18–20). Among the contemporary letters there are no real parallels to this.[118] There may be no direct connection between Paul's request and common epistolary usage, but a link may be conjectured with the requests for remembrance (in place of or in addition to the request for a letter) present in some of the common letters, usually in conclusion.[119] To be sure, Paul does not simply request to be remembered (but cf. Col 4:18), nor does he ask for letters; and yet prayer and remembrance are closely bound up in the Pauline letters.[120] But this is only a possible point of contact, not one to be pressed.

Finally, brief attention must be given to the strikingly unusual words which appear in the midst of the conclusion of 1 Corinthians, just after Paul's greeting and prior to the final wish: εἴ τις οὐ φιλεῖ τὸν κύριον, ἤτω ἀνάθεμα. Μαρανα θα (16:22). Both the content and the position of these words have given rise to a strong consensus that they are drawn from the primitive liturgy, where they functioned as formulae introductory to the eucharistic action.[121] The language is "un-Pauline" (esp. φιλεῖν) and traditional (Μαρανα θα), and partial parallels can be seen in Did 10:6 and Rev 22:15–21. The presence of ostensibly liturgical material at the conclusion of a letter would be well explained on the assumption that the letter was meant to be read before, and to lead into, the eucharistic celebration. It is unquestionable that the phrases in 16:22 are traditional formulae which Paul has taken up, but very dubious how far this judgment can be extended to the surrounding verses, in particular to the kiss-greeting and grace-benediction, both of which are standard items in the Pauline conclusion.[122] But it also deserves to be noticed that, whatever its

---

[116]"The Apostolic *Parousia*: Form and Significance," *Christian History and Interpretation: Studies Presented to John Knox* (ed. W. R. Farmer, C. F. D. Moule and R. R. Niebuhr; Cambridge, 1967) 249–268.

[117]See, for example, among the papyri: *BGU* 37, 1205; P.Fay. 109; P.Ryl. 604; in Cicero: *ad Fam.* viii.8, *ad Att.* i.19; v.3; vi.8; viii.11b; see also 1 Clem 65:1, and below, 87.

[118]Bjerkelund (*Parakalô*, 53–54) cites several Christian letters of the second to fourth centuries containing requests for prayer. The statement of W. G. Doty ("The Classification of Epistolary Literature," *CBQ* 31 [1969] 196) that "the προσεύχεσθε περὶ ἡμῶν of Heb 13:10 [correctly 13:18] is informed by the frequent mention of intercessory prayer in the non-Christian papyri" must refer to the proscynesis formulae, which, however, are introductory elements.

[119]On these see Koskenniemi, 123–26, with examples.

[120]Rom 1:9; Phil 1:3; 1 Thes 1:2; Phlm 4; Col 4:12.

[121]See the studies cited above, note 89.

[122]The parallels adduced in Revelation and the Didache pertain primarily to 16:22, and the only other formulaic element they contain is the reference to grace. This takes similar form in 1 Cor 16:23 and Rev 22:21, but has a different form and earlier position in Did 10:6. Yet the grace-benediction is always present in the Pauline letter conclusions, and in a form not duplicated elsewhere; but nowhere else is a liturgical or specifically eucharistic connection implied for it. Further, the supposed liturgical sequence in 1 Cor 16 is interrupted in vs. 21 with Paul's autographic greeting, a strictly epistolary feature which has no significance apart from the letter itself.

derivation, even the ban formula of 16:22 has parallels in the other Pauline conclusions. We may compare the conditional element of the ban formula with the conditional cast of Gal 6:16a, καὶ ὅσοι τῷ κανόνι τούτῳ στοικήσουσιν, and even more pertinently with 2 Thes 3:14a, εἰ δέ τις οὐκ ὑπακούει. . . .[123] The ban itself, ἤτω ἀνάθεμα, probably signifying separation from the community, is approximated by 2 Thes 3:14b, τοῦτον σημειοῦσθε, μὴ συναναμίγνυσθαι αὐτῷ, while in Gal 6:16 the condition, positively stated, is followed by a blessing instead of a curse.[124] 1 Cor 16:22 is not, then, out of character in purely epistolary terms. In any event, it is ill-advised to regard 1 Cor 16:20b–23 as a fixed and unitary liturgical sequence, or as serving a peculiarly liturgical function in the conclusion of the letter.

G. The Structure of the Pauline Conclusions

With the individual components of the Pauline conclusions in mind, we now inquire whether and to what extent these fall into a discernible pattern. A synoptic overview reveals that the primary formulaic elements are consistently ranged in a structural sequence.

We have seen that the grace-benediction always occupies the ultimate position, functioning as the final wish. The sole exception to this is furnished by 1 Corinthians, where the grace-benediction is followed by a wish of Paul's love (16:24). The latter is not a formal element, but only an *ad hoc* addition which is best regarded as a postscript.[125] The wish of peace, which we find in all but two of the undisputed letters, clearly belongs in the epistolary conclusions and nowhere else, and here this element always holds an earlier position. The greetings, absent only in Galatians, have their fixed place between the peace-wish and the grace-benediction when both are present. The request for the exchange of the kiss, when it appears, stands in immediate connection with the other greetings, so it too falls between peace-wish and grace-benediction. Even when the kiss request stands alone, as in 1 Thessalonians, it retains the position of the greetings, a fact which supports our understanding of the kiss-action as a concrete actualization of the epistolary greeting. Concluding hortatory remarks tend to precede all of these formulaic items, but the sequence of formal elements is occasionally interrupted by the insertion of a

---

[123]An interesting parallel among papyrus letters is furnished by P.Oxy. 1185 (second century), which toward the end reads εἰ δὲ μή γε ὃς ἂν ἀπειθήσει τούτῳ μου τῷ διατάγματι . . . (here the letter is broken off).

[124]See also the larger contexts of these verses (Gal 6:11–16; 2 Thes 3:6–15; and cf. 2 Cor 13:1–10). G. Delling ("Das Abendmahlsgeschehen nach Paulus," *Kerygma und Dogma* 10 [1964] 61–77, esp. 76), C. Spicq ("Comment comprendre φιλεῖν dans I Cor. xvi, 22?," *NovT* 1 [1956] 200–204, esp. 203–204), and E.-B. Allo (*Première Épître aux Corinthiens* [EBib; 2nd ed.; Paris, 1956] 468–69) have supposed that the use of the ban formula in 1 Cor 16:22 has its motivation in the epistolary situation and is meant to refer to definite persons in the Corinthian community. At least in the related texts specific motives are obvious. In a similar vein see C. F. D. Moule, "A Reconsideration of the Context of Maranatha," *NTS* 6 (1959–60) 307–310; he follows the lead of E. Peterson in wanting to regard the *maranatha* of 1 Cor 16:22 not as an invocation for the presence of the exalted Lord at the eucharist, but only as a sanction (reinforcement) of the preceding ban. See also Moule's remarks in his *Worship in the New Testament*, 43–44. Calvin Roetzel (*Judgment in the Community* [Leiden, 1972] 142–162) regards 16:22 as an "apostolic pronouncement" by means of which Paul reasserts the primary exhortation of the letter, referring to the epistolary situation as a whole.

[125]On the apparent deviation of Romans in this respect, see below, 88, 94.

brief warning or request.[126] Other less frequent and less formal items appear to have no fixed place. The pattern of the major components can be represented in the sequence:

 (1) Hortatory remarks
 (2) Wish of peace
 (3) Greetings
  (3a) Greeting with the kiss
 (4) Grace-benediction

No matter what else occurs in the conclusions or which of these formulaic elements is omitted, the sequence as such is never violated. The autograph, assumed to have been present in all the letters, does not regularly begin at any given point, so no constant scope can be assigned to it. The epistolary conclusions, then, show a high degree of regularity in components and structure. If this stylistic regularity is some-what less obvious in the conclusions than in the epistolary introductions, the con-clusions cannot be regarded as loose and disorderly conglomerations of random remarks. Yet despite their consistency, no two conclusions are alike in all respects—nor should we expect them to be. It is not their peculiarities, but their similarities which have importance for and explanation in epistolary style. This is the relatively constant factor in letter writing. The phenomenon of variations within a consistent pattern demonstrates the interaction of letter-style and letter-situation.

 Summarily, there is a perceptible similarity between the conclusions of the Hellenistic and Pauline letters. Yet this similarity is not mainly one of shared terminology or conventional formulae, but rather of general content, of functional correspondence between formal elements and of basic structure. In their conclusions as elsewhere, both the commonality and the distinctiveness of the style of the Pauline letters are illustrated. The distinctiveness reflects the freedom with which Paul elaborates or reforms the rather hackneyed conventions of the common letter. This free variation—we might say "creativity"—is scarcely to be paralleled among the papyrus letters, but finds interesting analogy in the "literary" letters, whose authors often found the stereotyped phraseology of the epistolary tradition in-adequate.[127] All the more did Paul, in adopting the letter form, also adapt it for the service of his gospel.

  [126] 1 Thes 5:25–27; Gal 6:17; 1 Cor 16:22; cf. Col 4:16–17. On Phil 4:10–20, see below, 94, 145–46. The injunctions of 1 Thes 5:27, Gal 6:17, and 1 Cor 16:22 have little or nothing in common by way of substance, but each is a solemn adjuration standing among the concluding formulae. Roetzel ("I Thess. 5:12–28: A Case Study," 376–77) considers them together as "apostolic pronouncements" which emphasize "the apostolic character of the letter itself." His observation gains force from the fact that the three letters containing such adjurations "lack a concluding reference to the arrival of the apostle himself," and to that extent we might suppose that these injunctions function to "underscore the importance of the letter as a whole as an apostolic event."

  [127] For reservations about the adequacy of common conventions and an inclination to improvise beyond them see, for example, Cicero's comment about the letter of recommendation (*ad Fam.* xiii.27): "It is permissible to use just the same terms again and again in sending you letters of this sort, thanking you for so diligently attending to my recommendations, which I have done in others and shall do again, I see. Nevertheless, I shall make every effort in my letters to do what you lawyers always do in your drafts, namely 'to do the same thing in a different way'" (*sic ego in epistulis de eadem re alio modo*). Cf. *ad Fam.* vii.6: "(In my letters) there is a recommendation of you, and not a conventional one, but one that expresses a clear sense of my high esteem for you" (. . . *commendationis tuae, nec ea vulgaris, sed cum aliquo insigni indicio meae erga te benevolentiae*). Cf. also *ad Fam.* xiii.15. The alteration or elaboration of standard formulae is often witnessed in Cicero, Pliny, and Fronto.

Romans 16 and the Pauline Conclusions

Thus far we have paid no particular attention to the Roman letter, having sought rather to base our description on letters for which, in their conclusions at any rate, there is no serious question of integrity.[128] Since Rom 16 is so often thought to have had no integral connection with the Roman letter, it must now be asked how Rom 16 appears by comparison with the other Pauline conclusions.

We must consider first the stylistic observations often brought into evidence for detaching ch. 16 from the Roman letter. It is frequently suggested that Romans in its present form exhibits several possible conclusions, and that one of these, 15:33, comprising the peace-wish, is to be regarded as the original and proper conclusion of the Roman letter, which is not supposed to have contained ch. 16. Yet our investigation has shown that the peace-wish of 15:33 cannot be understood as the final wish of the letter; everywhere else the peace-wish has a penultimate, never a final, position. Thus if ch. 16 is no original part of Romans, the conclusions of the Roman letter must have been either lost or displaced through redaction.[129] This is not impossible, but such an inference presupposes that Rom 16:1–20 was not an integral part of Romans, and is not necessary if the presupposition cannot be justified.

A second stylistic argument for the detachment of ch. 16 is the oft-noted resemblance between this chapter and the ancient letter of recommendation, a resemblance which would ostensibly allow ch. 16 to stand on its own as an independent piece.[130] It is easily and rightly recognized that in phraseology Rom 16:1–2 bears close affinity to the ἐπιστολὴ συστατική (*littera commendaticia*), many examples of which are to be found among the papyri and literary collections. Common to both are the mention of the person introduced, a brief statement of his identity (often referring to his relationship to the writer and giving other background information), and the request for a favor toward the letter-bearer (frequently with a purpose or motive).[131] In the common letters of recommendation the favor requested is usually of a quite general sort, just as in Rom 16:2: προσδέξησθε αὐτὴν ... καὶ παραστῆτε αὐτῇ ἐν ᾧ ἂν ὑμῶν χρῄζῃ πράγματι. With this structural similarity there is also close terminological resemblance, especially in the request formula.[132]

---

[128] A partial exception to this is Philippians, but see further below, 145–46.

[126] See above, 72 n. 79. The suggestion of Schmithals that 16:21–23 (the greetings from Paul's associates) formed part of the Roman letter and that these verses originally followed 15:32 is not adequate, since 15:33 would still be construed as the epistolary final wish. Moreover, we have found that greetings consistently fall between the peace-wish and the grace-benediction. If Schmithals had proposed that 16:21–23 originally followed 15:33, and if he had also wished to transfer the grace-benediction given by some witnesses at 16:24 back to a position after 15:33 + 16:21–23, his reconstruction would at least have accorded with the other conclusions. But such rearrangements of the texts are utterly needless, as will be shown.

[130] See above, 40 with n. 17.

[131] The structure and phraseology of the ancient letter of recommendation were discussed by C. W. Keyes, "The Greek Letter of Introduction," *American Journal of Philology* 56 (1935) 28–44, and have now been analyzed in greater detail by Chan-Hie Kim, *Form and Structure of the Familiar Greek Letter of Recommendation* (Missoula, Montana, 1972).

[132] Forms of δέχεσθαι and χρῄζειν (or χρείαν ἔχειν) such as we have in 16:2 are frequent in the common letters.

The resemblance between Rom 16:1–2 and the common letter of recommendation ought not be over-emphasized, however, since in some particulars Rom 16:1–2 departs from customary form. For example, the ancient letter of recommendation ordinarily refers to the one introduced with the formula, ὁ ἀποδιδούς σοι τὴν ἐπιστολήν. Further, the use of συνίστημι in 16:1 is striking, for though the term is

But the resemblance between Rom 16:1–2 and formulae of the ancient letter of recommendation provides no basis whatever for the frequent deduction that 16:1–2 together with 3–23 originally comprised an *independent* letter of recommendation. Such reasoning is immediately suspect when it is recognized that relatively discrete notes of commendation may frequently be found *within the conclusions* of lengthy ancient letters essentially devoted to concerns other than recommendation. Many examples are furnished by the Ciceronian correspondence. We have, of course, many independent *litterae commendaticiae* from Cicero; they are characteristically brief and to the point, and manifest the influence of the Greek letter of recommendation.[133] But sometimes Cicero incorporates notes of commendation into larger letters written for other purposes, and these commendations appear in the epistolary conclusion. Thus in *ad Fam.* iii.1 the closing lines are:

> *L. Valerium, iureconsultum, valde tibi commendo . . . Valde hominem diligo; est ex meis domesticis atque intimis familiaribus. Omnino tibi agit gratias; sed idem scribit, meas litteras maximum apud te pondus habituras. Id eum ne fallat, te etiam atque etiam rogo. Vale.*
>
> L. Valerius, a lawyer, I heartily recommend to you. . . . I am extremely fond of the man. He belongs to my household, and is one of my most intimate friends. He always mentions his gratitude to you, but he also writes that a letter from me would carry the greatest weight with you. I beg you over and over not to let that expectation be disappointed. Farewell.

Similarly, in the conclusion of *ad Fam.* xii.24, he writes:

> *T. Pinarium, familiarissimum meum, tanto tibi studio commendo, ut maiore non possim; cui cum propter omnes virtutes, tum etiam propter studia communia, sum amicissimus. Is procurat rationes negotiaque Dionysi nostri, quem et tu multum amas, et ego omnium plurimum. Ea tibi ego non debeo commendare, sed commendo tamen. . . .*
>
> T. Pinarius, my very good friend, I cannot commend to you more enthusiastically than I do. Both because of all his virtues and because of our common interests I am most friendly with him. He is agent of the accounts and transactions of our Dionysius, whom you love much and I more than anyone. I ought not have to make this commendation to you, but I commend him all the same. . . .

These concluding notes of commendation do not refer to the letter carriers but to others who are likely to come into contact with the addressees. But elsewhere concluding notes of recommendation refer clearly to the bearer of the letter. Thus *ad Quint.* ii.14:

> *His diebus (ignosces) cui darem, fuit nemo ante hunc M. Orfium, equitem Romanum, nostrum et pernecessarium, est quod ex municipio Atellano, quod scis esse in fide nostra. Itaque eum tibi commendo in maiorem modum, hominem domi*

---

widely used in literature with the sense "to introduce," it is not employed in the letter writing manuals and is very rare in actual letters of recommendation. In the 83 letters examined by Kim (*Form and Structure of the Familiar Greek Letter of Recommendation*) the indicative form is found only once (P.Strass. 174), while it occurs in periphrastic constructions several times. Keyes ("The Greek Letter of Introduction," 39) supposes that the term was neglected because it was "too bald." See note 137 below.

[133]Keyes ("The Greek Letter of Introduction," 44) remarks, "It seems quite clear that Cicero knew and adapted some Greek formulae for letters of introduction, and very probably that he possessed and used one or more Greek handbooks of letter writing." Cf. Koskenniemi, 32–33 (with literature).

splendidum, gratiosum etiam extra domum. Quem fac ut tua liberalitate tibi obliges. . . . Gratum hominem observantemque cognosces.

In recent days (forgive me) there has been no one to whom I could entrust a letter until this M. Orfius, a Roman cavalryman, my friend and close relation, and who comes from the town of Atella which, as you know, is in my protection. Thus I recommend him to you emphatically as an illustrious man in his own town and respected outside it. Please oblige him by treating him well. . . . You will find him a grateful, attentive man.

In *ad Fam.* xvi.21 a very brief phrase of recommendation, doubtless for the carrier, falls between the *formula valetudinis* and final wish:

Tu velim in primis cures, ut valeas, ut una συμφιλολογεῖν *possimus. Anterum tibi commendo. Vale.*

Above all, do take care of your health, so that we may have a friendly conversation together. I commend Anterus to you. Farewell.[134]

In Greek letters there are other examples. Plato *Ep* 13, a lengthy letter, ends with the recommendation:[135]

Ἰατροκλῆς ὁ μετὰ Μυρωνίδου τότε ἐλεύθερος ἀφεθὶς ὑπ᾽ ἐμοῦ, πλεῖ νῦν μετὰ τῶν πεμπομένων παρ᾽ ἐμοῦ. ἔμμισθον οὖν που αὐτὸν κατάστησον ὡς ὄντα σοι εὔνουν, καὶ ἄν τι βούλῃ, αὐτῷ χρῶ.

Iatrocles, who along with Myronides was set free by me, is now about to embark with those sent by me. Therefore give him some paid employment since he is well-disposed toward you; and use him for whatever you wish.

And Polycarp's letter to the Philippians concludes with the commendatory note (preserved only in Latin):

Haec vobis scripsi per Crescentum, quem in praesenti commendavi vobis et nunc commendo. Conversatus est enim nobiscum inculpabiliter; credo quia et vobiscum similiter.

I have written this to you through Crescens, whom I commended to you when I was with you and commend again now. Among us he has conducted himself blamelessly, and I am sure he will do the same with you.

All of these notes of recommendation are found in the conclusions of lengthy letters.[136] As a rule they conform closely in structure and phraseology to the

---

[134]Closing remarks commending the letter carrier are also found in *ad Fam.* viii.8: "I send you my freedman, Philo, and Diogenes, a Greek, and I have given them instructions and a letter for you. Please give them and the business on which I sent them your kind attention" (*eos tibi et rem, de qua misi, velim curae habeas*); likewise in *ad Att.* i.19: "This Cossinius, to whom I have given this letter, seems to me a good and reliable sort of man, and one devoted to you, just as you described him in your letter" (*Cossinius hic, cui dedi litteras, valde mihi bonus homo et non levis et amans tui visus est et talis, qualem esse eum tuae mihi litterae nuntiarant*). Among the papyri a closing commendation for the letter carrier is found in P.Oxy. 293 (first century). After asking for instructions about some clothes, the writer adds: τῷ δὲ φέροντί σοι τὴν ἐπιστολὴν θεωνᾶτι ἱκανὸν ποίησον περὶ οὗ ἐὰν θέλῃ.

[135]R. Hercher, *Epistolographi Graeci* (Paris, 1873) 531.

[136]In a reference to his inclusion of commendations in letters written for other purposes, Cicero comments in *ad Fam.* vii.6: "In all my letters to Caesar or Balbus there is a sort of statutory appendix, my recommendation of you" (*in omnibus meis epistulis . . . legitima quaedam est accessio commendationis tuae . . .*).

type of the ἐπιστολὴ συστατική. Taken out of their proper contexts they might be regarded as self-contained, but they are not independent pieces.[137]

Moreover, a look at the Pauline letters themselves shows that the commendation of a third party is not foreign to the epistolary conclusions as such.[138] A very close parallel to Rom 16:1–2 is provided by 1 Cor 16:10–11, where Paul commends Timothy to the Corinthians. In the expectation that Timothy will come to them, Paul makes a general request on his behalf, βλέπετε ἵνα ἀφόβως γένηται πρὸς ὑμᾶς, adding a motive for compliance, τὸ ἔργον κυρίου ἐργάζεται. This pattern of request-motive is then repeated in vs. 11. Such a repeated pattern is also present in Rom 16:1–2: προσδέξησθε αὐτὴν–ἀξίως τῶν ἁγίων–καὶ παραστῆτε αὐτῇ–καὶ γὰρ αὐτὴ προστάτις ἐγενήθη. We can see in 1 Cor 16:15–18 a similar commendation, this time probably on behalf of the letter carriers.[139] These several commendations in 1 Cor 16 appear immediately after Paul's ''travelogue'' (16:5–9) and prior to the final greetings (16:19–21), a position exactly like that of the recommendation for Phoebe in Rom 16:1–2 (travelogue in 15:22–32, greetings in 16:3–16).

Thus in the secular letter tradition and in Paul's own letters we have precise analogies for the commendation in Rom 16:1–2 in form, content and position within the letter's conclusion. We are thereby warned against detaching ch. 16 from the larger Roman letter on the grounds that it has the character of a note of recommendation. That vss. 1–2 have that character imposes no necessity and creates no likelihood that the chapter was originally independent. In expressing commendations in the letter's conclusion Paul had ample precedent.

Is Rom 16, then, to be understood merely as a fragment of some larger letter, now lost, which has been attached to Romans? We are now in a position to make a positive objection against the fragment hypothesis. When Rom 16 is placed alongside the conclusions of the other Pauline letters, this chapter can be seen to correspond with what we have found to be characteristic of the other conclusions, and this is true with regard both to individual elements and to the sequence in which they stand.[140] In 15:33 we have the formulaic wish of peace, followed by the

[137]Another observation on the style of the ancient letter of recommendation has bearing on the question whether Rom 16 might be regarded as an originally independent letter. We noted above (41, with n. 19) that those who find in Rom 16 a discrete note of commendation see no difficulty for their view in the extensive greetings which follow the recommendation in 16:1–2: McDonald points to comparably lengthy greetings in other rather brief letters, while Goodspeed sees the greetings as essential to the purpose of recommendation. These arguments lose their force, however, in view of the fact that greetings are very rare in ancient letters of recommendation. Of the eighty-three letters collected by Kim only three contain greetings (P.Oxy. 1767, 2630 and P.Ryl. 691, all third and fourth century), and these have only one greetings-phrase each. Also, Cicero's letters of recommendation characteristically lack greetings. This absence accords well enough with the very limited aim of such letters. They are all brief, and do not move beyond the immediate concern of introduction. From the point of view of letter-form, then, not only the extent but the very presence of greetings in Rom 16 militates against seeing here an independent letter of recommendation.

Furthermore, the presence of δέ in 16:1 must give some pause to the desire to regard this sentence as an *opening* statement.

[138]The commendation of a third party sometimes occurs at an earlier point, and not necessarily in conclusion: thus, e.g., Phil 2:25–30; 2 Cor 8:16–24.

[139]Cf. also Col 4:7–8 and Eph 6:21–22 as deutero-Pauline parallels. Kim (*Form and Structure of the Familiar Greek Letter of Recommendation,* 118ff.) also wishes to consider Phil 4:2–3 and 1 Thes 5:12–13a as passages of commendation, but the motive of these passages seems to be of a different sort.

[140]For the moment we continue to leave out of account the doxology (16:25–27), which is no original part of this conclusion. See below, 122–24.

recommendation of Phoebe, and then in 16:3–15 by the greetings. After these greetings to various persons and groups come the request for the exchange of the kiss and the general greeting from all the churches (16:16). The sequence is then "interrupted" by the hortatory remarks of 16:17–20,[141] and these are followed by the grace-benediction of 16:20b. It is a departure from the other conclusions when in 16:21–23 the greetings are resumed, but this section is discrete insofar as it contains only greetings from Paul's associates, greetings which have no specific objects. Following these some MS witnesses offer a second grace-benediction as 16:24. All of the elements which appear here are found elsewhere *only in the conclusions* of the Pauline letters. It is evident also that the progression of these elements from 15:33 to at least 16:20b is that which we discovered in the other letters, and it is to be noted that this sequence ties together chs. 15 (with vs. 33) and 16.

From the point of view of style, however, two aspects of Rom 16 require further attention. The grace-benediction which occurs in the MS witnesses variously as 16:20b, 16:24 and even 16:28 (after the doxology) is a style-critical as well as a text-critical difficulty, for on purely stylistic grounds Paul's custom of placing this benediction in letter-final position—which accords with its function as final wish—favors the position at 16:24, and yet the textual evidence is generally thought stronger for the position at 16:20b. But leaving aside the textual question for the moment, we can find very precise parallels in ancient letters both for the placement of greetings after the final wish in the manner of a postscript, as appears to be the case in Rom 16:21–23,[142] and for the doubling of the final wish if the benediction should perhaps be read at both 16:20b and 16:24.[143] In anticipation of evidence to be given later,[144] strong text-critical reasons favor the grace-benediction at 16:24 as an original reading, but not necessarily over against 16:20b, and this doubling of the final wish, though unique in Paul, is not unusual in the ancient letter. Thus in Rom 16 as elsewhere the grace-benediction retains its ultimate position. Yet it may be possible to account for its doubling in this case.

A second apparent stylistic difficulty is posed by the repetition of the peace-wish of 15:33 in 16:20a, ὁ δὲ θεὸς τῆς εἰρήνης συντρίψει τὸν Σατανᾶν ὑπὸ τοὺς πόδας ὑμῶν ἐν τάχει. What is unusual here is not that hortatory remarks such as we have in 16:17–19 interrupt the sequence of concluding elements, or even that these are rounded off with a prayer-wish, but only that the formula ὁ θεὸς τῆς εἰρήνης appears for a second time in the context. This, together with the doubling of the grace-benediction, could lead to the supposition that 16:1–20 is an interpolated section. As regards the peace-wish, what we have here is unique, but not without analogy. In Philippians the peace-wish with the formula ὁ θεὸς τῆς εἰρήνης appears rather early at 4:9. Between this and the greetings stands Paul's expression of thanks for the Philippians' gift (4:10–18), after which follows a prayer-wish of the same form to which the peace-wishes, with other prayer-wishes, belong, ὁ δὲ θεός μου πληρώσει πᾶσαν χρείαν ὑμῶν. . . . Of course the peace-wish as such is not repeated in Phil 4, but it is important nonetheless that we have here a structural parallel, within the letter-conclusion, to Rom 15:33–16:20a.[145]

[141]The form of this παρακαλῶ period is that appropriate to the conclusions; see above, 80.
[142]See n. 48 above.
[143]See n. 14 and n. 15 above.
[144]Below, 129–132.
[145]We might also compare 2 Thes 3:1–16. The requests and assurances of 3:1–4 are followed by a prayer-wish in 3:5; the particularized exhortations of 3:6–15 are closed off with the peace-wish of 3:16.

If Rom 16 is supposed to represent only a letter fragment, it could be only the concluding fragment of the presumed lost letter, since it contains those elements which elsewhere are met only in the conclusions and manifests the same basic structure as the other conclusions.[146] But if this is so, and if in the MS tradition Rom 16 is found only in connection with the Roman letter, and if without Rom 16 the Roman letter has no conclusion even remotely approximating the conclusions of the other Pauline letters, then it is questionable in the extreme whether in Rom 16 we have to do with a letter fragment at all. Is ch. 16 not rather the original and appropriate conclusion of Romans? Beyond the disposal of objections to this, several additional stylistic considerations indicate that this is indeed the case.

In Hellenistic letters the epistolary framework, that is, the introduction and conclusion, contains the greatest concentration of set formulae and the highest degree of structural consistency. In the case of Paul's letters this has long been recognized for the epistolary introductions, and can now be affirmed for the conclusions also. Despite the relative consistency of letter form and style, the Pauline letters are not composed strictly under this aspect. Rather, form and style suffer accommodation to, and so reflect the exigencies of, the particular epistolary situation. The *locus classicus* for illustrating the influence of the situation on form and style is Galatians. The introduction to this letter is peculiar among the letters of Paul. The prescript is formed on the usual pattern, yet here Paul does not merely refer to his apostolic status, but defends it polemically (1:1b).[147] The prescriptive salutation reproduces the customary Pauline formula, but is expanded by the addition of a confessional statement (1:4–5). And in the address Paul fails to connect the addressees in any way with God or Christ, as is his custom, and speaks only of "the churches of Galatia."[148] These departures from the usual style of the epistolary introductions appear, in the light of the whole letter, to be motivated by the situation. This is also why here alone Paul does not introduce the letter body with a thanksgiving, but immediately expresses his dismay (1:3ff.). The conclusion of Galatians has likewise been affected. The usual concluding elements are reduced to a minimum while the polemic has been extended, with the emphasis of Paul's own hand, almost to the end. General paraenetic remarks and greetings are completely omitted, and the peace-wish is cast in tersely conditional form.

Without entering into detailed discussion of the extent to which the frameworks of the other letters stand under the influence of their own situations, the letter to the Romans provides an instructive counterpart to Galatians in this respect. The epistolary situation, in which an obvious factor is the absence of mutual per-

---

There is probably a good explanation for the stylistic peculiarities shared by Philippians and Romans in their conclusions, on which see further below, 93–94.

[146]This was explicitly recognized already by Paul Wendland, *Die Urchristlichen Literaturformen* (HNT 1/3; Tübingen, 1912) 350–51: "Wäre die 'Ephesus-Hypothese' richtig, so könnte c. 16 jedenfalls nicht ein vollständiger Brief, sondern nur der Schluss eines solchen sein."

[147]Gyllenberg ("De inledande hälsningsformlerna i de paulinska breven," 28–31) has observed that in the prescript of 1 Thessalonians, written to a community whose respect Paul presumes, no personal credentials are provided; in Galatians and 1 and 2 Corinthians, written to communities in which his apostleship has been questioned, Paul speaks of his apostolic call through the divine will; in Philippians and Philemon, written from prison, Paul designates himself a slave or prisoner of Christ; in Romans also Paul speaks of himself as a slave but refers also to his apostolic call and mission. All of these variations seem to be contingent on aspects of the given situations.

[148]This failure and the absence of any honorific epithet is regarded by Schlier (*Der Brief an die Galater,* 30) as contributing to the "gewollte Distanz."

sonal acquaintance between Paul and the Roman Christians, and the anticipation of such acquaintance, is clearly expressed in 1:10–15 and 15:22–23. It has obviously been a formative influence on the construction of the expansive epistolary introduction. Here Paul provides a lengthy characterization of the basis of his apostleship, of the gospel with which he is entrusted, and of the task of his preaching—all this within the prescript (1:1–6).[149] Unique here among the prescripts is the emphasis placed by Paul on the universal ambience of his mission (1:5, ἐν πᾶσιν τοῖς ἔθνεσιν). The honorific designation of the addressees is richly filled out beyond what is usual (1:6–7, κλητοὶ Ἰησοῦ Χριστοῦ, ἀγαπητοῖς θεοῦ, κλητοῖς ἁγίοις).[150] It is of a piece with all this that the thanksgiving of Romans is conceived more formally than any other, and expresses Paul's esteem for the community as well as his earnest desire to come to them.[151]

It is often and rightly observed that the concerns of 1:8–15 are echoed toward the conclusion of the letter in 15:22–33. These sections of the letter are correlated not only by subject matter but also by stylistic features. The dominant formal element of the introduction, the εὐχαριστῶ period, has its counterpart in the παρακαλῶ period of 15:30–33, which culminates the section parallel in content to the thanksgiving. Despite the scope of the material intervening between these passages, this correlation of formal elements having a close similarity of content has led Bjerkelund to suggest that 15:30–33 plays a very important role in the letter as a whole, indeed, that precisely here is to be seen the particular purpose which Paul pursues in the Roman letter.[152] This means that 15:14ff. does not constitute merely a transition into the epistolary conclusion, as many have supposed. Rather, here the letter moves toward its epistolary—if not theological—climax, focusing directly on the epistolary situation, on Paul's plans and on what he desires of the addressees.[153] Thus in Rom 15:30–33 we have the conclusion of the letter body, but not conclusion of the letter as a whole.[154] Bjerkelund therefore expresses the opinion that Rom 16 has to be regarded as "the necessary and natural conclusion of Romans."[155] Whatever one makes of Bjerkelund's particular arguments—and they are not without

[149]It is generally recognized that Paul has incorporated into this prescript a pre-Pauline confessional formula (1:3–4); see the concise discussion of Ferdinand Hahn, *The Titles of Jesus in Christology: Their History in Early Christianity* (London, 1969) 246–251 (with literature). Even so, there is little agreement about the motivation of this inclusion. The majority of commentators think that Paul pursues an apologetic purpose, seeking through the use of a pre-Pauline formula (known in Rome?) to assure the addressees of his orthodoxy and establish a common ground with them, so to gain recognition; thus, e.g., Dodd, *The Epistle of Paul to the Romans,* 5; Michel, *Der Brief an die Römer,* 38; C. K. Barrett, *A Commentary on the Epistle to the Romans,* 19; Otto Kuss, *Der Römerbrief* (2nd ed.; Regensburg, 1963) I, 8. Others connect the use of the formula with the Roman situation and accord it something of a polemical character over against Gentile Christians; thus H. W. Bartsch, "Zur vorpaulinischen Bekenntnisformel im Eingang des Römerbriefes," *TZ* 23 (1967) 329–339, esp. 339. Others see here an appropriate, if not comprehensive, summary of the gospel, stressing its historical rootage; so P. Stuhlmacher, "Theologische Probleme des Römerbrief-präskripts," *EvT* 27 (1967) 374–389, esp. 383–84.

[150]Cf., however, the similarly full designations in 1 Cor 1:2.

[151]On the delineation and character of this thanksgiving see Schubert (*Form and Function of the Pauline Thanksgivings,* 31–33), who speaks of the "ruggedness and laboriousness of this thanksgiving's style."

[152]Bjerkelund, *Parakalô,* 158.

[153]Ibid., 159.

[154]This is confirmed by the presence of the peace-wish in 15:33, since, as we have seen, the peace-wish is the first formulaic item of the conclusions.

[155]*Parakalô,* 159.

force—the formal and stylistic parallelism between epistolary introduction and conclusion reflecting the nature of the epistolary situation, which on the basis of Galatians we might well expect, can be discovered in Romans only if ch. 16 is taken as a part of the original letter.

Ch. 16 has all the earmarks of an epistolary conclusion, as can be seen by comparing it with other conclusions. The same comparison, however, reveals the distinctiveness of Rom 16, a distinctiveness which can be accounted for only on the basis of the situation presupposed in the Roman letter. Of primary importance here are the greetings which make up most of the chapter. If many have found in these greetings a primary objection to the Roman address of the chapter, from the point of view of epistolary style the greetings strongly favor the integrity of the letter.

Here as elsewhere the greetings conform in large measure to common epistolary practice. But in several respects they stand apart from Paul's usage in other letters. First, the greetings of Rom 16 are far more numerous than in any other Pauline letter. Though unusual for Paul, we find among the papyri a number of letters with comparably extensive sections of greetings.[156] Greetings in general, and especially greetings of such length, belong to the style of the personal and private, not the official, letter. Beyond their number, the greetings of this chapter are particularized by being addressed to specific individuals and groups, which contrasts sharply with Paul's habit of communicating only a general and collective greeting. The particularization of the greetings is accomplished not only by the naming of names, but in many cases by supplying the names with rich descriptive characterizations.[157] This feature is not to be seen elsewhere in Paul, and although the usual greeting form in Hellenistic letters allows for such descriptive phrases, they are not so extensive as many of those in Rom 16. The assumption that greetings with such name-specifications and descriptive phrases would be natural if here Paul were writing to a community with which he was well acquainted, however reasonable on a priori grounds,[158] finds no support whatever in the rest of the Pauline correspondence.

Further, the descriptive phrases can hardly be motivated in this case by a concern for precise identification, as though there could be some doubt as to who was designated by a given name. Nor is it likely that the descriptions are meant to be informative. Would not the community addressed, whichever it may have been, already know these things of its own members? It is essential to recognize that many of these descriptive phrases have a clearly *commendatory character*.[159] To name the

---

[156]For example: P.Oxy. 1296 (12 lines of greetings in a letter of 20 lines), 1299 (8 lines of 20), 1581 (8 lines of 18), 1679 (12 lines of 29); *BGU* 601 (13 lines of 31), 632 (14 lines of 28); cf. also P.Oxy. 1769; *BGU* 332, 714; P.Mich. 207; P.Lond. 404. Thus the number of greetings in Rom 16 does not *in itself* speak against the possible independence of this chapter, so that Lietzmann's classic objection (above, 47 n. 51) is invalid. Yet if Rom 16 is construed as a letter of recommendation, one must come to terms with the general absence of greetings in common letters of this type (above, n. 137).

[157]This is especially to be seen in 16:3–13. In vss. 14–15 descriptive phrases lack. Even within vss. 3–13 there is a noticeable movement from more elaborate to simpler characterizations.

[158]Even on a priori grounds this assumption is questionable: would not the singling out of some inevitably give offense to others?

[159]This conclusion was also reached independently by Kim (*Form and Structure of the Familiar Greek Letter of Recommendation*, 133–39), though he came to it by a different route and construes its significance in a somewhat different way from that in which we shall. Kim sees a similarity of structure between the greetings of 16:3–16 and the elements of what he terms the "Pauline commendation formula," which he abstracts from the various passages commending third parties. But in fact the

obvious examples, the description of the self-sacrificial service of Prisca and Aquila, to whom not only Paul but all the Gentile churches are indebted, the description of Epaenetus as ἀπαρχή, a distinction we know to have been respected (cf. 1 Cor 16:15–16), the description of the apostolic work of Andronicus and Junias which involved them in imprisonment and for which they are "esteemed among the apostles," all carry laudatory force. Other descriptions can also be viewed in this light.[160] Thus the greetings are invested with the function of commendation; but why is this? This peculiarity is difficult to explain on any supposition other than that of a Roman address, for it is especially striking how, in the descriptive phrases, a heavy emphasis is placed on the relationship between the individuals mentioned and Paul himself.[161] He ties them to himself, and himself to them. From these features it can be seen that Paul's commendatory greetings to specific individuals serve to place those individuals in a position of respect vis-à-vis the community, but also, by linking the Apostle so closely with them, place Paul in the same position. At the same time, those singled out for greeting are claimed by Paul as his advocates within the community. That epistolary greetings should be turned to this effect would hardly be comprehensible if they were addressed to a community whose recognition of himself Paul could have presumed. Only if addressed to the Roman church, where such recognition could not be assumed—a fact acknowledged in Paul's cautious and apologetic approach to it (15:14–21)—does the peculiar character of the greetings of Rom 16 make any sense.

There is a further notable aspect of these greetings. We saw above how little significance or emphasis is attached to Paul's personal greeting in other letters, and found this corroborated by the absence of first person indicative and imperative forms of the verb of greeting. Apart from Phil 4:21 and the requests for the exchange of the kiss, there are no imperative greetings in the other letters. Yet in Romans the imperative form is found sixteen times in succession! There can be no question here, any more than in the case of the kiss-greeting, of the imperative forms meaning that the greetings are addressed to persons outside the actual readership.[162] Even if the readership as a whole can still be regarded as the agents of

structure of these greetings conforms very closely to the common Hellenistic greeting formula. Yet he is right in seeing the preponderance here of complimentary phrases, which function very much as the "credentials" phrases in the passages of commendation.

[160]Thus the references to "laboring" on behalf of Christ and the church in vss. 6 and 12 (cf. 9); in the commendation passages of 1 Cor 16:10, 16 such activity is mentioned as a motive for respect (cf. also 1 Cor 4:12; Gal 4:11, where Paul, so to speak, commends himself). The term "fellow worker" (16:3, 9) is used with similar force. On the term, see A. Harnack, "κόπος (κοπιᾶν, οἱ κοπιῶντες) im frühchristlichen Sprachgebrauch," ZNW 27 (1928) 1–10.

[161]16:3–4, 5, 7–9, 13, all emphasize the personal relationship. In other cases where the relationship is not seen in terms of activity and/or affection we should reckon also with the designation συγγενεῖς. It is hard to see what significance this could have apart from the effort to draw out some kind of relationship. Never outside of Rom 16:7, 11 (cf. 21) does Paul use συγγενεῖς as descriptive of a particular individual. See the remarks of Käsemann, An die Römer, 396–97.

[162]Mullins ("Greeting as a New Testament Form," 418, 420–21) contends that in the second person imperative type of greeting it is a matter of the writer asking the addressee to greet for him someone standing outside the immediate readership of the letter. Kim (Form and Structure of the Familiar Greek Letter of Recommendation, 139–140) takes a similar view. This is true enough as regards Hellenistic private letters generally, but does not hold good for the Pauline letters or for Rom 16, as the requests for the kiss show: the kiss-greeting is to be exchanged among the readership (certainly not to be given by the reader to the congregation!), which is the sense of the reciprocal ἀλλήλους. Likewise, in Phil 4:21 "every saint" means simply "every member of the community." Thus we must assume that

these greetings, the recipients of the greetings stand within the circle of readers. This means, however, that the imperative form of the greeting verb functions here as a surrogate for the first person indicative form, and so represents a direct personal greeting of the writer himself to the addressees.[163] Thus in Rom 16 it is Paul's own greetings which hold the first and dominant place, and are clearly emphasized, while the greetings of others (16:21–23) are by comparison brief in scope and by position of secondary importance.

A further observation may be drawn in here. In the prescripts of all his other letters Paul names others as senders together with himself.[164] This is not the case only in Romans (and Ephesians!) where none stands beside the Apostle in the letter introduction (even though Timothy is present, according to 16:21). This, together with the concentration of the prescript and thanksgiving on Paul himself, suggests at the outset the highly personal character of the Roman letter, a character equally evident in 15:14–33 and in the greetings of ch. 16.[165]

It is to be admitted, of course, that there is a certain disjunction between 15:33 and 16:1ff., but this results above all from the transition in thought and the movement from the body to the conclusion of the letter. Still, it is an attractive conjecture that the Pauline autograph began with 16:1 and that this has contributed to the disjunction. Several observations favor this conjecture. There is no reference

the recipients of the second person imperative greetings in Rom 16 are members of the community, and therefore also are among the addressees of the letter. Käsemann (*An die Römer,* 400) tentatively considers the second person form of the greetings to support the independence of ch. 16 as a letter of recommendation, since the readers would, assumably, have to pass the greetings on to their rightful recipients. But this assessment is clearly mistaken.

[163]The conclusions of Mullins ("Greeting as a New Testament Form," 425–26), on the basis of the greetings of Rom 16, that Paul "had close enough rapport with that congregation to let them act for him" and that "the use of the second person type greeting means that the persons greeted might not be among those who read the letter," as well as the suggestion of Kim (*Form and Structure of the Familiar Greek Letter of Recommendation,* 139–140) that there may have been "several congregations . . . and one of these must have been the recipient of the letter," place too much reliance on the second person greeting in private letters and do not allow for the difference of situation when a "private" letter is addressed not to an individual but to a large group and so takes on a more "public" character. That the congregation should "greet" the persons named really means that Paul himself greets them; yet the agency of the community as a whole in these greetings is tantamount to a "recognition" of those greeted.

[164]Paul and Sosthenes: 1 Cor 1:1; Paul and Timothy: 2 Cor 1:1; Phil 1:1; Phlm 1:1 (also Col 1:1); Paul, Sylvanus, and Timothy: 1 Thes 1:1 and 2 Thes 1:1; Paul and "all the brethren who are with me": Gal 1:1–2.

[165]Koskenniemi, in his study of Greek epistolography, has sought to illumine the use of the various epistolary phrases and formulae from the point of view of the intended function of letters. He has shown that the purpose of letters is not always primarily or exclusively the communication of information, but can also include the cultivation of the personal relationship between the correspondents (88–95). On the basis of this insight the letters of antiquity can be divided into three types: (a) letters of which the sole intention is to convey information, (b) letters which convey information but also aim at forging a bond between the writer and addressee, and (c) letters of which the only or dominant purpose is to foster a closer personal relationship between writer and addressee (92). The first type of letter is the most heavily evidenced among ancient letters, but there is no want of examples of the second and third types, granting that the distinction between these types is not absolute. What is important for us is that the use of epistolary formulae and personal references is closely correlated with and reflective of epistolary intention (in Paul we have already noted this for Galatians); thus, in letters of the first type, established formulae and personal references are absolutely minimal (usually only the brief prescript and the final wish), while in the other types, especially the third, these elements are profuse (92–94). Koskenniemi has called these phrases and formulae "philophronetic," expressing and intending φιλία between the correspondents. The *formula valetudinis,* greetings, requests for letters, the proscynesis formula, and general expressions of concern for the circumstances of the addressee are all philophronetic in character (128–154).

to the presence of an autographic conclusion in Romans, but we have discovered good reasons to suppose that all of Paul's letters originally revealed his own hand toward the end. We have also found that the extent of the autographic portion can be determined only by internal criteria. Galatians shows that in some cases it could be fairly extensive. The close structural correspondence between the conclusions of Romans and Philippians would be well accounted for if both Phil 4:10–20 (or 4:10–23) and Rom 16:1–20 were autographic. In each case the section in question is set off by reason of content from what precedes, and each commences just after the wish of peace (Phil 4:9b, Rom 15:33), just as in 2 Thes 3:16–17 the autograph follows immediately on the wish of peace. There are, moreover, good reasons why Paul should have written these sections himself. It is in the nature of the case in dictated letters that the autographic portion is the most personal and intimate—here the writer is in immediate touch with the readers. In this respect it is easily understood why in Philippians Paul has reserved to the end his expression of thanks for the Philippians' gift, for in that position his gratitude could be communicated firsthand. The delay of this note of thanks, however inappropriate it may seem to us, can therefore be explained from the perspective of epistolary style without resorting to literary-critical operations which wish to see here an independent letter.[166]

It would have been quite fitting for much of Rom 16 to be in Paul's hand, since the matter here is highly personalized and aims at establishing a degree of intimacy between the writer and the addressees. In particular, the commendation of Phoebe would seem to require this, and the greetings, in view of their function, hardly less so. It is clear from the first person greeting of Tertius the scribe in 16:22 that the whole chapter was not written by Paul.[167] The autograph, then, most likely broke off with 16:20, for the greetings from Paul's companions appear as something of an afterthought. Vss. 21–24 were written by the scribe. If the autograph embraced 16:1–20, this would go far toward explaining the "doubled" features of this epistolary conclusion in comparison with others; Paul originally meant to bring the letter to a close with the autograph, and so finished writing with the benediction of 16:20b, having reiterated the peace-wish just beforehand, as elsewhere. But then he decided to add the greetings of his associates in 21–23 (a postscript), after which it was necessary to repeat the final wish, 16:24. As we have seen, all of this can be closely paralleled in extant ancient letters.

Thus, even though many have found considerations of content to be prohibitive of a Roman destination for ch. 16, in terms of letter-form and style everything

---

It may be questionable how useful or pertinent such a general classification of letters according to intention is for the understanding of the Pauline letters. It relates to our concern insofar as it is based on the recognition of the influence of intention and situation on the letter's form and style. In particular, we may say that the elaborate introduction and conclusion of Romans, which abound with what we may term philophronetic elements and center so strongly on the relationship, actual and anticipated, between Paul and the addressees, are exactly what we should expect in view of ancient epistolary style, Paul's own epistolary style and the situation presupposed by the Roman letter.

[166]On the various partition theories for Philippians, for which the note of thanks in 4:10–20 is an important piece of evidence, see below, Appendix II.

[167]It seems to be implicit in this remark of Tertius that some of the conclusion was written by Paul himself. For a postscriptive greeting by someone other than the sender of the letter see P.Oxy. 1067, and also above, 59 with n. 16. An appropriate analogy is furnished by Cicero (ad Att. v. 20): "I am pleased that Alexis (Atticus' secretary) so often sends greetings to me, but why can he not put them in a letter of his own, as Tiro, who is my Alexis, does for you?"

speaks in favor of the integrity of the letter. That Paul had some acquaintances in Rome—and only a limited number of firsthand acquaintances need be supposed—is a smaller and more reasonable assumption than that ch. 16 was no original part of the Roman letter. If judgments based on content are inevitably somewhat subjective and inconclusive, the evidence of epistolary style is a much more demonstrable and reliable index for deciding literary-critical issues.[168] In the case of Romans it provides as much certainty as can be had that Rom 1–16 preserves the original extent of Paul's letter to the Romans. This judgment will be all the more decisive if it can be shown that the shorter forms of the letter attested in the textual tradition are attributable to motives in the later church and are not to be set down to Paul himself.

[168]On the relation of literary-critical theories to the form- and style-criticism of the letters, see below, 137–39.

CHAPTER IV

TEXTUAL HISTORY:
THE ORIGIN OF THE SHORTER FORMS

If, as we have tried to show, Paul's letter to the Roman church is represented in the full sixteen-chapter form of the text, we must now seek to determine when and for what reasons the shorter forms of the letter, composed respectively of chs. 1–14 and 1–15, emerged. Prior to the discovery of P[46], the only textual witness to the fifteen-chapter form of the letter, this question was entertained for the fourteen-chapter text alone. The influence of the Ephesian hypothesis for ch. 16 has up to now prevented the fifteen-chapter text from being drawn into consideration as a secondary short form of the Roman letter. But having rejected the Ephesian hypothesis, we are in a position to treat the fifteen-chapter form in connection with later textual developments and to find in it useful additional evidence for a solution of the larger problem of the origin of the shorter recensions.

The Fourteen-Chapter Recension

The existence at an early time—certainly by the middle of the second century but quite possibly earlier than that—of a text of Romans ending with ch. 14 is clearly demonstrated by the textual evidence. The many and varied attempts to account for this form of the letter must now be critically evaluated.

A. The Fourteen-Chapter Form as a Pauline Product

Several scholars have on occasion supposed that Paul himself was the originator of the fourteen-chapter form of Romans. J. B. Lightfoot[1] argued for the integrity of the letter in sixteen chapters, but without the doxology. Being intended for the Roman church, the letter naturally had specific motivations—Paul's plans to visit the Roman community, to establish a "diplomatic relation" with it, and to provide a conciliatory theological statement to a congregation of mixed elements, Jew and Gentile. According to Lightfoot, these motives required that the letter should have a general and comprehensive cast. It represents in large part the fruit of the Apostle's reflections on the Jew-Gentile problem with which he had recently dealt in Galatia and Corinth. This is taken by Lightfoot as a key to the origin of the fourteen-chapter form of the letter. At a later period of his life, perhaps even in Rome itself, Paul wished to have the letter circulate more widely on account of its general pertinence for the Jew-Gentile issue.[2] To this end he removed the references

[1] *Biblical Essays,* 315–16, 319.
[2] Lightfoot (ibid., 319) suggested that the short text "perhaps was circulated to prepare the way for a personal visit in countries into which Paul had not yet penetrated (1:11ff.)."

96

to Rome in 1:7 and 1:15 and the personalia of the final two chapters, and then added the doxology to bring the resultant fourteen-chapter text to a suitable conclusion. Thus Paul put the letter into circulation in a more general form. The various features of the textual tradition are to be explained, then, as the consequence of later attempts to combine two *Pauline* forms of the letter.

This is a simple explanation, and its value is enhanced by its capacity to explain the facts of the subsequent tradition without positing intervening factors. Among its weaknesses,[3] the most obvious is the way in which the abridgment, leaving nothing after 14:23, slices in half the argument which begins at 14:1 and does not conclude until 15:13, and makes for a singularly abrupt ending. Paul himself would scarcely have made such a division, even for Lightfoot's proposed motive, for 15:1–13 is as suitable for general circulation as what precedes. Cognizant of this problem, Kirsopp Lake proposed that the history of the textual forms is best explained by an inversion of Lightfoot's theory.[4] For Lake, the fourteen-chapter form of the letter could be understood only as a *precursor* of our Roman letter. This earlier, general letter was composed, he thought, about the time of Galatians as a broad treatment of the Jew-Gentile issue to be sent to churches not yet visited by Paul. This letter originally had nothing whatever to do with Rome. Only at a later time did Paul provide this general letter with the specific Roman address and the final chapter (i.e., ch. 15[5]), which served as a covering letter.[6] The virtue of Lake's hypothesis, as opposed to Lightfoot's, is its ability to offer a plausible reason why there is a continuous thought-connection between chs. 14 and 15 despite the textual hiatus: ch. 15 *is* a continuation of ch. 14, but one added only later when the previously general letter was adapted for a Roman destination.[7]

The idea of a general letter lying behind our Romans has had more recent advocates. As we saw earlier, this is also the conviction of T. W. Manson, who speaks of a letter "to the Romans—and others" summarizing Paul's mature understanding of the relation of the church to Judaism, a manifesto which Paul tried to circulate as widely as possible.[8] A similar understanding has been developed by John Knox, who seeks further considerations in its favor.[9] In particular, Knox

[3]The motive for the generalization proposed by Lightfoot is of questionable sufficiency, as we cannot assume that the Jew-Gentile issue possessed such wide interest and urgency to call for a general treatment. On the problem of motives for a general letter, see further below, 98–99. Hort (*Biblical Essays,* 348) criticized Lightfoot's appeal to Ephesians as a parallel case, pointing out that even if Ephesians is Pauline and circular, it was apparently sent to several communities simultaneously, and was general in essence and origin. Against the forging of a general letter from a specific letter, Hort suggested that "if for any purpose Paul needed an impersonal treatise on the old subjects, he would surely have written it anew."

[4]Kirsopp Lake, *The Earlier Epistles of Saint Paul* (London, 1911), 362–65. Lake acknowledged that his hypothesis was an adaptation and simplification of E. Renan's view. For a thorough summary and critique of Renan's view see Lightfoot, *Biblical Essays,* 287–320, and, more briefly, Sanday and Headlam, *The Epistle to the Romans,* xcii–xciii.

[5]Lake tentatively regarded ch. 16 as addressed to Ephesus.

[6]Lake, too, supported his argument by reference to Ephesians, in which he saw the same features characteristic of the short form of Romans (the lack of attention to a concrete situation), and to Galatians, which bears an obvious similarity to Romans in primary concerns.

[7]Lake fails to explain, however, why such a continuation was made, supposing only that "Aquila had told him this was desirable" (365). But note how this conflicts with Lake's regard for ch. 16 (the only mention of Aquila in Romans)!

[8]See above, 41–43.

[9]John Knox, "A Note on the Text of Romans," 191–93. See also his later article, "Romans 15:14–33 and Paul's Apostolic Mission," *JBL* 83 (1964) 1–11, esp. 10. Knox's view has been approved,

thinks it is striking that in ch. 1 Paul neither mentions a projected journey to Spain nor even promises a visit to Rome. This peculiarity, if it is such, is best accounted for in Knox's view if the letter to the Romans is an adaptation of an earlier general letter "originally composed for a type of Gentile church with which Paul is seeking to establish contact—a letter intended not to announce a visit but to take the place of a visit which was having to be postponed."[10] Thus we can understand why Paul mentions his intention to go to Spain via Rome only at the end of the Roman letter: the only alteration in the fourteen-chapter form was the addition of the Roman address and ch. 15.

It is certainly appropriate, in the light of the textual evidence for a fourteen-chapter form of the letter omitting the Roman address, to consider the possibility that there may have been a general letter of which our Romans (in fifteen or sixteen chapters) is but a particularized version. But this possibility deserves more rigorous scrutiny than it has received; its plausibility has been greatly over-estimated, and there are numerous obstacles to it.

First, a general or "circular" letter, though not having an exclusive desti-nation, requires a compelling motive, just as does a letter to a specific community. But what motive might have existed for a general letter comprising roughly Rom 1–14? That in leisurely reflection Paul worked up a systematic statement on past issues and sent it out for the edification of some of his churches—such seems to be Manson's view of the matter—is an explanation wholly lacking in the compulsion of real occasion and purpose and gives us a cause inadequate to the effect and incongruous with Paul's methods. The same must be said of Knox's suggestion that the letter was only a means "to establish contact" and perhaps "to validate and interpret his role as apostle to the Gentiles."[11] M. Jack Suggs properly criticizes these proposals, which suggest that the (general) letter was worked up, as it were, for Paul's own benefit, and points out that mere retrospection will not suffice as the occasion of a general letter embodying Paul's considered views. Even less does it explain why a form of such a letter should have been sent to Rome.[12] But Suggs retains the idea of a general letter, seeking only a better motive for it. He therefore allows the anticipated encounter in Jerusalem to be the dominant factor in the situation, and from that perspective comes to regard the substance of Romans as a "brief," a statement of Paul's case on the matters which will be central in Jerusalem. This brief is "not prepared as a mere summary of controversies now ended, but in anticipation of a situation in which they may break forth afresh."[13] He believes, further, that this "brief" was circulated among Pauline churches "as a letter which states the Pauline 'party line' . . . ," and that it was necessary to do this prior to the collection's delivery to make it clear to all concerned that Paul's position on the issue "is independent of Jerusalem and consistent with his previous procla-mation."[14] Although in this way Suggs is better able to understand the occasion and

---

with some differences, by Funk, *Language, Hermeneutic and Word of God*, 265 n. 66, and "The Apostolic *Parousia*," 267–68, and by Suggs, " 'The Word is Near You,' " esp. 289–298.

[10] "A Note on the Text of Romans," 192.

[11] Ibid.

[12] Suggs, " 'The Word is Near You,' " 289–294.

[13] Ibid., 296; in a similar vein see also Jacob Jervell, "Der Brief nach Jerusalem; Über Veranlas-sung und Adresse des Römerbriefes," *ST* 25 (1971) 61–73.

[14] " 'The Word is Near You,' " 297.

purpose of a general letter, even his premises do not convincingly show why a form of this letter was sent to the church in Rome.[15] Thus efforts to rationalize the Roman letter as a particularized form of a general letter which Paul also sent elsewhere, however adequately they may postulate a motive for a general letter, are most tenuous precisely at the point of the most rudimentary fact, that whatever else it might have been, the letter was at least a letter to Rome.

It cannot be disputed that the textual tradition attests a generalized form of Romans at an early time. But these hypotheses take it for granted that this generalized form of the letter must be directly connected with Paul. And so we must ask, what is the actual evidence for a *Pauline* general letter, of which our Romans is supposed to be but one specific form? It is in fact quite small.

The textual evidence itself is the point of departure for the general letter theories, in particular the omission of the address in some witnesses. But it must be emphasized that we have to do here only with the *absence* of the address; nowhere is an alternative specific address to be found. This would be strange if Paul is thought to have directed his statement to communities other than Rome, for we would expect the tradition to have preserved a trace of some other address.[16] The omission of ch. 15 is also part of the evidence of a generalized form of the letter, but this fact has not been seriously reckoned with by advocates of a *Pauline* general letter. Not only does ch. 14 lack an epistolary ending; the textual break at the end of ch. 14 also does not coincide with any break in the movement of thought which begins at 14:1 and reaches its conclusion only at 15:13. Given this unbroken continuity between chs. 14 and 15, it is difficult to maintain that the text concluding with 14:23 represents a general form of the letter devised by Paul. If we wished to posit a Pauline general letter we would naturally seek its conclusion no earlier than 15:13.[17] Yet there is absolutely no textual evidence for a form of the letter ending with 15:13.[18]

There are reasons apart from this textual evidence for the assumption that there is a general Pauline letter lying behind our Romans. One is that the content of Romans is, or at least appears to be, unconditioned by any circumstances of the Roman church itself. That it has no concrete relevance to the situation of the Roman church is assumed equally, and perhaps more so, because Paul had not previously visited the Roman community, and *therefore* cannot have known anything of its internal character. The other reason for the supposition of a general letter is the attachment of allegedly Ephesian matter in ch. 16 which, in the compositional form

[15]Suggs (ibid., 296–97) can say only that through this letter "the strategic and perhaps powerful church in Rome is tactfully reminded that Paul has an apostleship to all the Gentiles...." But the purpose or necessity of such a "reminder" is not shown.

[16]The deutero-Pauline Ephesians, for example, was almost certainly put out as a general letter, but it was apparently meant to include specific addresses. The omission of a specific address in Eph 1:1 leaves a nonsensical sentence, and although it is omitted in numerous witnesses, the tradition does preserve at least one specific alternative: Marcion knew Ephesians as Laodiceans.

[17]This is admitted by John Knox ("A Note on the Text of Romans," 193) who calls it an unresolved mystery "why the 'shorter form' of the letter ended apparently with 14:23 rather than with 15:13." Funk ("The Apostolic *Parousia*," 268) says that "Rom 1:1–15:13 may well have been conceived by Paul as a general letter," and apparently feels no constraint by the absence of textual evidence for this form.

[18]One might hold, as Lake does, that the general letter did end at 14:23, and that Paul, in adapting the letter for Rome, picked up the line of argument in ch. 14 and carried it to 15:13, but this would be special pleading.

of the Ephesian hypothesis, is taken to show that Paul dispatched a copy of the letter to Ephesus.[19] But if we reject the Ephesian destination of ch. 16 as implausible, or even if its Ephesian destination is maintained but its attachment to Romans is not attributed to Paul, then we have no indication that the letter was sent elsewhere than to Rome.

Thus if it has to be admitted that there was once a generalized form of Romans, the very evidence that compels this conclusion also speaks against attributing that general text to Paul. The conjectures about a general *Pauline* letter which was adapted and particularized for Rome may begin from the textual evidence, but the textual evidence has not been permitted to control the directions of those conjectures. Even if we wish to maintain that the body of the Roman letter is entirely general and has no clear relation to the actual situation of the Roman church, the fact remains that we have no indication that the letter was sent by Paul to any other community.[20]

In sum, no interpretation of the evidence is satisfactory which traces *both* the fourteen- and the sixteen-chapter forms of the letter to Paul himself. Seeing this, many have sought in the later history of the text the occasion for the emergence of the shorter form of the letter.

B. The Fourteen-Chapter Form as a Marcionite Product

The most influential and indeed the earliest of these attempts traces the creation of the fourteen-chapter form to Marcion, a view which on account of its wide advocacy requires extended discussion.[21]

The question of Marcion's influence on the text and canon of the NT has

---

[19]In the redactional form of the Ephesian hypothesis the presence of ostensibly Ephesian matter in ch. 16 is not the work of Paul but of a later redactor, and so intimates nothing about the letter's circulation *by Paul*.

[20]Knox interprets the statements of 1:8–15 as broadly as possible, certainly with too much latitude. These verses can hardly be said naturally to mean that no visit is anticipated and that in fact the letter is meant to take the place of a visit. There is a very close parallelism between 1:8–15 and 15:14–33, and the former must be understood just as specifically as the latter. The removal of the specific address in 1:7 and 1:15 only partially mitigates the particularity of 1:8–15. It is most unlikely that these sections of the letter were conceived independently or with respect to different situations.

Funk ("The Apostolic *Parousia*," 266–68) seeks to provide additional evidence for the general letter theory by pointing out that elements of the parousia section (or travelogue), which normally occurs toward the end of a letter, are incorporated in the thanksgiving of Romans, but without being particularized (here he follows Knox). But the force of this observation is uncertain. Paul does not do this elsewhere, but then we have from him no letters except Romans which were written to communities he had not visited. Granted that Rom 1:8–15, omitting the specific address, *might* have been appropriate to other churches not visited by Paul, we have no evidence that it was ever destined for another church, and cannot simply assume it.

[21]Among many who have approved this explanation we mention de Bruyne, "La finale marcionite," 136–142; E. Riggenbach, "Textgeschichte," 580–591; A. Bludau, *Die Schriftfälschungen der Häretiker* (NTAbh 11/5; Münster, 1925) 19; F. J. Leenhardt, *The Epistle to the Romans,* 26; Sanday and Headlam, *The Epistle to the Romans,* xcvi–xcvii (see below, n. 98); R. Schumacher, *Letzten Kapitel,* 135; G. Zuntz, *The Text of the Epistles,* 226–27; T. W. Manson, "St. Paul's Letter to the Romans—and Others," 230–31; M. Goguel, *Introduction au Nouveau Testament,* IV/2, 252–54; E. Kamlah, *Traditionsgeschichtliche Untersuchungen zur Schlussdoxologie des Römerbriefes* (Dissertation, Tübingen University, 1955) 22–23 (hereinafter *Schlussdoxologie*); H. J. Vogels, "Der Einfluss Marcions und Tatians auf Text und Kanon des NT," in *Synoptische Studien, Alfred Wikenhauser zum siebzigsten Geburtstag dargebracht* (Munich, 1953) 278–289.

long intrigued scholarship.[22] It is a question as necessary to pose as it is difficult to answer. The facts that Marcion was active in the very period when the NT gained a relatively fixed form, that his Scripture is the first explicitly authoritative collection of Christian writings of which we have evidence, and that he made textual emendations in the interest of his dogmatic persuasion, all require that it be asked what effect, if any, Marcion had on the text and canon of the catholic church. The answer is not immediately apparent. The difficulty of finding an answer lies primarily in the paucity of source materials for the whole period, and this is compounded by problems inherent in the sources we do have. Thus, despite the concentrated efforts of a number of scholars, the problem of Marcion's influence has remained largely intractable.

Of course, research has fostered a wealth of hypotheses and inferences, but little which can claim compelling evidence or common consent. Previous studies at least prompt the recognition that a direct and wholistic approach to the question will not suffice. It is no longer justifiable or profitable in terms of method to proceed from general a priori judgments.[23] Rather, what is required is a careful sifting and testing of the evidence on particular points which, taken together, may eventually provide a firm basis for a more precise estimate of Marcion's importance in matters of text and canon.

The issue of Marcion's influence on the text of the NT obtrudes itself directly into a discussion of the textual history of Romans through the testimony of Origen, mentioned earlier, which now must be examined more closely. The evidence of Origen's explicit statement is usually supported by reference to other aspects of the textual tradition of Romans and of the Pauline letters generally, in particular to the doxology (Rom 16:25–27) and the so-called Marcionite prologues to the Pauline letters, but also to generally recognized proclivities of Marcion in doctrine and textual alteration. We must therefore consider these supporting arguments as well.

Foremost among the evidence favoring Marcion's impact on the text of the letter is the clear declaration of Origen that Marcion eliminated from Romans the concluding doxology and everything after 14:23, that is, that Marcion himself produced the fourteen-chapter form of the letter. We reproduce Origen's statement in full:

> Marcion, by whom the evangelical and apostolic writings were falsified, completely removed this section (16:25–27) from this letter; and not only this, but also from that place where it is written 'all that is not of faith is sin' (14:23) he cut it away up to the end. Indeed, in other copies, that is, in those which are not contaminated by Marcion, we find this same section differently placed. For in some manuscripts, following the place which we mentioned above, that is, 'all that is not of faith is sin' [the words] 'now to him who is able to strengthen you' have a consistent position; yet other manuscripts have it at the end, as it is now placed.[24]

[22] On the whole question see Harnack, *Marcion;* John Knox, *Marcion and the New Testament; An Essay in the Early History of the Canon* (Chicago, 1942); E. C. Blackman, *Marcion and His Influence* (London, 1948); and Campenhausen, *The Formation of the Christian Bible,* 147–165.

[23] Cf., e.g., the opinion of Zahn, *Geschichte,* I, 681: "Der bewusste Hass der Kirche gegen den Antichristen und Schriftenverfälscher Marcion macht es undenkbar, dass man in kirchlichen Kreisen dem marcionitischen Bibeltext einen positiven Einfluss auf die Gestaltung der kirchlichen eingeräumt habe."

[24] *PG* XIV, 1290 AB.

In our earlier treatment of this testimony we concluded that it does derive from Origen and that, despite questions raised about its possible meanings, its sense is clear: Marcion did not simply make selective excisions from chs. 15 and 16, but removed them completely along with the doxology.[25] Before evaluating this statement further we must set beside it another comment found in Jerome's commentary on Ephesians apropos Eph 3:5, concerning the mystery of Christ "which was not made known to the sons of men in other generations as it has now been revealed to his holy apostles and prophets by the Spirit." In Jerome's exposition we have an attempt to refute the notion that the prophets of the OT did not know the meaning of what they said:

> Those who suppose that the prophets did not understand what they said, as though they spoke in ecstasy, take for the confirmation of their doctrine, along with the present testimony (Eph 3:5), that which *in most manuscripts is found in Romans* and says, 'Now to him who is able to strengthen you according to my gospel and the preaching of Jesus Christ according to the revelation of the mystery kept secret for long ages but now manifested through the prophetic writings and the coming of our Lord Jesus Christ, etc.' (Rom 16:25–27). To these it is briefly to be replied that in times past the mystery of Christ was hidden not to them who promised that it would be, but to all nations to whom it was afterward revealed. And it is likewise to be noted that the mystery of our faith ought not to have been revealed except through the prophetic writings and the coming of Christ. Therefore, as for those who do not understand the prophets and do not wish to know, asserting that they are content with the gospel alone, let them know that they are ignorant of the mystery of Christ which was always unknown to the nations.[26]

The relevance of this statement for a proper estimate of the testimony of Origen becomes apparent with the recognition that Jerome in his commentary on Ephesians relies heavily on Origen's (lost) exposition of the same letter. Jerome himself acknowledges his indebtedness,[27] and the extent of it can be rather precisely determined by a comparison of Jerome's work with the Catena fragments of Origen's commentary. At virtually every point where comparison is possible Jerome gives words and ideas modelled on those of Origen.[28] Though Origenic fragments lack in this particular case, there are nevertheless clear indications that this passage was

[25] See above, 22–23.

[26] *PL* XXVI, 512 D–513 A: *Qui volunt prophetas non intellexisse, quae dixerint, et quasi in ecstasi loquutos, cum praesenti testimonio (Eph 3:5) illud quoque, quod ad Romanos in plerisque codicibus invenitur, ad confirmationem sui dogmatis trahunt legentes: 'Ei autem qui potest vos roborare juxta evangelium meum et predicationem Jesu Christi secundum revelationem mysterii temporibus aeternis taciti, manifestati autem nunc per scripturas propheticas et adventum domini nostri Jesu Christi et reliqua' (Rom 16:25–27). Quibus breviter respondendum est, temporibus praeteritis tacitum Christi fuisse mysterium non apud eos, qui illud futurum pollicebantur, sed apud universas gentes, quibus postea manifestatum est. Et partitur annotandum, quod sacramentum fidei nostrae nisi per scripturas propheticas et adventum Christi non valeat revelari. Sciant igitur qui prophetas non intelligunt nec scire desiderant, asserrentes se tantum evangelio esse contentos. Christi nescire mysterium, quod temporibus aeternis gentibus cunctis fuerit ignorantum.*

[27] *PL* XXVI, 472 B.

[28] The Catena fragments of Origen's commentary on Ephesians were collected by J. A. F. Gregg, "The Commentary of Origen on the Epistle to the Ephesians," *JTS* 3 (1901–02) 233–34, 398–420, 554–576. Some comparisons between Jerome's commentary and the fragments of Origen were made by A. Souter, *The Earliest Latin Commentaries on the Epistles of St. Paul* (Oxford, 1927) 112–13; a long list of parallels is given by Zahn, *Geschichte*, II, 427 n. 2. Rufinus, questioning Jerome's attitude toward Origen on doctrinal points, made capital of Jerome's dependence on Origen in his commentary on Ephesians. In his *Apologiae in Sanctam Hieronymum* (*PL* XXI, 563B ff.) Rufinus selected some seven-

taken from Origen, as early suggested by Hort.[29] The variant reading in the doxology, *et adventum domini nostri Jesu Christi,* is found nowhere else in Jerome but frequently in Origen.[30] Further, when Origen deals with the problems envisioned in this passage he appeals to the doxology.[31] In addition, the concern with Montanism[32] obvious in the passage is symptomatic of the early third century, not the fourth. All of this leaves no doubt that in this statement of Jerome we have ultimately to do with the testimony of Origen.

What do these two testimonies intimate about the textual history of Romans? Clearly, in his commentary on Romans Origen regards Marcion as the creator of the fourteen-chapter text. According to him, the Marcionite text lacked the doxology and the final two chapters, whereas all the catholic texts known to Origen had the doxology and the final two chapters, though in the catholic MSS the doxology was variously to be found, either at the end of ch. 14 or at the end of ch. 16. In the Origenic testimony preserved by Jerome, however, while it is explicitly observed that MSS are known which lack the doxology, the impression is left that these are catholic texts; it is not said that they are heretical products (or are affected by such), much less of Marcionite origin. We are thus confronted by two testimonies not easy to reconcile: on the one hand texts without the doxology are thought Marcionite, while on the other hand they are apparently considered catholic.

As a means of explaining the inconsistency much discussion has aimed at determining who is being polemicized in the passage from Jerome's commentary on Ephesians. The Montanist movement seems to be in view when it is said that some think the prophets were ignorant of what they said because they prophesied in ecstasy, and this accords with the explicit rejection of such teaching as Montanist which shortly precedes this section.[33] Such a notion is not one ordinarily associated with Marcion or his disciples. Yet the following polemical thrust against those who do not understand the prophets and do not wish to, and who prefer to have the gospel only, apparently reflects a Marcionite tenet. Efforts have been made to exclude any reference to the Montanists and to reserve the whole polemic for the Marcionites, in the hope of gaining some confirmation of Origen's other testimony.[34] That reference to the Montanists can be excluded does not seem possible, but even if we should think in the whole context of Marcionites alone, the fact

---

teen passages from Jerome's commentary in order to prove that Jerome used the exact words of Origen at many points without repudiating Origen's interpretations.

[29]*Biblical Essays,* 333–34, and later with B. F. Westcott in *The New Testament in the Original Greek* (2 vols.; New York, 1882) II, "Appendix: Notes on Selected Readings," 112–14. Fuller proof was adduced by Zahn, *Geschichte,* II, 428–29. Cf. also Dupont, "L'histoire de la doxologie," 13–14.

[30]Thus *Comm. in Joh.* vi.2 (*PG* XIV, 205C), xiii.17 (*PG* XIV, 424B), *Contra Celsum* ii.4 (*PG* XI, 802A). The reading is confirmed for Origen also by codex 1739, for which the text of Romans was transcribed from the lemmata of Origen's commentary. See Bauernfeind, *Der Römerbrieftext des Origenes nach dem Codex von der Goltz,* 119.

[31]See Dupont, "L'histoire de la doxologie," 14, and Zahn, *Geschichte,* II, 428.

[32]See further below. It is possible that Marcionites are also (only?) in view, but that does not make a difference for referring these remarks to Origen.

[33]*PL* XXVI, 510C: *Aut igitur juxta Montanum, patriarchas et prophetas in ecstasi locutos accipiendum, et nescisse quae dixerint.*

[34]Thus Riggenbach, "Textgeschichte," 593; Zahn, *Geschichte,* II, 428–430; and Dupont, "L'histoire de la doxologie," 15–17 with further considerations. This explanation requires that the allegation that the prophets did not know what they said because they spoke in ecstasy be attributed to the Marcionites. The arguments for ascribing this view to Marcionites are interesting but hardly convincing.

remains that MSS lacking the doxology appear—through the concise parenthetical mention—to be considered quite as catholic as others. Nor does it suffice to assume that a Marcionite origin of these is implied,[35] for in a polemical statement of this kind it would have been almost mandatory to point up the anomaly of heretics appealing for dogmatic support to a passage they did not accept as part of the text, if this were known to be the case. Thus even if only Marcionites are in view the discrepancy between the testimonies is not resolved, but only shifted to another point: in the commentary on Romans the omission of the doxology is said to be the work of Marcion, while in the commentary on Ephesians Marcionites are found citing the doxology as a proof of their position. This conflict might be escaped by supposing that the doxology emerged in Marcionite circles after Marcion, but this would go against Origen at yet another point since he accuses Marcion of removing the doxology![36] Beyond that, the statement in Jerome's commentary on Ephesians cannot be used to confirm Origen's assertion that Marcion created the fourteen-chapter form of Romans; all it really offers is further evidence of a form of Romans in which the doxology was absent.

The cost of harmonizing these two statements from Origen is too high, especially since efforts to harmonize them produce no positive result, and the inconsistency should be allowed to stand. De Bruyne saw the necessity of this and concluded that when Origen wrote on Ephesians he was simply better informed than when he wrote on Romans, and was no longer willing to impute to Marcion the removal of the doxology.[37] Whatever the reason for it, we may here leave open the problem of the inconsistency between Origen's testimonies.

It remains for us to evaluate in itself Origen's accusation that Marcion created the fourteen-chapter text of Romans. Even within the testimony *ad Rom* 16:25–27 there is a curious feature. The fourteen-chapter form of the text is seen as the work of Marcion, and yet it is asserted that the doxology is found at the end of ch. 14 in texts which do not stand under Marcionite influence (*in his quae non sunt a Marcione temerata*). But as we observed earlier, the placement of the doxology after ch. 14 in any MS is clear evidence that at some point in the history behind that MS there existed a text of the letter without chs. 15 and 16.[38] If Marcion bears the responsibility for the fourteen-chapter form of the text, then MSS with the doxology after ch. 14, which Origen reckoned as catholic and not influenced by Marcion, are in fact "tainted" by a Marcionite streak in their ancestries. Conversely, if Origen can speak of MSS with the doxology after ch. 14 as not being influenced by Marcion, that can only cast doubt on Origen's opinion that it was Marcion who first omitted the final chapters.[39] Taking Origen's testimony on its own terms, we are

---

Even if Origen on occasion combats the (Marcionite?) view that Moses failed to grasp the true sense of the Law he announced, that does not justify ascribing to Marcionites a view which Jerome unambiguously imputes to Montanists.

[35]Such is the judgment of Hort, *Biblical Essays,* 334; Zahn, *Geschichte,* II, 430; Schumacher, *Letzten Kapitel,* 128; and Dupont, "L'histoire de la doxologie," 18.

[36]Zahn (*Geschichte,* II, 429) sought to overcome the difficulty by suggesting that we have here a case in which Marcionites, in disputing with the orthodox, used a text which the orthodox had to recognize, even if the Marcionites themselves did not have it.

[37]"La finale marcionite," 140 n. 1.

[38]See above, 24.

[39]Origen cannot, of course, have been aware of this problem, but could have been awakened to it by an encounter with catholic MSS lacking the doxology.

It is possible that Origen correctly thought that Marcion omitted the doxology and the last two

brought to the alternative: either MSS with the doxology after ch. 14 are not without Marcionite influence, or Marcion did not foster the fourteen-chapter text. Origen provides no rationale for his opinion that Marcion excised the final chapters of the letter—there is no mention of historical evidence or tradition. This does not of itself make the testimony any less important, but it does compel an effort to discover elsewhere support, or lack of it, for Origen's stated conviction.

Many have sought to substantiate Origen's witness by discovering motives for a Marcionite elimination of chs. 15 and 16. This is achieved mainly by identifying features of these chapters which would have offended Marcion's dogmatic sensibilities. As such we might consider the numerous quotations of the OT in ch. 15 (vss. 3, 9–12, 21), the commendation of Scripture (i.e., the OT) as valuable for the Christian (15:4), the description of Christ as a "servant to the circumcised" (15:8), the warning against false teachers in 16:17–20, and perhaps even the historical specificity of the letter (15:22–33; 16:1–23).[40] It is fairly obvious that the first three of these items would have run counter to Marcion's theological persuasion, and that had he known ch. 15 he might well have removed such elements from the text. On the other hand, neither of the last two features can be given any weight. The warning against false teachers could have been construed by Marcion as a vindication rather than an indictment of himself, as he may have done in similar polemical passages. And that Marcion was primarily a theoretician who had no interest in specific groups of readers, and so preferred an abstract theological treatise to a historically particular letter,[41] is scarcely convincing, since it appears that Marcion did not excise the personalia of Col 4 or make any alterations in Philemon, and since in his *Apostolikon* he retained the superscription "To the Romans."[42]

Granting, however, that Marcion could have taken dogmatic exception to some elements of ch. 15—the conflict of ideas is manifest—it must still be asked whether he would have found it necessary on that account to eliminate *everything* after 14:23. An omission of such extent is unparalleled in Marcion's work on the epistles.[43] His customary practice was to remove only the specific passages which

---

chapters, and simply failed to recognize that Marcion's text had influenced the catholic texts. Yet texts which could then be considered to stand under Marcionite influence (those with the doxology after ch. 14) must have been well represented to Origen. There is no numerical comparison, but the juxtaposition of *nonnulli* and *alii* gives the impression of an almost equal number of texts with the doxology after ch. 14 and those with it after ch. 16.

[40]A representative statement is that of Sanday and Headlam, *The Epistle to the Romans,* xcvi–xcvii. Vogels ("Der Einfluss Marcions und Tatians auf Text und Kanon des NT," 282) adds that Marcion wished his text to be suitable for reading in worship, and for this ch. 16 was of no value.

[41]Thus, in one way or another, de Bruyne, "La finale marcionite," 137; Corssen, "Überlieferungsgeschichte," 35–36; Zahn, *Geschichte,* I, 649. De Bruyne saw such a tendency expressed also in the short benediction which he found in several MSS after 14:23 (see above, 24).

[42]Also, even if Marcion did not have the words "in Ephesus" in Eph 1:1, he still accepted for this letter the specific address of Laodicea. Corssen ("Überlieferungsgeschichte," 36) counters these observations with the remarks that Marcion believed these letters were addressed to individual communities, but were not meant exclusively for them. If the Vulgate prologues to the Pauline letters are Marcionite products (see below, 111–13), by providing concise statements as to the historical circumstances and addressees of the letters, they speak against the assumption that Marcion would not tolerate specific addresses. Regarding the alleged abstract and general interests of Marcion, Harnack (*Marcion,* 160* n. 1) rightly stated that "the text of Marcion available to us provides no sufficient basis for such generalizations."

[43]The only analogous case would be the omission of much of Rom 9–11, but it is uncertain that this section was removed *in toto*. Cf. Tertullian *Adv. Marc.* v.14 (*PL* II, 539B), and Harnack, *Marcion,*

he disapproved, allowing the rest to stand. Thus both the paucity of assured motives and the divergence of the omission in extent and method from Marcion's other editorial work create doubt that the fourteen-chapter text originated with Marcion.

In addition, we must reckon with the fact that among patristic writers Origen stands alone in holding Marcion responsible for the short-text of Romans. Tertullian and Irenaeus not only fail to cite anything from Rom 15 and 16, a fact indicating that they themselves used the short form, but neither they nor Epiphanius implies that Marcion deleted these chapters. The absence of any such notice is especially striking in Tertullian, who says that Marcion mutilated Romans more than other letters and who is always ready to comment on Marcion's textual mutations at points where he knew them to exist.[44] Further, the fourteen-chapter form of the text must have been extremely influential in the early period in East and West. It was well represented to Origen in the form of MSS with the doxology after ch. 14, a placement characteristic of virtually all our Byzantine witnesses. Its prevalence in the West is shown by the Old Latin tradition. Such broad dispersion is hardly to be expected of a heretical product, and would be the more remarkable at this early time when the catholic opposition to Marcion was at its zenith.

Indirect light is shed on the question by the character of the Marcionite text in general, a reconstruction of which is one of the most important results of Harnack's study of Marcion.[45] On this basis Harnack came to see that a very close relation pertains between the text of Marcion and the text of the Pauline bilingual MSS, witnesses to the Western text of the epistles. Of these Harnack found Codex Boernerianus (G) to stand nearest Marcion's text.[46] Harnack isolated approximately 100 readings in which Marcion and the Western witnesses stand together against the major text-types. Of these he considered only about ten to be *possible* results of tendentious (Marcionite) alterations, but only six of these as *probable* results of such.[47] After a lengthy examination of the possibilities of dependence Harnack was forced to the conclusion that there is no basis for the assumption that the Western text actually rests on the Marcionite text.[48] This conclusion, which is soundly based, means that many readings which might have been regarded as specifically Marcionite are not Marcionite, but only characteristic Western variants.[49] In both Marcion and the major Western witnesses we have (indirect) attestation of a fourteen-chapter text of Romans which originally lacked the doxology.[50] Given the extensive affinity

---

150*. Moreover, it is much easier to see why Marcion could not tolerate Rom 9–11, and may have removed it as a whole, than why he should have omitted Rom 15–16.

[44]*Adv. Marc.* v.13 (*PL* II, 536A). Epiphanius, *Adv. Haer.* i.3.42 (*PG* XLI, 720D–721A), notes only eight small omissions made by Marcion in Romans, among which the doxology and the last two chapters do not figure.

[45]*Marcion,* 67*–127* (Apostle), 183*–240* (Gospel).

[46]Ibid., 151*–52*.

[47]Ibid., 153*–55*. Among these six Harnack included the doxology of Rom 16:25–27, which should not be counted, as we shall see.

[48]Ibid., 166*, cf. 135*ff., 222*ff., 247*ff.

[49]A. Pott ("Marcions Evangelientext," *Zeitschrift für Kirchengeschichte* 42 [1923] 202–203), using Harnack's reconstruction of Marcion's text, was able to show through a comparison with the apparatuses of Tischendorf and von Soden that the relation between the Marcionite and Western texts was closer than even Harnack supposed, to the extent that some readings Harnack thought unattested outside Marcion are in fact to be found elsewhere. Harnack's perception of the close relation between the Marcionite and bilingual texts was anticipated to some extent by Corssen.

[50]See above, 16–29.

among these witnesses and the impossibility of regarding the Marcionite text as the *Vorlage* of the Western, it is even more dubious that Marcion created the short text of Romans.

The availability of the testimony of Origen has in the past led to a search for other traces of Marcionite influence on the text of Romans, and these have been supposed to be present above all in the doxology itself (16:25–27).

The debate about the authenticity of the doxology has not yet come completely to rest, but it is now widely recognized that aspects of its style, language and thought weigh against Pauline authorship. The decisive argument for its non-Pauline origin lies elsewhere, however, namely in the fact that the doxology was attached originally to the fourteen-chapter text of the letter, which is not to be attributed to Paul.[51] But, having made a judgment against the authenticity of the doxology, many scholars have thought it to be a composition of Marcion or of his followers. A Marcionite origin of the doxology, if demonstrable, could be taken to support, but not to prove, the contention of Origen that Marcion created the short form of the letter. Still, it must be noted that the doxology can be thought Marcionite only at the expense of part of Origen's own testimony, which has it that Marcion removed the doxology.[52]

Corssen was the first to suggest that the doxology exhibits features of Marcionite doctrine, and on that basis he assigned its composition to Marcionite circles.[53] His major arguments for this were the following. Although the affirmations of the doxology, that the gospel rests on revelation and not human reason and that its content was determined before creation but remained hidden, are certainly in accord with the Pauline perspective, Paul never did and never could insist with the doxology that the revelation was always concealed in time. Paul understood the secret to have been early proclaimed by the prophets (Rom 1:2; 3:21, etc.). This peculiar and un-Pauline idea Corssen discerned especially in the term σεσιγημένον, which has a distinctly stronger nuance than ἀποκεκρυμένον. Since Paul appeals for evidence of the gospel to the Law and the prophets, the doxology contradicts Paul's understanding. Further, the statement of the doxology that the secret is made known διὰ γραφῶν προφητικῶν cannot be understood as a reference to the prophetic books of the OT; this is excluded, according to Corssen, both by the hiddenness of the secret in time and by the absence of the article, which would have been necessary if a complete and recognizable group of books were meant. The reference is rather to the Pauline writings themselves: Paul is the "prophet" who mediates the revelation. Thus Corssen found in the doxology two fundamental Marcionite conceptions: the revelation was eternally concealed before Paul, and Paul is the bearer of the revelation.

Corssen's attribution of the doxology to Marcionite circles was taken up and developed by Harnack.[54] Whereas Corssen had dealt with the doxology in its

---

[51] On this see below, 123–24.

[52] Corssen ("Überlieferungsgeschichte," 34) took Origen's testimony seriously enough not to speak of Marcion himself, and supposed that Origen had only heard that Marcion removed everything after 14:23 and misunderstood this to refer to the doxology also.

[53] "Überlieferungsgeschichte," 32–34.

[54] "Über I Kor. 14,32ff. und Röm. 16,25ff. nach der ältesten Überlieferung und der marcionitischen Bibel," *Studien zur Geschichte des Neuen Testaments und der Alten Kirche*, I, *Zur neutestamentlichen Textkritik* (Berlin, 1931) 180–190. Harnack's estimate of the doxology has more recently

traditional form, Harnack, persuaded of its Marcionite origin, endeavored to show that the present form of the doxology is secondary, the result of an ecclesiastical editing of an older Marcionite text. He judged a number of elements in the doxology as superfluous and/or inconsistent. In reconstructing the "original" (Marcionite) form Harnack eliminated as corrective editorial additions the phrases καὶ τὸ κηρύγμα Ἰησοῦ Χριστοῦ,[55] and διά τε γραφῶν προφητικῶν . . . γνωρισθέν-τος.[56] This allowed a stricter consistency of thought and a simpler structure in which only two clauses are correlated (σεσιγημένον—φανερωθέντος).[57] Thus the reconstructed doxology contained two basic Marcionite emphases: on the previous absolute inaccessibility of the revelation and on the ultimacy of the Pauline gospel. For support Harnack referred also to the divine attributes mentioned in the doxology (μόνος, σοφός, αἰώνιος) as indicative of a Marcionite perspective.[58] Thus Harnack felt he had conclusively shown the purely Marcionite character of the doxology. According to him, the present form of the doxology arose when the Marcionite piece had gained a foothold in the catholic tradition but was felt to be dogmatically unsatisfactory. It was then (mistakenly) assumed that Marcion had perverted an originally Pauline text, and the effort to restore the supposed Pauline original led to the editorial additions(!).[59]

It requires no special acumen to see that Harnack's argument is a pure *petitio principii;* his conclusion is not surprising, for it was also his premise.[60] Harnack rightly observed, however, that the doxology is constructed with a certain awkwardness and pleonastic style. But whether this warrants a reconstruction of the text is quite another question, and one which can be answered only through a form-critical study of doxologies generally.

These efforts to find in the doxology of Romans a distinctly Marcionite coloring are shown to be misguided by several more recent form-critical studies which effectively demonstrate that the conceptuality and terminology of Rom 16:25–27 are characteristic of a clearly defined pattern of early Christian proclamation.[61] The doxology is but one of several texts which embody a "revelation scheme" marked by the idea of a mystery previously hidden but now revealed.[62]

---

been endorsed by Zuntz, *The Text of the Epistles,* 227–28. Harnack's argument and conclusion are summarized in *Marcion,* 165*.

[55]"Über I Kor. 14,32ff. und Röm 16,25ff. nach der ältesten Überlieferung und der marcioniti-schen Bibel," 186, for the reason that it is pleonastic to mention the *kerygma Christi* after "my gospel."

[56]Ibid., 187, because this idea stands in contradiction to the main statement ("kept secret for long ages"), once it is recognized that the "prophetic writings" are indeed those of the OT.

[57]Ibid., 188.

[58]Ibid., 189: μόνος meaning the only true God, the creator-God being the κοσμοκράτωρ, σοφός showing Marcion's special interest in the divine σοφία, and αἰώνιος contrasting with the temporal life of the creator-God.

[59]Ibid., 189–190.

[60]Note that one of the two phrases which led Corssen to the notion of a Marcionite origin, the reference to "prophetic writings," is set down by Harnack to a catholic editor!

[61]See N. A. Dahl, "Formgeschichtliche Beobachtungen zum Christusverkündigung in der Gemeindepredigt," in *Neutestamentliche Studien für Rudolf Bultmann* (ed. W. Eltester; BZNW 21; Berlin, 1954) 3–9. His conclusions are taken up and elaborated by Dieter Lührmann, *Das Offenbarungsverständnis bei Paulus und in paulinischen Gemeinden* (WMANT 16; Neukirchen-Vluyn, 1965) 124–133 (hereinafter *Offenbarungsverständnis*). Also, independently of these, see Kamlah, *Schlussdoxologie.*

[62]The relevant texts are 1 Cor 2:6ff., Col 1:26, Eph 3:4–7, 8–11, Rom 16:25–27; cf. also 2 Tim 1:9–11, Tit 1:2–3, and, outside the Pauline material, 1 Pet 1:18–21; Ign Mag 6:1; Herm Sim 9:12. In

The turning point between the concealment and the revelation is marked by νῦν, referring to the eschatological time of salvation.[63] The presence within this pattern of such terms as εὐαγγέλιον, κήρυγμα (Rom 16:25), εὐαγγελίζεσθαι (Eph 3:8), λόγος τοῦ θεοῦ, καταγγέλλειν, διδάσκειν (Col 1:25–28), shows that the revelation scheme had its *Sitz im Leben* in primitive preaching.[64]

The close similarity between the doxology of Romans and the related texts demonstrates that the notion of a revelation concealed for eternity but now made known was very much at home in early Christianity, but especially popular in Pauline circles, and that the antithesis "hidden-revealed" in Rom 16:25–27 does not of itself suggest a Marcionite tendency. Even if the idea of hiddenness is perhaps more strongly expressed through the use of σεσιγημένον, we still stand in the same conceptual environment.[65] Decisive weight was placed by Corssen and Harnack on the phrase χρόνοις αἰωνίοις, but this is not a significant departure from the modifying phrases in the related texts: cf. ἀπὸ τῶν αἰώνων καὶ ἀπὸ τῶν γενεῶν (Col 1:26), ἀπὸ τῶν αἰώνων (Eph 3:9), ἑτέραις γενεαῖς (Eph 3:5). The mention of prophetic writings in Rom 16:26 is somewhat more difficult to explicate. In the other texts concerned with the revelation of the mystery there is sometimes mention of prophets. In Eph 3:4–5 we have the mystery revealed τοῖς ἁγίοις ἀποστόλοις αὐτοῦ καὶ προφήταις ἐν πνεύματι, and in Rev 10:7 the mystery is to be fulfilled ὡς εὐηγγέλισεν τοὺς ἑαυτοῦ δούλους τοὺς προφήτας. Yet nowhere outside our doxology are prophetic *writings* mentioned. It is conceivable that at least in Eph 3:5 *Christian* prophets are meant, as is suggested by the correlation of προφῆται with the preceding ἀπόστολοι as recipients of the revelation, and the fact that the revelation belongs to the eschatological period. This is possibly true of Rev 10:7 also.[66] It may be, therefore, that Christian prophets were generally considered recipients of the mystery as the content of their revelations, and so figure naturally in the mystery formulae. Even so, this does not explain why in Rom 16:26 we hear of prophetic *writings,* which can scarcely mean the writings of Christian prophets in general. One possibility, as we have seen, is that Paul himself is the (Christian) prophet in this instance, and that for this reason writings are mentioned.[67] The only

---

these three groups of texts Dahl ("Formgeschichtliche Beobachtungen," 4–5) sees two variants of one basic scheme, the first speaking of a hidden mystery, the latter lacking these terms and being more freely formulated. Lührmann (*Offenbarungsverständnis*, 125) wishes to reserve the designation "revelation scheme" for Col 1:26, Eph 3:4–7, 9–11 and Rom 16:25–27, since the term "mystery" which Lührmann regards as fundamentally important appears only in these places.

[63]Lührmann (*Offenbarungsverständnis*, 125) observes that the νῦν has no historical precision and that therefore the real point is not so much "when" as "through whom" and "where" the revelation occurs.

[64]Dahl, "Formgeschichtliche Beobachtungen," 4–5.

[65]Elsewhere we have ἀποκεκρυμμένον (1 Cor 2:7; Eph 3:9; Col 1:26) and οὐκ ἐγνωρίσθη (Eph 3:5). We know of course of a σιγή speculation in Gnosticism, and Lührmann (*Offenbarungsverständnis*, 122–23) thinks this Gnostic concern lies behind the doxology. But a very similar notion can be seen in Hellenistic and apocalyptic Judaism in Wis 18:14–16; Apoc Bar 3:6–7; 4 Ezra 6:38–39; 7:30, as Kamlah has pointed out (*Schlussdoxologie*, pp. 122ff.). Michel suggests that the emphasis lies not so much on the idea of silence as on the epoch during which the saving plan was concealed (*Der Brief an die Römer*, 390 n. 1).

[66]Kamlah (*Schlussdoxologie*, 50) supposes that OT prophets are meant here. The question is very difficult to decide.

[67]Thus, in addition to Corssen (see above, 107), Lührmann, *Offenbarungsverständnis*, 123–24, referring to the σιγή idea in 16:25 understood in a Gnostic way and recalling the Gnostic denial of revelatory value to the OT prophets.

other possibility is to think of the prophetic literature of the OT, as do most recent commentators.

The solution of this problem lies in the observations made by Kamlah on the composition of the doxology. In his highly detailed investigation he has shown that the doxology was compiled from originally distinct materials. This is obvious from the fact that two independent formal patterns, the doxological formula and the revelation scheme, are here fused together.[68] Beyond conflating these two forms, the author of the doxology added some phrases modelled on Pauline statements. The phrase in the doxology εἰς ὑπακοὴν πίστεως (16:26) is a verbatim reproduction of a phrase found in Rom 1:5. This close connection with the prescript of Romans makes it very likely that the phrase in the doxology, διὰ γραφῶν προφητικῶν, is conceived with reference to Rom 1:2, ὃ (εὐαγγέλιον) προεπηγγείλατο διὰ τῶν προφητῶν αὐτοῦ ἐν γραφαῖς ἁγίαις ("which [gospel] he promised beforehand through his prophets in holy scriptures").[69] If this is so, then the phrase γράφαι προφήτικαι of 16:26 must refer to the prophetic books of the OT.[70] This is certainly the most natural understanding of the words, and the idea that the revelation is revealed in the eschatological period through prophetic writings of a previous period is not the contradiction in terms which many have found in it, as the Qumran literature has taught us.[71] On the other hand, that Paul himself should be thought of as a prophet, or that his writings should be characterized primarily as "prophetic," goes against the dominant aspects of Paul's self-understanding, not to mention later regard for him, and against the real nature of his letters.[72]

Finally, neither do the divine attributes mentioned in the doxology, μόνος and σοφός, favor a Marcionite origin of the doxology, as Harnack urged. A comparison of the doxological elements in Rom 16:25–27 with other doxological texts reveals how closely our passage corresponds to customary form and terminology. The designation μόνος is very frequent in doxologies,[73] and other attributes are often added,[74] even though only here do we find the combination of μόνος and σοφός. Yet the divine wisdom is not an uncommon theme in Hellenistic Judaism or the NT and in no way points to a Marcionite dogmatic interest.[75]

[68]Kamlah, *Schlussdoxologie*, 28ff., 66ff., 77ff. and *passim* speaks of a "hymn to the mystery" rather than of a revelation-scheme.

[69]Ibid., 58ff. The syntactical difficulties and pleonastic style which Harnack observed in the doxology are quite real for the most part, but result from the compilation of the doxology from originally independent materials, not from the sort of secondary editorial reworking of an originally unitary composition that Harnack supposed. On the relation of the doxology to Romans see further below, 122–23.

[70]Ibid., 45–52. He concludes that even if the mention of prophets belonged to the revelation-scheme which lay before the author of the doxology, he altered it by reference to Rom 1:2 in order to connect the doxology more closely with Romans.

[71]That the divine plan was not made known to the prophets but that it is nevertheless revealed in the prophetic writings is a fundamental presupposition of Qumran's *pesher* hermeneutic: the true meaning of the prophetic scriptures emerges only in the light of events of the end-time. Cf. 1QpHab 7:1–5; 2:8–10.

[72]It can also be asked whether Marcion or Marcionites would have described Paul's writings with a phrase so liable to an interpretation inimical to their view of the OT.

[73]1 Tim 1:17; Jude 25; 2 Clem 20:5; cf. 1 Tim 6:15; Rev 15:4.

[74]1 Tim 1:17 (ἄφθαρτος, ἀόρατος), 2 Clem 20:5 (ἀόρατος). Those terms are at home primarily in a Hellenistic milieu, and the use of μόνος has its impact vis-à-vis a polytheistic (Hellenistic) context. On these and other doxological attributes see Deichgräber, *Gotteshymnus und Christushymnus in der frühen Christenheit*, 97ff.

[75]Kamlah, *Schlussdoxologie*, 83ff., citing several parallels from Philo, e.g., *Sacr. Abr.* 64.120, *q. Deus imm.* 102, *Phant.* 46.138, *Conf. ling.* 39.94, etc., for Philo's use of μόνος and σοφός as divine

Thus nothing in the doxology is suggestive of an origin in Marcionite circles.[76] Even if Marcionite ideas were to be found in it, that would say nothing about whether Marcion created the short text of Romans, but would be evidence only that this form of the letter was *used* by Marcionites, which is not disputed.

The case is similar with the prologues to the Pauline letters preserved in numerous Vulgate MSS which, since the early studies of de Bruyne and Corssen, have been widely thought to be Marcionite, and so are customarily called the Marcionite prologues to the Pauline letters.[77] The evidence for this opinion is considerable, but falls short of decisive proof.

In addition to providing concise statements about the geographical locations of the recipients and the place from which each letter was written, the prologues betray a strong interest in juxtaposing Paul, called *apostolos,* with others, termed *falsi- (pseudo-) apostoli,* who subvert the "word of truth" (*verbum veritatis*). Under this aspect the Pauline letters are regarded as means either of recalling the communities to the true faith or of commending them for their steadfastness against deceit. That Paul appears here as *the* apostle and that the doctrine espoused by the false apostles has a clearly Jewish character are both features that accord very well with Marcionism.[78]

Equally important is the order of the Pauline letters presupposed by the prologues. The prologue to 1 Corinthians can be understood only if the prologue to Galatians preceded it. The latter reads *hi verbum veritatis primum ab apostolo acceperunt* ("These first received the word of truth from the apostle"), and that to 1 Corinthians *et hi similiter ab apostolis audierunt verbum veritatis . . .* ("these too likewise heard the word of truth from the apostles . . .").[79] Further, in the prologue to Colossians the phrase *et hi . . . sunt Asiani* must point back to the prologue to Ephesians, the only other one to describe the recipients as *Asiani.* Hence the order of the letters lying behind the prologues placed Galatians before Corinthians and Ephesians before Colossians, and this is just the order in which Marcion had the letters, although he knew Ephesians as Laodiceans.[80] There is, in addition, every reason to suppose that the prologue to Romans is based on the short text of Romans.[81] Thus the ideology of the prologues, the order of the letters which they presume, and the use of the short text of Romans might all be expected if the prologues were composed in a Marcionite setting. It is clear that they must have had

---

attributes. On the phrase see also J. Dupont, "Μόνῳ σοφῷ θεῷ (Rom. XVI, 27)," *ETL* 22 (1946) 362–375.

[76]Curiously, Lührmann (*Offenbarungsverständnis,* 123 n. 4) continues to think the doxology originated in Marcionite circles.

[77]Donatien de Bruyne, "Prologues bibliques d'origin marcionite," *RBen* 24 (1907) 1–14, and, independently, Corssen, "Überlieferungsgeschichte," 36–45, with "Nachtrag," 97–100. A convenient summary of the debate is given by Gustave Bardy, "Marcionites (prologues)," *Dictionnaire de la Bible, Supplément* (Paris, 1957) V, 877–881.

[78]The false apostles induced believers *in lege et circumcisione* (Gal), *in lege et prophetis* (Rom), and some were deceived *a secta legis Iudicae* (Cor), etc.

[79]The prologue to Romans takes a completely different line and is not a candidate for first position among the letters in this case.

[80]The beginning of the prologue to Colossians (*Colossenses et hi sicut Laodicenses sunt Asiani*) led de Bruyne ("Prologues bibliques d'origin marcionite," 4ff.) to suppose that there was originally a separate prologue to Laodiceans (=Ephesians), which he proceeded to reconstruct. Others are content simply to regard the prologue to Ephesians as having suffered only a change in the name of the letter's recipients.

[81]See above, 19–20.

an early origin. Certainly they antedate the Vulgate, and were very likely taken up into Vulgate MSS from Old Latin MSS.[82]

In spite of all this, the conjecture of a Marcionite origin is not absolutely compelling and can be contested on several grounds.[83] Since there is no extant prologue to Ephesians *as* Laodiceans, and since the mention of the Laodiceans in the prologue to Colossians can be accounted for merely by reference to Col 4:12ff. without assuming an original Laodicean prologue, it is doubtful whether the author of the prologues knew Ephesians as Laodiceans, and so questionable that he was a Marcionite.[84] We also have to reckon with the existence of prologues to the Pastorals, which were not part of Marcion's canon. But this can be explained by assuming either that later Marcionites admitted the Pastorals and provided them with prologues,[85] or that the prologues to the Pastorals are later catholic additions to the original Marcionite matter.[86]

Further, if we cannot doubt that Marcion had the letters in the order presupposed by the prologues, it still has to be asked whether this order originated with Marcion or was uniquely possessed by him.[87] For a long time it has been axiomatic that Marcion created this order of the letters, but the evidence for this is slight. Marcion is supposed to have elevated Galatians to the head of the collection for dogmatic reasons: in Galatians the Pauline opposition to Judaism is most sharply expressed. But if this were so, why did Romans not occupy at least second position in Marcion's order, for a similar reason? For the rest, Marcion's arrangement of the letters is usually thought to be determined by the principle of decreasing length.[88] But it is equally, and in some respects more likely that the order attested by Marcion—but not by him alone[89]—rests on chronological considerations, that is, is governed by a conception of the order in which the letters were written.[90] In this case a Marcionite origin of this order is scarcely to be considered above any other.

[82]It is difficult to date the origin of the prologues. Those favoring a Marcionite origin naturally assume their composition in the second century, but there is no clear evidence for this, especially if we deny that the Muratorian canon alludes to them. Though extant only in Latin, it is possible that at least some of them were composed in Greek; the prologues to the letters to seven churches (the shape of the original collection?) are more easily converted into Greek than the others.

[83]Early opposition was mounted by W. Mundle, "Die Herkunft der 'marcionitischen' Prologe zu den paulinischen Briefen," *ZNW* 24 (1925) 56–77, and M. J. Lagrange, "Les prologues prétendus marcionites," *RB* 35 (1926) 161–173. The most recent and cogent counterargument is that of Frede, *Altlateinische Paulus-Handschriften*, 171–78.

[84]But it is possible that the present prologue to Ephesians is secondary; it is almost identical with the prologue to Philippians.

[85]Thus Corssen, "Überlieferungsgeschichte," 43, and Harnack, *Marcion*, 127*–134*.

[86]Thus de Bruyne, "Prologues bibliques d'origin marcionite," 8.

[87]Here as elsewhere it is important to maintain the distinction between "earliest evidence" and "origin."

[88]See, e.g., Harnack, *Marcion*, 168*–69*, J. Finegan, "The Original Form of the Pauline Collection," *HTR* 49 (1956) 85–104, esp. 94.

[89]More or less the same order, with Galatians, Corinthians and Romans at the head and minor variations for the rest, is attested for the Syrian church by the *Catalogus Sinaiticus* and by Ephraem. For the evidence for this and other orders of the Pauline collection see the recent and very useful discussion by H. J. Frede, "Die Ordnung der Paulusbriefe und der Platz des Kolosserbriefes im Corpus Paulinum," *Vetus Latina. Die Reste der altlateinischen Bibel*, XXIV/2: *Epistulae ad Philippenses et Colossenses*, Lieferung 4 (Freiburg, 1969) 290–303.

[90]So Zahn, *Geschichte*, I, 623; W. Hartke, *Die Sammlung und die ältesten Ausgaben der Paulusbriefe* (Bonn, 1917) 73; W. Hadorn, "Die Abfassung der Thessalonicherbriefe auf der dritten Missionsreise und der Kanon des Marcion," *ZNW* 19 (1919–20) 67–72; and now Frede, "Die Ordnung der Paulusbriefe," 295–96. Zahn was willing to allow for the possibility that the chronological principle was ignored in placing Galatians at the head; but that Galatians should have stood at the head of a strictly

Finally, none of the anti-Marcionite polemicists reveals any acquaintance with these prologues, but if they belonged to the *Apostolikon,* or were otherwise especially associated with Marcion, we would expect them to be cited.[91]

Nevertheless, the conceptuality of the prologues provides a strong argument for their Marcionite connection, though this cannot be conclusively established. As far as their significance for the textual history of Romans is concerned, however, the prologues, if they are Marcionite, can show only that the fourteen-chapter text was used by Marcionites, not that Marcion created this form of the text.

It is significant that although Corssen, followed by Harnack, thought both the doxology and the prologues to be Marcionite, neither felt justified in ascribing the creation of the fourteen-chapter form of the text to Marcion or his disciples. Corssen accepted as the most probable explanation "that the exemplar of the Roman letter used by Marcion was mutilated at the end."[92]

Summarily, the widely held view that the origin of the fourteen-chapter text of Romans is to be traced to Marcion, a view occasioned primarily by the testimony of Origen, has no firm foundation in the available evidence and must be set aside in favor of some other explanation. At best the evidence indicates that Marcion employed the short form of the text, and, given the wide use of this text during the same period, it must be assumed that Marcion took over a text of Romans which was already in circulation.[93] The testimony of Origen need not stand in the way of

---

chronological order is both possible and even likely in view of the extensive information about Paul's early career in Gal 1–2. Nor can it be objected that in a chronological order Romans would have occupied final position, for the matter which would have required such a position, Rom 15, was not at hand.

[91]Harnack ("Die marcionitischen Prologe zu den Paulusbriefen, eine Quelle des muratorischen Fragments," *ZNW* 25 [1926] 160–63) tried to show that the writer of the Muratorian canon knew the prologues as part of the text of the letters, and for this reason was able to say *epistolae autem Pauli quae a quo loco vel qua ex causa directae sint, volentibus intelligere ipsae declarant* ("But the epistles of Paul themselves make clear to those who wish to know it which there are [i.e. from Paul], from what place and for what reason they were written," lines 39–41). However, this statement could as easily refer to the letters themselves without the prologues (cf. *volentibus intelligere*), as shown by Dahl ("Welche Ordnung der Paulusbriefe wird vom muratorischen Kanon vorausgesetzt?" 51ff.), who also points out that the geographical notices of the prologues have little or no effect on the notices of the Muratorian fragment itself. That the prologues were actually present in the catholic text of the letters requires the fantastic assumption that a Roman edition of the NT contained anti-Marcionite prologues to the Gospels, but Marcionite prologues to the letters! Dahl is willing to allow that the Muratorian canon polemicizes the prologues, but even that seems unnecessary.

[92]"Überlieferungsgeschichte," 45, and similarly Harnack, *Marcion,* 165*. It should be pointed out that many have misread Corssen, supposing that he attributed the origin of the short text to Marcion. This misunderstanding arises in part from the ambiguity of his statements (cf., e.g., p. 34), but mainly from a failure to read his study closely. Others not accepting the view that Marcion himself shortened the letter are Lake, *The Earlier Epistles of St. Paul,* 354–55, Knox, *Marcion and the New Testament,* 51, and Frede, *Altlateinische Paulus-Handschriften,* 156.

[93]It goes without saying that Marcion's fourteen-chapter form of the text must have lacked the specifically Roman address in 1:7 and 1:15, as does G(g); cf. Harnack, *Marcion,* 164*, and Zuntz, *The Text of the Epistles,* 228 n. 1. The opinion of Manson ("St. Paul's Letter to the Romans—and Others," 230) that the omission of the address in Romans (and Ephesians) was made by Marcion because of his rebuff at the hands of the Roman (and Ephesian) church, has no likelihood whatever. The same holds for Corssen's assumption ("Überlieferungsgeschichte," 35–36) that Marcion removed the address because of *his* generalizing interests; see above, 105 and n. 42. Of course it is improbable that Origen, who did not have the Roman address in ch. 1, was indebted for this to a Marcionite text, and though Origen pointed out what he considered Marcion's tampering with the conclusion of Romans, he says nothing of an excision of the address by Marcion. For this a Marcionite dogmatic interest is not to be conjectured. In the absence of the address Marcion only preserved an older variant. If Marcion, as we suppose, took over an already existing form of Romans, this runs counter to the view that Marcion edited his NT in Rome (Harnack, *Marcion,* 152*). Could he have had his NT already in Asia Minor?

this judgment: being aware of Marcion as a falsifier of the NT text and having knowledge of the short text of Romans, Origen made the natural but certainly erroneous inference that Marcion himself removed the doxology and the final two chapters.[94] Origen's chief importance for this and for other text-critical problems remains that of being a witness, not a judge.[95]

C. The Fourteen-Chapter Form as the Result of Liturgical Usage or Accidental Mutilation

Brief attention must be given to two further hypotheses which seek to account for the omission of chs. 15 and 16 without reference to Marcion. The first explains the truncation of the letter as a consequence of liturgical usage. As much is initially suggested by the doxology itself as a liturgical formula closely associated with the fourteen-chapter text. Is it not possible that the final two chapters of Romans were omitted because of their specialized nature, consisting in the main of Paul's missionary plans and personal greetings, which rendered them unsuitable for public reading in worship?[96] Even if the doxology stood first after ch. 16, its value for reading might have led to its preservation and association with a part of the letter which was customarily read in worship; thus a movement of 16:25–27 from the supposedly original to an earlier position is explained.

But this hypothesis encounters insurmountable difficulties. The assumption that already in the early second century there was a fixed use of lectionary texts is purely gratuitous and improbable, especially for the *Apostolos*. And while an omission of ch. 16 on liturgical grounds might explain the position of the doxology after 15:33,[97] it does not rationalize the placement of the doxology after 14:23, which would require the omission of ch. 15 as well.[98] But the elimination of ch. 15, or at least of 15:1–13, is as inconceivable for liturgical as for other reasons. Beyond these

[94]As much could be supposed simply from the way in which Origen introduces his testimony: the reigning idea is that Marcion was a falsifier of Scripture.

[95]Origen's citation of different texts in Romans is characteristic of his testimony to the text of the NT generally. Sometimes he expresses his clear preference for one or another attested reading, but at other times he rests content to allow variants to stand without himself making a choice among them. On his methods of citation and evaluation see the study of Frank Pack, "Origen's Evaluation of Textual Variants in the Greek Bible," *Restoration Quarterly* 4 (1960) 139–146, and also Bruce M. Metzger, "Explicit References in the Works of Origen to Variant Readings in New Testament Manuscripts," in *Biblical and Patristic Studies in Memory of R. P. Casey* (ed. J. N. Birdsall and R. W. Thomson; Freiburg, 1963) 78–95. It is quite impossible to speak of *the* text of Origen if a constant and closely defined textual tradition is meant. We have to consider that in the extent of his writings and movements Origen employed different MSS at different times and places, with the result that his testimony to the text of the NT is not consistent or indicative of a completely homogeneous tradition (e.g., see above, Ch. I, n. 78). Still, it can be said with Zuntz (*The Text of the Epistles*, 82) that in matters of text Origen provides "a characteristic, if variable, norm."

[96]So Hort, *Biblical Essays*, 341–44; Sanday and Headlam, *The Epistle to the Romans*, xcvii (see also below, n. 98); M. J. Lagrange, *L'Epître aux Romains* (EBib; 2nd ed.; Paris, 1950) lxv; R. Steinmetz, "Textkritische Untersuchung zu Röm. 1,7," *ZNW* 9 (1908) 177–189, with reference to the address also. These assume the authenticity of the doxology and its original place after ch. 16.

[97]Chrysostom, *Homilia in epistolam ad Romanos* xxi.i.3 (*PG* LX, 663), says that in his time 16:1–24 was considered less suitable for public reading, but this cannot be referred without further ado to an earlier period, and he does not say that the chapter was omitted from MSS.

[98]Zahn (*Introduction*, I, 410) has pointed out that our oldest lectionaries do in fact contain readings from Rom 15. Sanday and Headlam (*The Epistle to the Romans*, xcvii) attempt to account for the placement of the doxology after 14:23 by reference to Marcion as well. Assuming that the *Apostolikon* enjoyed wide circulation in the West and did affect the catholic text at some points, but also that there was a need in catholic circles to shorten the text of Romans for liturgical purposes, they proposed that the

problems we may doubt whether a liturgical use of chs. 1–14 or 1–15 only would have led to a failure to transcribe in continuous-text MSS portions which were not read in worship. And even if that is granted, it is exceedingly doubtful that such a lectionary system could have exerted so strong an influence—indeed the dominant influence so far as extant MSS are concerned—on the textual tradition of the letter. For all of these reasons the conjecture of a liturgical shortening of Romans is untenable.

Another explanation of the short text of Romans is born more of dissatisfaction with the foregoing alternatives than of a positive evaluation of the evidence. It is that the fourteen-chapter text arose not through any intentional modification of the text but simply through a fortuitous loss of several of the final leaves of an early MS.[99] The value of this explanation is great in one respect, for it alone among the various possibilities can give a good account for the abrupt breaking off at 14:23. So obviously does this interrupt the argument that in order to assume an intentional deletion of chs. 15 and 16 a solid measure of carelessness, even obtuseness, must be credited to the editor. It is inviting to be rid of this problem by appealing simply to the mutilation of some ancient archetype.

But this explanation also must be discounted. We have seen that the fourteen-chapter text of Romans was very widely diffused in East and West. It is unthinkable that all the numerous and varied traces of this form of the text are ultimately derivative from a single defective MS.[100] But it is even more significant that the evidence associates the absence of chs. 15 and 16 with the omission of the Roman address in ch. 1. These phenomena belong together in our witnesses, and certainly always belonged together. The coincidence of these omissions, far from suggesting some paleographical mishap, indicate a conscious and deliberate revision of the text of the letter. And finally, if we are correct in assuming that P^{46} gives evidence of a form of the Roman letter which lacked only ch. 16 and that this cannot represent the original extent of Paul's letter, then in framing a hypothesis we must reckon with *two* short forms of Romans. It would be preposterous to suppose that the fifteen-chapter text was also the result of an accident; the break after 15:33 is acceptable and without the offense of the break after 14:23. If the fifteen-chapter text does not derive from a mutilated archetype, this is all the less likely for the fourteen-chapter text.

D. The Fourteen-Chapter Form as the Result of Catholic Generalization

We come, then, to a final possibility, namely, that Romans was subjected to conscious revision with a single intention, to convert the letter from a specific

---

catholic text was adapted for reading by leaving off the final matter. Though there was no necessity in breaking off the letter after 14:23, "It was natural to make the division at a place where in a current edition the break had already been made" (i.e., by Marcion). The plausibility of so accounting for the textual tradition is nil. The Marcionite hypothesis renders the liturgical hypothesis superfluous; nothing is gained by trying to correlate the two.

[99]Or, perhaps, the outer portion of a roll. This has at various times been seen as a possibility; cf. Hort, *Biblical Essays*, 350–51; C. W. Emmet, "Romans XV and XVI: A New Theory," *Expos*, eighth series, 11 (1916) 275–288. The most recent advocate is Frede, *Altlateinische Paulus-Handschriften*, 156–57.

[100]Of course, the plausibility of this theory is much reduced if accidental mutilation is supposed to have been the fate of more than one MS.

communication to a particular community into a document suitable for a wider and general audience, or, in a word, to "catholicize" the letter.[101]

This explanation lies ready to hand at least for the omissions of the Roman address in 1:7 and 1:15, for which no other assumption is satisfactory.[102] The motive must be judged by the effect, and the effect is not ambiguous. Moreover, the assumption of a generalizing or catholicizing intention is capable of providing a cogent reason for the coincidence in the tradition of the omission of the address and the final two chapters. However plausible the other theories are judged to be with regard to the omission of the last two chapters, none of them is able to make the excision of the address comprehensible; they deal with only half the problem. If, further, the fifteen-chapter form of the text inferred from P[46] cannot be regarded as a Pauline product, then an account of the textual history of Romans must take into consideration not one but two shorter forms of the letter. Of the available options the idea of a liturgical revision[103] could theoretically satisfy this requirement, but for the letter conclusion only, quite apart from the difficulties inherent in the liturgical hypothesis. The other hypotheses can entertain only one short form. Thus only on the theory of generalization can two such similar and yet distinct results be set down to a single motive.

Beyond the level of the textual facts and the prerequisites they pose for any explanation, it is clear that certain conceptions were current in ecclesiastical circles of the second and later centuries which can only have been formulated if the specific addresses of Paul's letters had been felt as problematic. One of the earliest and best-known—certainly also the most peculiar—statements of such a conception is found in the Muratorian canon:

> ... the blessed apostle Paul himself, imitating the example of his predecessor (!) John, wrote to seven churches only by name . . . . But although he wrote twice to the Corinthians and Thessalonians, for reproof, it is nevertheless obvious that one church is known to be dispersed throughout the whole globe of the earth. For John also, while he wrote in the Apocalypse to seven churches, nevertheless speaks to all.[104]

Here the fact that Paul wrote to seven communities allows a correlation between Paul and John, who wrote to seven communities and therefore addressed the whole church. Whatever questions there may be about the "logic" of this statement— there are hidden premises—the argument is formulated to speak to a particular issue:

[101]Thus Nils A. Dahl, "The Particularity of the Pauline Epistles as a Problem in the Ancient Church," in *Neotestamentica et Patristica* (Cullmann Freundesgabe; Leiden, 1962) 261–271.

[102]This was recognized by Lietzmann, *An die Römer*, 27. John Knox ("The Epistle to the Romans," 363–64) also advances this explanation with regard to the address, but for him this motive was operative only in relation to the whole *Corpus*, in such editions as began with Romans. Cf. also Ernst Käsemann, "Epheserbrief," *RGG* (3rd ed.) II, 520.

[103]We emphasize that a strict distinction must be made between the liturgical hypothesis and the hypothesis of generalization. The hypothesis of generalization makes no presumptions about liturgical usages or their requirements, and makes no appeal to lectionary texts.

[104]*Cum ipse beatus apostolus Paulus, sequens prodecessoris sui Johannes ordinem non nisi nominatim septem ecclesiis scribat . . . verum Corinthiis et Tessalonicensibus, licet pro correptione, iteratur—, una tamen per omnem orbem terrae ecclesia diffusa esse dinoscitur. Et Johannes enim in Apocalypsi, licet septem ecclesiis scribat, tamen omnibus dicit* (lines 47–59; we follow the text given by A. Souter, *The Text and Canon of the New Testament*, rev. by C. S. C. Williams [London, 1965] 191–94). On the structure and precise sense of the whole passage there has been much discussion. See especially Zahn, *Geschichte*, II, 65–75.

how can the letters of Paul, addressed to individual communities and dealing for the most part with matters of specific and local interest, be relevant to the church catholic? Although we nowhere else encounter precisely the same argument, we do find quite similar conclusions which aim to meet the same problem. Thus Tertullian, denouncing Marcion's use of Ephesians as Laodiceans, declares, "Of what significance are the titles, since in writing to a certain church the Apostle in fact wrote to all?"[105] Emphasis on the number seven in this connection is shared with the Muratorian canon by Victorinus of Pettau, who comments on Rev 1:20 that

> Those seven stars are the seven churches which he (John) names by name in his addresses, and calls them to whom he wrote letters. Not that they are themselves the only or even the principal churches, but *what he says to one he says to all*. . . . In the whole world Paul taught that all the churches are arranged by sevens, and that the catholic church is one. And first of all, certainly in order that he too might maintain the type of seven churches, he did not exceed that number. But he wrote [to seven communities].[106]

Even if here the catholic pertinence of John is argued by reference to Paul, the type of thinking is the same and is widely found in one or another respect.[107]

All such arguments are quite obviously *post facto* rationalizations, at once sophisticated and naive.[108] It must have taken some time, not to mention ingenuity, for this sort of rationalization to develop, and yet the problem which these arguments meet *post facto*, of the general pertinence and validity of Paul's letters, must have existed almost from the very beginning. It is not difficult to suppose, therefore, that at an early time Paul's letters were adapted for more general use in an unsophisticated and rather mechanical way by textual revision which aimed at omitting specific matter. The short form of Romans which omits the address can be understood as a consequence of this interest, and we probably have to do with the same cause for the variants in the addresses of 1 Corinthians (1:2) and Ephesians (1:1), as Dahl has suggested.[109] According to evidence, precisely these three letters enjoyed

---

[105]*PL* II, 545A: *Nihil autem de titulis interest, cum ad omnes Apostolus scripserit, dum ad quosdam.*

[106]*PL* Supplementum I, 109–110 (Editio Victorini): *Septem autem ecclesiae, quas nominatim vocabulis suis vocat, ad quas et epistolas facit, non quia illae solae sint ecclesiae aut principes, sed quia quod uni dicit, omnibus dicit; . . . in tote orbe, septem ecclesias omnes et septem nominatas unam esse catholicam Paulus docuit; primum quidem, ut servarit ipse et ipsum, septem ecclesiarum non excessit numerum, sed scripsit [ad Romanos, ad Corinthos, etc.].*

[107]The major evidence is conveniently assembled by Zahn, *Geschichte*, II, 73 n. 2.

[108]Krister Stendahl, "The Apocalypse of John and the Epistles of Paul in the Muratorian Fragment," in *Current Issues in New Testament Interpretation* (ed. W. Klassen and G. F. Snyder; New York, 1962) 239–245, esp. 243.

[109] "The Particularity of the Pauline Epistles as a Problem in the Ancient Church," 266–67, 270. It is important to note that Dahl's argument for 1 Corinthians does not require that the phrase expanding the specific address, "together with all those who in every place call on the name of our Lord Jesus Christ, both their Lord and ours," be regarded as a catholicizing interpolation, as suggested by J. Weiss (*Der erste Korintherbrief* [Meyer; 10th ed.; Göttingen, 1925] xli, 2–4) and often supposed by others. Dahl's theory rests instead on the strictly textual observation that in some witnesses (P46 B D F G etc.) the specific address, "which is in Corinth," follows rather than precedes the words "sanctified in Christ Jesus." From this Dahl concludes that the specific reference to Corinth fell out at one time and then later reentered the text at the wrong place, or, possibly, that the two were regarded as alternative readings, which amounts to the same motive. On this variant see also Zuntz, *The Text of the Epistles*, 91–92. The fact that this inverse ordering of the phrases is attested in East and West in distinct traditions implies the antiquity of the disorder and its cause.

the greatest ecclesiastical use in the late first and early second centuries, and so would seem to have called for some resolution of the problem of particularity.[110]

Of course this hypothesis too must reckon with possible objections. It may be asked, for example, whether this is the simplest explanation of the phenomena. The omission of a specific address in Romans, 1 Corinthians and Ephesians might be as well accounted for on the assumption that at one time or another each of these letters occupied first position in the collection of Paul's letters, and that in each edition the head letter was generalized by excising the geographical destination. But neither of these assumptions carries conviction. We can be absolutely certain only that there was an early order of the Pauline letters in which Romans held first place. This has firm and ancient support and is attested by all extant MSS. On the basis of some ancient witnesses and a principle of order according to letter length, it is widely accepted today that there once was an arrangement of the letters in which the Corinthian correspondence was given first position.[111] The evidence for this is far from conclusive,[112] but the possibility is not to be rejected out of hand. The existence at one time of an order of the letters with Ephesians at the head is an assumption growing out of the hypothesis of E. J. Goodspeed that Ephesians was composed as an introduction to all the Pauline letters when the *Corpus* was initially published.[113] Such an order is therefore as doubtful as Goodspeed's understanding of Ephesians, and is completely without any sort of attestation in the tradition.[114] Thus to explain the generalized addresses of these three letters by appealing to various editions of the *Corpus Paulinum* is problematic in its own right.

It must be specified, furthermore, to what extent Ephesians really provides

[110]For the evidence on the use of the Pauline letters in this period see Albert E. Barnett, *Paul Becomes a Literary Influence* (Chicago, 1941).

[111]The Muratorian canon gives the orders: (a) Corinthians, Galatians, Romans (this listing, which from the context appears to be chronologically intended, is quickly given up after naming only three letters); (b) Corinthians, Ephesians, Philippians, Colossians, Galatians, Thessalonians, Romans. Tertullian (*Adv. Marc.* iv. 5 [*PL* II, 395C]) lists the letters in the order: Corinthians, Galatians, Philippians, Thessalonians, Ephesians, Romans. In neither case is it certain that an actual canonical order is reproduced. The principle which would seem to underlie such an order, at least an order with Corinthians at the head, is one of relative length, with the double letters (Corinthians and Thessalonians) counted as units. On the evidence for the order with Corinthians at the head see Frede, "Die Ordnung der Paulusbriefe," 294–95 and 292; also Zahn, *Geschichte,* II, 346–48.

[112]That the Muratorian list as it stands represents an actual canonical order has been strongly disputed by Dahl ("Welche Ordnung der Paulusbriefe wird vom muratorischen Kanon vorausgesetzt?" 39–53), who wishes to find presumed here the customary canonical order; cf. also Finegan ("The Original Form of the Pauline Collection," 91–92), who also points out that Tertullian, in the same context where he lists the Pauline letters, names the Gospels in a non-canonical order. Therefore the primary evidence for the order with the Corinthian letters at the beginning must be regarded with caution. See further below, n. 127.

[113]E. J. Goodspeed, *The Meaning of Ephesians* (Chicago, 1933); *idem,* "The Place of Ephesians in the First Pauline Collection," *ATR* 12 (1930) 189–212; *idem,* "Ephesians and the First Edition of Paul," *JBL* 70 (1951) 285–291; see also the systematic statement of the argument by C. L. Mitton, *The Formation of the Pauline Corpus of Letters* (London, 1955).

[114]The considerations advanced by John Knox (*Marcion and the New Testament,* 39ff.) as favoring Goodspeed's hypothesis are only *a posteriori* arguments for a thesis proposed on other grounds. Working with the idea that the *Corpus* was published in two rolls, Knox supposed that if the rolls were to be of approximately equal length one of the shorter letters would have stood with the Corinthian letters in the first roll, while Romans and the other letters would have occupied the second roll (arranged according to length). He observes that Marcion substituted Galatians for the short letter which originally stood with Corinthians. This shorter letter, accordingly, must have been Ephesians, both because of its general and introductory character and because in Marcion's (rearranged) order Ephesians stands in the place which Galatians would have held in an order according to length.

a parallel to Romans and Corinthians in respect of the omission of the address. Hardly anyone will suppose that the absence of τῇ οὔσῃ ἐν Κορίνθῳ in 1 Cor 1:2 or of ἐν 'Ρώμῃ in Rom 1:7 and 1:15 represents an original Pauline reading.[115] Everything suggests that each of these letters was directed to the single and specific congregation. Ephesians is another case altogether, for it is impossible to think that this letter originally had a specific community primarily or exclusively in view. For the question of the omission of the address the issue of authenticity is more or less irrelevant, except that apart from Ephesians we have no evidence that Paul himself wrote "encyclical" letters. In Eph 1:1 some of the oldest and best witnesses omit the words ἐν 'Εφέσῳ.[116] In addition, our Ephesians was known to Marcion as Laodiceans, a difference not to be attributed to Marcion's peculiar interests. To this it must be added that the address without a place name, τοῖς οὖσιν καὶ πιστοῖς, is nonsensical. It can only be concluded that this reading is not original; some geographical designation, or at least the possibility of such (as furnished by a blank space), must be assumed.[117] The important point for the question at hand is that for Ephesians there was not an *exclusively* correct original address, and this accords very well with the general cast of the letter as a whole. In this Ephesians stands on a different footing from Romans and 1 Corinthians, and inferences about the latter are not immediately to be made from the former. Whether it is thought that Eph 1:1 originally manifested a blank space for the insertion of the address, or that there was some specific address which was later deleted in some parts of the tradition, makes no difference for the conclusion that in Ephesians we have evidence of an interest in generalizing the Pauline letters. In the former case it would have to be assumed that Ephesians was *composed* as a sort of catholic compendium of Pauline thought, while in the latter case, regardless of the compositional intent, the letter was *converted* into a catholic letter by omitting the address.

There is no good reason, however, to draw into connection with the publication of the *Corpus* the omissions of the address in Ephesians, Romans or 1 Corinthians. That the head letter of the *Corpus* would as a matter of course be deprived of its address also stumbles against the more general consideration that "the edition of Paul's collected letters would in itself imply the general importance of all of them. In order to show that Paul was speaking to all churches when he wrote to one it would neither be necessary nor sufficient to give the first letter in the collection a general address."[118] Also, even if the possibility is held out that the omission of the Roman address might be due to Romans having held first place in an early edition of the *Corpus,* such an explanation is not at all adequate to the removal of the last two chapters, and the two omissions are not to be separated.

All of this means that in order to account for the variants in the addresses of

[115] Yet this was suggested for Romans by W. B. Smith, "Address and Destination of St. Paul's Epistle to the Romans," *JBL* 20 (1901) 1–21, whose thesis was approved by Harnack, "Zu Röm. 1,7," *ZNW* 3 (1902) 83–86. The same view was held, but for Rom 1:7 only, by Zahn (*Introduction*, I, 378; *Der Brief des Paulus an die Römer*, 51, 615).

[116] P46 א* B* 1739 Origen.

[117] It makes no difference for our purposes whether the letter was put out with a blank space into which the address might be inserted; in favor of such a possibility see Zuntz, *The Text of the Epistles*, 228 n. 1, but against it see Nils A. Dahl, "Adresse und Prooemium des Epheserbriefes," *TZ* 7 (1951) 241–264, esp. 241–250.

[118] Dahl, "The Particularity of the Pauline Epistles as a Problem in the Ancient Church," 270. Cf. Lucetta Mowry, "The Early Circulation of Paul's Letters," *JBL* 63 (1944) 73–86, esp. 80.

these letters, and in the case of Romans for the omission of the concluding chapters, we must look not to any supposed archetypal edition of the *Corpus*, but to the early period when Paul's letters circulated individually, then perhaps in small groups, among the communities. Goodspeed and others have presumed Paul's letters early fell into obscurity and suffered a prolonged period of neglect, but this is unlikely in terms of historical probabilities and cannot explain the availability in great number and variety of textual variants which are hardly the consequence simply of the transmission and corruption of a single early edition of the *Corpus*. Even Zuntz, who has not surrendered the conception of a definitive edition of the collected letters of Paul, was compelled by the existence of major variants to admit "some use and circulation—*ergo* copying—of the, or some, Epistles prior to the production of the *Corpus*...."[119] If we do not follow Zuntz in his theory that the editing of the *Corpus* was a highly technical undertaking in the tradition of the best Alexandrian criticism, it is nevertheless important that he allows in his conception of the origin of the *Corpus* a possibility often regarded too lightly, namely, that the *collecting* of the Pauline letters and the editing of them are not without further ado to be collapsed into one and the same moment. The failure to make this distinction is frequent in modern treatments of the problem, and so it must be emphasized that the idea of a published "edition" of the letters does not *ipso facto* exclude their early circulation or early small collections or even a complete collection, but in some respects seems to require these. The recent and rather grandiose reflections on the emergence of the *Corpus* which propose that the letters endured decades of disuse and that the collecting and editing were so closely tied together, even to the extent of being the work of a single individual,[120] are appealing more for their ingenuity than for their realism. That Paul's letters did circulate prior to any edition of the *Corpus* as a whole is persuasively shown by the data given in the textual history of Romans.[121]

We noted above that the omission of the address and final chapters of Romans is not adequately explained as a result of Romans having occupied first place among the collected letters. This phenomenon becomes intelligible on the hypothesis of generalization. Even though in 1 Corinthians and Ephesians we do not

---

[119]Zuntz, *The Text of the Epistles*, 278.

[120]In addition to Goodspeed and his followers, cf. Schmithals, "On the Composition and Earliest Collection," 253–274.

[121]The question ought to be more seriously investigated whether the impetus toward early circulation was not already implicit in the letters themselves, given the status and authority which Paul claimed for himself. Paul's letters are not "private letters" which can be put on a par with the private correspondence among the papyri; they have an "official" cast which is not absent even in the most "private" of them, Philemon, as properly emphasized by U. Wickert ("Der Philemonbrief—Privatbrief oder apostolisches Schreiben?," *ZNW* 52 [1961] 230–38). Even during his lifetime the impressiveness of Paul's letters had to be conceded by his opponents (2 Cor 10:10). Such a directive as we have in Col 4:16, if authentic, indicates that Paul to some extent encouraged the exchange of his letters; but even if Colossians is not authentic, 4:16 at least presumes that such exchanges were in fact made. The arguments often marshalled for an early and continuing neglect of the letters down to the time of a "publication" of the *Corpus* are all *e silentio:* the post-Pauline literature of the first century seems to make no use of Paul. As far as the theological content of Paul's letters is concerned, that is true enough, but what of the non-Pauline letters of the NT? Are they not indebted to Paul at least for the *form*? On the failure of Acts to make use of the letters—by all counts the most important of the arguments from silence—see Günter Klein, *Die zwölf Apostel. Ursprung und Gehalt einer Idee* (FRLANT 77; Göttingen, 1961) 189–201, supposing that the author of Acts knew but chose not to use the letters; also Mowry ("The Early Circulation of Paul's Letters"), who discounts non-use by Acts as "irrelevant" and brings further considerations favoring the early circulation of the letters.

have to reckon with any textual revision beyond the address, in the case of Romans more extensive revision can be understood in terms of the letter itself, for in it the only matter which bears a *prima facie,* necessary, and exclusive relation to the Roman community is to be found in the opening address and the final two chapters. The interior, the body of the letter, can be understood—we do not say was intended, which is another question—in a completely general way. Thus in purely structural terms this letter alone of all the letters invited and permitted a thoroughgoing sort of generalization to be simply effected.[122]

Furthermore, the textual evidence requires us to reckon with two basic shorter forms of the letter, one in fourteen chapters and widely attested, one in fifteen chapters evidenced only by P^{46}. Even within the fourteen-chapter form there are several small variations: it appears originally to have contained nothing after 14:23; then the short benediction and/or the doxology were appended. We cannot be sure whether the fifteen-chapter form originally had the doxology in conclusion, but this is probable.[123] The fourteen-chapter form had a very strong impact on the whole tradition, as is clear above all from the various placements of the doxology and the benedictions of ch. 16.[124] The number, diversity and influence of these forms make it inconceivable that they arose either within or subsequent to any "publication" of a "first edition" of the Pauline *Corpus*. Rather, such forms must have had an earlier existence and continued for a long time to affect the textual tradition which even now preserves their traces. Indeed, this state of affairs has the effect of exploding the very notion of a single archetypal edition of the *Corpus Paulinum*. Lietzmann's investigation of the textual history of Paul's letters led him to the conclusion that "all the textual forms of the Pauline letters go back to a single collection. No letter has its own separate tradition."[125] But with this assumption it is extremely difficult, even impossible, to reconcile the existence not merely of small variant readings but of *distinct recensions of one entire letter*. At least it must be said that if there was such an edition, it was not of such type or significance as to suppress previously current Pauline texts.

That the shorter form of Romans emerged prior to the *Corpus* as a whole, during the period when this letter circulated independently, can be perceived from yet another vantage point, namely, the doxology (16:25–27). It is sometimes thought that the doxology, rightly assumed to be inauthentic, functioned originally to bring the entire collection to a conclusion, having been added by the editor of the whole.[126] This supposition requires, of course, that Romans stood last in an early collection. The possible existence of an early order with the Corinthian letters at the head has allowed 1 Cor 1:2, with its expansive address, to be drawn into considera-

---

[122]Thus we can agree with some of the basic observations such as led Lightfoot, Lake, Knox and others to the idea of a general letter converted into a specific letter or vice versa. But we come to another conclusion, and do not regard Paul himself as the agent of changing a specific letter into a general letter.

[123]See below, 124–26.

[124]See below, 129–132.

[125]Hans Lietzmann, "Einführung in die Textgeschichte der Paulusbriefe," *Kleine Schriften,* II, *Studien zum Neuen Testament* (ed. K. Aland; TU 68; Berlin, 1958) 138.

[126]Thus, e.g., Schmithals, "On the Composition and Earliest Collection," 258–59; Dodd, *The Epistle of Paul to the Romans,* xvii; and earlier J. Weiss, *Earliest Christianity* (2 vols.; New York, 1959) II, 684.

tion here. On this basis, some have reached the conclusion that an early collection beginning with Corinthians and ending with Romans was given a redactional introduction (1 Cor 1:2b) and conclusion (Rom 16:25–27). But this view of the matter is too easily gained and will not hold up under scrutiny.

Not only is the order of the letters required by this hypothesis an unlikely conjecture[127] and the redactional character of 1 Cor 1:2b very questionable;[128] the hypothesis also misconstrues the doxology of Romans. Even if we concede that the *Corpus* might have required some formal conclusion—and this is by no means self-evident—the need for a conclusion must have been even more strongly felt in the case of the truncated Roman letter which ended so abruptly with 14:23, and we can recognize on text-critical grounds that the doxology was originally appended to the fourteen-chapter text of Romans. But this means either that the *Corpus* in question must have contained only the fourteen-chapter text, or, if it contained the full sixteen-chapter text, that the doxology was not formulated to bring the whole collection to a close.

Internal criticism of the doxology shows that it was composed with a view not to the whole *Corpus* but to Romans alone. The opinion that "the doxology presupposes the collection of (seven) letters running from I Corinthians to Romans"[129] has no basis in the doxology itself and can appeal only to an alleged final position of Romans in the collection. Reference might be made to the phrases in the doxology, τὸ εὐαγγέλιόν μου ("my gospel," 16:25), interpreted as a designation of the Pauline proclamation generally, and γραφαὶ προφητικαί ("prophetic writings," 16:26), taken as a comprehensive reference to the Pauline letters. We need not dispute the sense of the first of the phrases, but in itself it says or implies nothing about any written materials. We saw earlier that the second phrase would be most unusual and unnatural as a description of the Pauline letters.

On the other hand, some commentators, often in a desire to demonstrate the authenticity of the doxology, have pointed out parallels in thought and terminology between the doxology and the Roman letter.[130] Most of the suggested parallels are

[127]In the lists of the Pauline letters provided by the Muratorian canon and Tertullian (see above, n. 111) Corinthians stands first and Romans last. We have already observed how uncertain it is that these lists reflect an actual canonical order. That aside, it is equally important to ask what principle of arrangement is supposed to have informed an order of Paul's letters with Corinthians at the beginning and Romans at the end. One of the strongest arguments for the Corinthian correspondence having stood in first place is that in an order based on letter length, the Corinthian letters, counted as a unit, would have stood first because they are longest. Yet the very same principle of order according to length contradicts a placement of Romans at the end. Romans, even in its short fourteen-chapter form, is of such length that it would necessarily have followed immediately on the Corinthian letters when the latter were counted together, and that it would have preceded the Corinthian letters when these were counted separately. Now, of course, it would be possible to account for a final position of Romans on the basis of an arrangement of the letters which aimed at ordering the letters chronologically or even geographically, but these principles fail to explain why Corinthians should stand at the beginning. Therefore, in addition to the uncertainty of the documentary evidence, there is no single principle of arranging the letters which can account both for a first position of Corinthians and a final position of Romans, and this makes the suggested order improbable. The effort of Schmithals ("On the Composition and Earliest Collection," 254–57) to discover such an order in the oldest witnesses is completely arbitrary. See my essay, "The Redaction of the Pauline Letters and the Formation of the Pauline Corpus," *JBL* 94 (1975) 403–418.

[128]Cf. Hans Lietzmann and W. G. Kümmel, *An die Korinther I–II* (HNT 9; 4th ed.; Tübingen, 1949) 5.

[129]Schmithals, "On the Composition and Earliest Collection," 259.

[130]For drawing comparisons between the doxology and Romans as a whole see, among others, Hort, *Biblical Essays*, 324–28; Sanday and Headlam, *The Epistle to the Romans*, 432–36; Lönnermark,

tenuous indeed and carry no force, but at least two are important for the issue at hand. The first is the striking, verbatim repetition in the doxology of the phrase εἰς ὑπακοὴν πίστεως ("to bring about the obedience of faith"),which also appears in Rom 1:5. Since this is a unique expression in Paul, its appearance in the doxology can be explained only through direct dependence on Rom 1:5, the more so because in each place it is referred to "all the Gentiles" (1:5, ἐν πᾶσιν τοῖς ἔθνεσιν; 16:26, εἰς πάντα τὰ ἔθνη). This precise echo adds to the likelihood that the phrase διὰ γραφῶν προφητικῶν ("through prophetic writings") in the doxology is a deliberate, if not verbatim, allusion to Rom 1:2, διὰ τῶν προφητῶν αὐτοῦ ἐν γραφαῖς ἁγίαις ("through his prophets in holy writings"). In each instance these "writings" are accorded a positive though not identical role in the salvation-history scheme. These two phrases alone make it clear that in building up the basic doxological form, in addition to incorporating the revelation-scheme, special attention was paid to the Roman letter, in particular to the prescript. At the same time the doxology discloses no similar connections with other individual letters or with the letters as a collection.[131] Thus there are no good grounds for supposing that the doxology was formulated to conclude, or ever did conclude, the whole collection of letters.

Nevertheless, the doxology is not for these reasons to be considered authentic; stylistic and textual observations point to the opposite conclusion. In terms of style, the conclusion of a letter with a doxology stands in clear contrast to Paul's habit of concluding with the grace-benediction.[132] And, apart from the conscious allusions to the prescript of Romans, the terminological and conceptual affinities of the doxology lie mainly with the deutero-Pauline letters (Ephesians, the Pastorals). Since Paul himself cannot be credited with devising the shorter form of the letter, neither can the doxology be attributed to him, for textual observations demonstrate that the doxology was originally appended to the fourteen-chapter text of Romans. If the doxology were originally read at the end of ch. 16, there would be no reasons by which to account for its transposition to the end of ch. 14 and the wide adoption of this placement in the tradition. But if the doxology was first present after 14:23, the position at the end of ch. 16 is easily seen as the consequence of a natural tendency to remove it to the end of the letter, especially since it interrupts the continuity between chs. 14 and 15. An original position after 14:23 can also account for the strong manuscript attestation for this placement. There is, further, no reason why the doxology should have been placed at the end of ch. 14 unless the letter actually ended there, in which case it was hardly derived from ch. 16.

Only the Alexandrian witnesses staunchly favor the position of the doxology after ch. 16. But early in that tradition we have Origen, who knew the doxology in both positions and certainly regarded the position after ch. 14 as well attested, even if he himself favored the later position.

Also in favor of the doxology's original position after ch. 14 is that the

---

"Till frågan om Romarbrevets integritet," 143–44; Kamlah, *Schlussdoxologie,* 29–65. Hort and Sanday and Headlam speak of the doxology as an appropriate conclusion to Romans, one which sums up all the leading ideas of the letter, but that is clearly not the case.

[131]Such connections should not be sought in the revelation-scheme formula, for this does not betray literary dependence.

[132]The letters Jude, 2 Peter, 2 Clement all conclude with doxologies.

witnesses placing it after 14:23 consistently read the last phrase as εἰς τοὺς αἰῶνας. The more expansive final phrase, εἰς τοὺς αἰῶνας τῶν αἰώνων, is found only when the doxology is placed at the end of ch. 16. MSS which offer the doxology in both places attest the short phrase in the early position and the long phrase in the later position. If we assumed that the doxology originally stood after ch. 16, it would be difficult to account for a shortening of the final phrase in moving the doxology back to the end of ch. 14; but the expansion of the final phrase is easily understood if the movement was in the other direction.

Thus an original placement of the doxology at the end of ch. 14 has the support of the MS evidence, accords with transcriptional probabilities, and is capable of explaining both the position after ch. 14 and that after ch. 16.[133] Therefore, the doxology must be judged an editorial product added to the short form of Romans in order to provide that form of the letter with a suitable conclusion.[134]

The Fifteen-Chapter Recension

Once the possibility has been excluded that the fifteen-chapter form of the letter preserves the original extent of Paul's letter to the Roman church—and we have found substantial reasons for rejecting this view—it becomes necessary to integrate this form of the text into the textual tradition at another and later point. Since we are compelled to regard the fifteen-chapter text as a second shortened form of the letter, its emergence can be rationalized only on the hypothesis of catholic generalization; the other explanations cannot individually be construed in such a way as to account for *two* abbreviated texts of the letter.

Beyond this, the only firm argument that the fifteen-chapter text was a generalized text is that the omission of ch. 16 is analogous in kind with the omission of chs. 15 and 16, the latter being closely coincident in the tradition with the deletion of the specific address in ch. 1. The motive for the omission of ch. 16 is, if anything, less ambiguous than the excision of the last two chapters, for ch. 16 contains little or nothing of general interest. The removal of these personalia is thoroughly consonant with a catholicizing intention.[135]

Conclusive evidence that the fifteen-chapter text was in fact a generalized text would be provided by the absence of the specific address in 1:7 and 1:15. Unfortunately, this information is denied to us by the sole witness to this form of the text, for P[46] lacks folios 1–7 and commences only with Rom 5:17.[136] But some light may be shed on this problem from another angle.

A close scrutiny of MS 1739, which substantially preserves the text used by

[133]An original placement of the doxology after 14:23 is also proven by the variations of the grace-benedictions at the end of ch. 16. On this, see below, 129–132.

[134]It is futile to seek the identity of the author-compiler of the doxology. The suggestion of Kamlah (*Schlussdoxologie*, 129–130) that the author of the Pastorals composed the doxology is only a little more satisfactory than that Marcion did.

[135]For a possible parallel to the omission of specific names, probably for the same reason, see Lietzmann, *An die Korinther I–II*, 136–37, on 2 Cor 8:18.

[136]But even if P[46] were known to contain the address, that would not necessarily show that this form of the text was not originally general. The presence of the address could be seen as a later correction, just as ch. 16 was added, and just as witnesses for the fourteen-chapter form sometimes show the specific address as a consequence of the tradition.

Origen in his commentary on Romans, together with the Latin version of the commentary made by Rufinus, yields some hints that Origen may have commented upon a text of the letter with the same form as that offered by P[46], that is, with the doxology following ch. 15. One of the most interesting features of 1739 in the Pauline letters consists of scholia indicating those points in the text at which the various *tomoi* of Origen's commentaries began. There are fifteen such scholia for Romans, which accords with the statements of Rufinus and Jerome that this commentary extended to fifteen *tomoi*.[137] E. von der Goltz, the first to investigate the MS carefully, was struck by the peculiar fact that the scholion marking the beginning of Origen's fifteenth and last *tomos* stands, in the margin of 1739, at Rom 14:10. This means that in terms of the amount of text included the final *tomos* would have been unusually extensive, covering almost three entire chapters of the letter. This is unparalleled not only in Romans but in all the other letters for which Origen's *tomoi* divisions are noted. This is a matter, however, of the biblical text only, yet we may assume a certain proportionality between length of text and extent of exegesis. Goltz therefore offered the conjecture that Origen provided no commentary on the greetings and personalia contained in Rom 16.[138] In support of this suggestion Goltz appealed to two marginal notes occurring outside of Romans: ad Phil 4:1, ἕως ὧδε ἐξηγήσατο, and ad Col 4:12, ἕως ὧδε ὁ τρίτος τόμος περιεῖχεν. ἡ δὲ ἐξήγησις ἕως τοῦ ἵνα σταθῆτε τέλειοι. In Philippians and Colossians the text was not taken directly from Origen's commentaries, but notes comparing Origenic readings were provided in the margins. These scholia state clearly that Origen's exegesis left off at the stated points, so that he did not comment upon the personal and specific remarks at the end of these letters. On this basis Goltz concluded that Origen characteristically did not comment on the concluding matter of Paul's letters because it lacked value for doctrine or edification.[139]

There is, however, one peculiarity which distinguishes the commentary on Romans from those on Philippians and Colossians. In the latter we must suppose that there was no commentary on any part of the text after the places at which the exegesis is said to have ended (Phil 4:1; Col 4:12). But in Romans we may be sure that Origen did comment upon the doxology which stands in 1739, as in modern editions, at the end of ch. 16. It is hardly likely that Origen neglected to comment on 16:1–23 but then commented on the doxology, *if the doxology stood at the end of ch. 16.* The format of his commentaries, interspersing text and exegesis, would seem to preclude this procedure. If, however, the doxology had stood at the end of ch. 15, then we could easily understand how Origen might have commented on it, but passed over 16:1–23, just as he neglected the concluding matter in Philippians and Colossians.[140] So the likelihood that Origen did not comment on 16:1–23 carries with it the probability that in the text he used the doxology was found at the end of

---

[137]Rufinus, "Praefatio in epistolam ad Romanos," *PG*, XIV, 831–32; Jerome, Ep. xxxiii (ad Paulam), *CSEL*, LIV, 255–56 (the relevant portion is omitted in Migne).

[138]*Eine textkritische Arbeit des zehnten bezw. sechsten Jahrhunderts*, 94.

[139]Ibid.

[140]Bauernfeind, following the lead of Goltz, reconstructed the text of Romans as it appeared in Origen's commentary as 1:1–15:33 + 16:25–27, and supposed that the text of ch. 16 in the ancestor of 1739 was therefore derived from the "most ancient copy" used for the rest of the *Corpus* (*Der Römerbrieftext des Origenes nach dem Codex von der Goltz*, 118).

ch. 15. P⁴⁶ not only proves the existence of a form of the letter which read the doxology after ch. 15 (and at one time omitted ch. 16); it also localizes this form of the text in chronological and geographical proximity to Origen.[141]

The surmise that Origen relied on a text with the doxology after ch. 15 gains support from the recollection that MS 1739 is a chief witness to Origen's omission of the Roman address at the beginning of the letter. We have seen that evidence for the absence of the final two chapters almost always occurs in company with the absence of the specific address. That Origen is a prime witness to the generalized address can only heighten our suspicion that the text he used gave evidence of a generalizing intention in placing the doxology after ch. 15. But the evidence, though suggestive, will not support a firm conclusion.[142]

It is nevertheless highly likely by analogy with the fourteen-chapter form of the text that the fifteen-chapter form also is the result of a generalizing intention. While it may be conceivable that the two shortened recensions of the letter, neither original with Paul, are to be set down to entirely different causes, we should not multiply causes unnecessarily. Both forms of the text can be, and in the absence of evidence to the contrary ought to be, accounted for on the basis of a single purpose.

[141]That the commentary was composed in Caesarea is no hindrance to the possibility that Origen used a text form such as we have in P⁴⁶, since while in Alexandria he sometimes used Caesarean texts, and in Caesarea sometimes used "Egyptian" texts. The commentary is probably no later than 247. We recall in this connection the close affinities which Zuntz has discovered between 1739 and P⁴⁶ on the basis of Hebrews and 1 Corinthians (*The Text of the Epistles*, 68ff.), although this cannot without further ado be assumed for Romans, since the ancestor of 1739 derived its text of Romans from another exemplar.

There is some reason to conjecture that Clement of Alexandria also employed such a form of the text, for he cites Rom 15:29 and the doxology as though the passages were continuous (*Strom.* v.10, *PG*, IX, 100A).

[142]In the Latin version of the commentary we possess, of course, a commentary on the entire text, including ch. 16. We should not make too much of this fact, however, because it is clear that much material in the commentary comes from Rufinus himself, and not Origen. Rufinus admitted that he made additions; a complete copy of the commentary was not available to him, for he says that *desunt enim fere apud omnium bibliothecas—incertum sane quo causa—aliquanta ex ipso corpore valumina* ("Praefatio in epistolam ad Romanos," *PG*, XIV, 831–32); thus he found it necessary "to fill out what was lacking" (*explere quae desunt*) ("Peroratio in epistolam ad Romanos," *PG*, XIV, 1293–94). Thus Henry Chadwick rightly emphasizes that "the question is not . . . the degree of freedom which Rufinus allows himself in his paraphrase, but rather how much he has suppressed which is essential to a true estimate of Origen's work, and, above all, how much he has added out of his own head which has no counterpart whatever in the original" ("Rufinus and the Tura Papyrus of Origen's Commentary on Romans," 16).

CHAPTER V

CONCLUSION

Having examined the major aspects of the problem of the textual history of Romans, it remains now to summarize the results we have gained and to sketch the development of the textual tradition. Subsequently and in conclusion it will be appropriate to draw out the implications of this study for two related questions, first, the problem of the occasion and purpose of the Roman letter, and second, problems of methodology in the literary analysis of the letters of Paul.

The Textual History of the Letter

A close investigation of the textual tradition of Roman shows clearly that as early as the second century the letter was current in several textual forms. Disregarding minor variations, we may speak of three basic forms distinguished by length, one in fourteen, one in fifteen and one in sixteen chapters. Which of these forms represents the text of Paul's letter to Rome cannot be determined on the basis of the textual evidence alone, though the textual evidence does demonstrate that the fourteen-chapter text cannot be so regarded: all explicit reference to Rome is absent from this form through the omission of the specific address (1:7; 1:15) and of ch. 15. The Roman form of the letter must therefore be preserved in the fifteen- or sixteen-chapter texts, but the textual evidence itself does not indicate which.

The longer text has been suspect chiefly by reason of the content and form of ch. 16, and more recently with reference to textual evidence furnished by P^{46}. These features have been taken by many to demonstrate that ch. 16 was originally independent of the fifteen-chapter text and had as its proper address a community other than Rome. But careful analysis of the traditional arguments for this view reveals them to be poorly founded and lacking probative force. Decisive arguments for the original unity of the sixteen-chapter text have emerged, however, through our examination of the style and structure of the Pauline epistolary conclusions. We have shown that all of the elements in ch. 16 are typically concluding elements, that without this chapter the fifteen-chapter text lacks an epistolary conclusion, and that the unusual aspects of some elements in ch. 16 find cogent explanation only on the assumption of its Roman address. Thus the unity of the sixteen-chapter text and its Roman address are established.

The primacy of this form of the text might, however, still be questioned if it were assumed that the sixteen-chapter text represents only a particularized form of an earlier general letter of Paul. But we have tried to show that the idea of an earlier general letter lying behind the Roman letter is a fragile fabrication with little to commend it. It generally assumes the original independence of ch. 16 (or at least a difference in its address), cannot find a convincing motive or occasion for a general

127

letter or a Roman particularization of it, and is not even adequate to the textual evidence. Therefore the emergence of both the fourteen- and the fifteen-chapter forms of the text must be sought at a later point in the tradition of the letter, and we have seen that of the various possibilities only an early effort to "catholicize" the Roman letter suffices to explain the origin of the shorter and generalized textual forms. On the basis of these results it is now possible to outline the development of the textual tradition, and in the process to clarify the residual difficulty of the benedictions at the end of ch. 16.

Paul's letter to the Roman church comprised Rom 1–16. At an early time, probably in the late first century, when Paul's letters circulated individually and then perhaps in small collections among the various communities, there arose the problem of how the letters of the Apostle, addressed to particular communities and dealing with specific questions of concern to those communities, could be relevant to and valued by others than their first recipients. That this was a real and not merely imagined issue is seen in that even in the late second century and afterward the question called for an answer. In this later period it was answered in a manner that did not dispute the particularity of the letters but affirmed their general pertinence, their "catholicity," by way of a "nevertheless." This was permitted by the availability of the letters in a collection composed of letters to seven communities, the number seven providing a clear sign, even of Paul's own intention, that the letters speak to Christendom at large. But before this mode of rationalization was at hand it was less easy to maintain both specific address and catholic relevance. The latter was achieved at the expense of the former by the mechanical, but natural and effective method of textual emendation. The Roman letter was not alone in being subjected to such revision, but most invited and was most affected by it. As a result, shorter forms of the Roman letter came into being.

The first of these was the fourteen-chapter text in which the address in ch. 1 and the historically and locally specific matter in chs. 15 and 16 were left aside. Yet the full sixteen-chapter text did not disappear but continued to exist alongside. The fourteen-chapter text exercised a broad influence on the tradition, and this suggests its priority to the fifteen-chapter form of the text, which by comparison had very limited impact on the tradition. Whether the fifteen-chapter text arose independently of the fourteen-chapter text is impossible to say with certainty. The probability, however, is that the fifteen-chapter text is a modification of the fourteen-chapter text on the basis of the sixteen-chapter text, but a modification respecting the aim of the short text; that is, the generalizing interest was maintained but thought not to require the omission of ch. 15, which was accordingly taken over from the long text. Chapter 16 remained intolerable in a generalized form of the text, so the doxology was transposed from the original position after 14:23 to the new position after 15:33. Only later did the text presently offered by P[46] emerge, when the fifteen-chapter text interacted once again with the full text, thus gaining ch. 16, yet without transferring the doxology to the end of the whole.[1]

---

[1]This reconstruction is suggested by some features of our only witness to the fifteen-chapter form, P[46]. The fact that in the doxology P[46] reads the short final phrase εἰς τοὺς αἰῶνας indicates that the doxology was appropriated from a text which offered it after ch. 14 (see above, 124). Further, P[46] lacks the benediction at 16:24, concluding with 16:23, even though the doxology is placed earlier, after 15:33. As we will show (see below, 129–132), this suggests that in the text from which ch. 16 was derived the doxology stood at the end of ch. 16.

The age and importance of the fourteen-chapter text are evident in the way it has penetrated the tradition, no branch of which failed to be affected by it eventually. It is attested for us in the West (Europe and Africa) primarily through patristic usage and scriptural aids together with the Old Latin bilingual MSS, while in the East it is evidenced by the overwhelming propensity of Byzantine MSS to place the doxology at the end of ch. 14 and by forms of the text known to Origen.[2] That the secondary doxology is now found in almost all MSS is yet another sign of the agglomerative nature of the textual tradition.

On the interaction of the fourteen- and sixteen-chapter texts, then, the whole complex textual tradition, including the fifteen-chapter form, rests. Basically we have to reckon with the following steps. The fourteen-chapter text seems to have ended originally with 14:23, lacking a formal conclusion of any sort.[3] This lack was soon made up by the addition of the doxology.[4] The form 1–14+16:25-27 met with the form 1–16, which originally lacked the doxology, and from this encounter resulted the forms of the letter attested by extant texts:

    (a) 1–14+16:25-27+15–16
    (b) 1–14+15–16+16:25-27
    (c) 1–14+16:25-27+15–16+16:25-27,

but also, according to our reconstruction,

    (d) 1–14+15+16:25-27+16:1-23.

The Benedictions at the End of Chapter 16

In our effort to disentangle and describe the various forms of the text of Romans we must deal, finally, with the benedictions attested at the end of ch. 16. The picture here is confusingly complex, for benedictory elements are variously attested in three different positions at 16:20b, 16:24, and also at 16:28 (i.e. after the doxology).[5] Previous discussions of the textual history of the letter have regarded these variations as being virtually random and without importance for the major textual issue. But this is incorrect: not only are the variations in the benedictions intelligible, but they also confirm our reconstruction of the development of the textual forms.

The Textus Receptus reads two benedictions at the end of ch. 16, as 16:20b and 16:24. Modern editions are unanimous, however, in rejecting the benediction of 16:24 and retaining only the one at 16:20b, and this decision is justified by the relative strength of the witnesses for each. Even so, it still must be asked how the tradition came to furnish two benedictions at the conclusion of the letter. By way of explaining this it has been pointed out that the form of the benediction attested at 16:24 is exactly like that of 2 Thes 3:18, which then makes it possible to suppose

---

[2]The short text, so far as we can judge, seems to have had a longer existence in Europe and Africa than in Alexandria, for already in the early third century Origen implies the increasingly normative character of the longer text.

[3]This is not certain, but that there was a short form of the text without the doxology is to be assumed on the basis of the testimony of Origen and the Fuldensian *capitula*.

[4]On the basis of the Latin MSS which offer a short benediction after 14:23 and before the doxology we may suppose that this benediction results from an independent effort to provide a conclusion for the fourteen-chapter text, though now the benediction is encountered only in connection with the doxology. See above, 24.

[5]See above, 35.

that 16:24 is secondary, having been added on the model of 2 Thessalonians in order to bring the letter to a formal close when the doxology was not at hand.[6] Alternatively, it has been suggested that originally the benediction was read only at 16:24, but that when the doxology was transposed from the end of ch. 14 to the end of ch. 16 the letter possessed too many concluding elements, and that as a result 16:24 was pushed back to 16:20b, thus producing the sequence 16:20b+21-23+25-27.[7] Yet neither of these explanations is adequate. As to the first, if in the absence of the doxology a more usual conclusion was sought for ch. 16, the simplest and most natural recourse would have been to move the benediction of 16:20b to the later position of 16:24 rather than to formulate a new benediction and allow the old to stand. Moreover, the formal identity between 16:24 and 2 Thes 3:18 gives no presumption whatever that 16:24 might be secondary. The second explanation, that the position at 16:20b is secondary, must be discounted for two reasons. First, the position at 16:20b is very well supported, even by MSS which read the doxology only at the end of ch. 14 and in which, therefore, the doxology has not influenced ch. 16. Secondly, we cannot speak merely of the displacement of a single benediction, since the witnesses attest two different benedictions. The benediction placed at 16:20b has the consistent form ἡ χάρις τοῦ κυρίου ἡμῶν Ἰησοῦ μεθ' ὑμῶν, the only variant being the occasional addition of Χριστοῦ after Ἰησοῦ. But the benediction at 16:24 is consistently read ἡ χάρις τοῦ κυρίου ἡμῶν Ἰησοῦ Χριστοῦ μετὰ πάντων ὑμῶν. ἀμήν, with no significant variants.[8] This is also the form of the benediction sometimes placed at 16:28 (after the doxology).

A solution to the problem posed by the variations of these benedictions in form and position becomes immediately obvious when it is recognized that the witnesses are grouped in a particular way in reading these benedictions, as the chart shows. It can be seen that witnesses which either lack the doxology altogether or place it only at the end of ch. 14 almost always offer the benediction at 16:24. Within this group of witnesses those reading the doxology after ch. 14 also read the benediction at 16:20b. On the other hand, texts which contain the doxology at the end of ch. 16 always offer the benediction at 16:20b, but almost never provide the benediction at 16:24, and only occasionally do they offer the benediction of 16:24 as 16:28, that is, after the doxology.[9] Thus we can see that the benediction of 16:24 is lost (or displaced to 16:28) *only when the doxology is found at the end of ch. 16.* Thus even if the benediction at 16:20b is very well attested, this is no way impugns the authenticity of 16:24, which is actually strongly supported. To the contrary, once the intrusion of the doxology is recognized as the *cause* of the omission of 16:24—and this is exactly what the alignment of the witnesses shows—then 16:24 has to be judged an original reading.[10]

[6] Aland, "Glosse, Interpolation, Redaktion und Komposition in der Sicht der neutestamentlichen Textkritik," 46, with the assertion that "all the forms with this verse show late influence."

[7] Corssen, "Überlieferungsgeschichte," 11–12.

[8] A slight exception is posed by the Gothic, reading "with your spirit."

[9] Even the minor variants appear to be closely correlated with the main types. Thus minuscule 630, which reads the doxology after ch. 16 only, has a unique text in providing the benediction in the same form at 16:20b and (after the doxology) at 16:28.

[10] This fact appears to have been recognized only by Zahn (*Introduction,* I, 408–409), and he noticed it only because he argued so strenuously for the authenticity of the doxology and an original position for it after ch. 14. Of course the peculiar features of the benedictions do confirm that the doxology originally stood after ch. 14.

Relative Placements
of the Doxology and Benedictions

MSS and versions	Position(s) of Doxology				Positions of Benedictions		
	post. 14	post. 14 & 16	post. 16	om.	16:20b	16:24	16:28
L	x				x	x	
ψ	x				x	x	
0209	x				x	x	
181	x				x	x	
326	x				x	x	
330	x				x	x	
451	x				x	x	
614	x				x	x	
1241	x				x	x	
1877	x				x	x	
1881	x				x	x	
1984	x				x	x	
1985	x				x	x	
2492	x				x	x	
2495 (with most min.)	x				x	x	
syr[h]	x				x	x	
A		x			x		
P		x			x		x
.5		x			?		?
33		x			x		x
104		x			x		x
arm		x			x		x
P[61]			x		x		
ℵ			x		x		
B			x		x		
C			x		x		
81			x		x		
436			x		x		
630			x		x		
1739			x		x		
1962			x		x		
2127			x		x		
vg			x		x		
syr[p]			x				x
cop[sa,bo]			x		x		
G(g)				x		x	
(D,F)				x		x	
E26 inf				x		x	
629				x		x	

(P[46], with doxology after 15:33, reads only the benediction at 16:20b.)

Therefore, Paul's letter to the Romans contained a repetition of the grace-benediction in the conclusion. We saw earlier that the doubling of the final epistolary wish is to be found rather often in ancient letters, and not infrequently do greetings fall between these wishes, just as in Rom 16:21–23.[11] If we are correct in the way we understand ch. 16 to have been written, with the autograph extending from 16:1–20b, an original doubling of the grace-benediction is easily understood.[12]

In witnesses placing the doxology at the end of ch. 14 the double benediction at the end of ch. 16 has, as a rule, been allowed to stand. Witnesses offering the doxology twice (after ch. 14 and after ch. 16) also attest the double benediction, though in this case the second benediction is usually read as 16:28, standing after the doxology. Typically, in the Old Latin tradition where the doxology was altogether absent, 16:20b has been omitted while the benediction of 16:24 stands alone. This is easily understood since the double benediction is difficult and does not conform to Paul's customary usage.

Once the doxology began to find a firm place at the end of ch. 16 the benediction of 16:24 became problematic: there were too many concluding elements. There was a growing tendency to omit 16:24, but 16:20b was satisfactory enough to be retained. Yet the fact that 16:24 already had a strong foothold in the tradition is shown by the many witnesses which give the doxology at the end of ch. 16 but continue to retain the benediction of 16:24, often after the doxology.

Thus the primary form of the text at the conclusion of the letter was 16:20b+21–23+24, without the doxology. Of all extant texts, only one preserves this sequence, and it probably by accident: MS 629, a fourteenth-century minuscule. Apart from this the tradition contains no extant witnesses to either the pure long form or the pure short forms of the Roman letter.

The Textual History of Romans and the Purpose of the Letter

A long-standing *crux* in the interpretation of Romans is the difficulty of specifying with confidence its occasion and purpose. The problem is sharply posed if we formulate the question in this way: why did Paul write this letter to the Roman church? Our reconstruction of the letter's textual history does not finally settle this issue, but it does rule out some possibilities and lend support to others.

Paul's other letters, because they speak so obviously and directly to the specific situations of their addressees, lead the interpreter to define their respective *Sitze im Leben* by juxtaposing the concrete circumstances of the recipients (the "occasion") and the aims of Paul with regard to those circumstances (the "purpose"). The particularity of Paul's letters—their emergence from and concern with definite historical situations—makes it necessary for the backgrounds of the letters to be understood if we are to understand the letters themselves. But since the backgrounds can be defined only through the letters, the exegete must always move in a circle of inference and deduction, from the letter to the situation and back. In this respect the letter to the Romans is not different from the other letters: we will understand it fully only by recognizing the historical circumstances which called it forth.

[11] See above, 59 with n. 14.
[12] See above, 93–94.

132

Yet it is precisely when the interpreter of Romans attempts to proceed on this principle that he receives an immediate rebuff. The expectation evoked by the other letters, that we will be able to discern something of the readers' situation from the letter and so be able to perceive why Paul says what he says, seems to be flatly disappointed by Romans. If in the other letters the occasion of writing appears to lie in the situation of the readers, at least in the main, in Romans it is not at all clear that Paul responds to the circumstances of the addressees. Rather, in Romans not only the "purpose" but also the "occasion" seems to rest entirely with the Apostle. At least this is generally taken for granted on the basis of the few explicit remarks which bear on the question of the occasion and purpose of the letter.

From these remarks we learn that at the time of writing Paul has not been to Rome; he did not found nor has he visited this church. Only now, despite a long-standing intention, does Paul at last have a realistic prospect of coming to Rome, and it is clear that he really does mean to come (1:10–15; 15:22–24, 28–29). Yet according to Paul's statements, the visit to Rome is rather incidental to another intention, the inauguration of a mission in the West, in Spain (15:23–24, 28). Thus Paul will not go to Rome merely for the sake of going to Rome, but will go only "in passing" (διαπορευόμενος, 15:24), only "by way of" Rome to Spain (ἀπελεύσομαι δι' ὑμῶν, 15:28). Paul is able now to contemplate this because he has fulfilled his missionary task in the East (15:18–23)—almost. It remains for him to convey to Jerusalem the offering of the Gentile churches. Certainly this was no mere "tying up of loose ends," for the delivery of this contribution was a crucial milestone in Paul's work, temporally, of course, but even more in a theological sense. It is difficult to overestimate the significance of this event for Paul: here was a sign and seal of Gentile Christianity's concern for and indebtedness to the Jewish Christian mother church and thus, on acceptance, of the unity of the whole church. Paul informs the Roman community that his journey to Jerusalem takes precedence over his desire to come to them, and asks their prayers that the offering be found acceptable and—what was surely of less importance—that he himself be preserved from his opponents in Judaea (15:25–32). So much do we know of Paul's situation.

On the other hand, the Roman letter seems not to divulge explicit or unambiguous references to the actual circumstances in Rome, apart from the general commendatory remarks to the effect that their faith is renowned and that they are full of goodness and knowledge (1:8, 11–12; 15:14; cf. 16:19). Such ostensibly meager occupation with the readers themselves is perhaps all that should be expected, since Paul had not been to Rome and did not know the community firsthand.

The interpretation of Romans must proceed at the most basic level from these given data: first, Paul's statements about his situation and plans; second, the Roman letter as such. But with these data we are given the problem: how to correlate satisfactorily the content of the letter with its ostensible occasion. Put differently, why did Paul write *this* letter to the Romans? The question has been variously answered. While we cannot undertake a full discussion of the problem, we can show the relevance of our findings for it.

Starting from the notices about Paul's situation, the seemingly general cast of the letter as a whole, and some facets of the textual tradition, it has been a common view that Romans is only one form of a general letter which was sent, or was in principle capable of being sent, to other communities also. On this view

Romans is construed more as a "manifesto" or "position paper" or "tract for the times" than as a letter in the strict sense. The letter form is taken to be almost incidental. Yet the textual history of the letter, properly evaluated, shows beyond doubt that Romans was originally a letter sent specifically and exclusively to the Roman church, and that the shorter forms of the letter and/or the omission of the address may not be used to support the notion that the letter in its present form or in any other form was ever directed *by Paul* to a community other than Rome. In this sense, Romans is as "particular" and "occasional" as all the rest of Paul's letters.

But other possibilities remain. Most views of the occasion and purpose of the letter have in common one element, the assumption that the body of Romans has little or nothing to do with Roman Christianity as such and was not called forth by the circumstances of that community, even if it was sent exclusively to Rome. But from this point of departure several paths may be followed. One of these looks especially to the notices about Paul's plans, and specifically his plan to come to Rome. The simplest and most immediate conclusion is that Paul's purpose in writing was to announce to the Roman church his impending visit. Since he had not been to Rome, this required that he "introduce himself." Thus the announcement of the visit frames the body of the letter which, accordingly, is understood as Paul's self-introduction. In the letter Paul seeks to give the readers an understanding of his preaching, hoping in this way to establish rapport with an unknown congregation, to insure a welcome in Rome and to gain the support needed of Rome for the projected Spanish mission.[13] But this understanding of the matter, far from solving the problem of how to correlate the occasion of Romans with the content of the letter, only makes the problem stand out more sharply, for it reveals how inadequate are the supposed motives for the nature of the letter itself. Surely a letter of such extent and weight goes far beyond what would have been required to let the church know of his coming and assure its support of his Spanish mission.[14] And when all is said, Romans really does not offer a "summary" of Paul's theological views, but only an aspect; many distinctive themes and emphases are absent or minimally noted. If this understanding of Romans can explain why Paul wrote *a* letter to Rome, it offers no reason why he wrote *this* letter, which is far more than an introduction, though at least that.

Another opinion, especially advocated recently, is more attentive to Paul's anticipation of the Jerusalem visit. There was, it is said, every reason why Paul's thoughts should be oriented in that direction, and not without anxiety, since the failure of the Jerusalem church to accept the collection and acknowledge its significance would be tantamount to a denial of the most basic premise of Paul's apostolic work, that the gospel is offered to all alike on the basis of faith alone, that Gentile and Jewish believers share equally in it, and that the church therefore is one. Thus it is suggested that Romans, as a defense of Paul's preaching of justification and of the unity of Jewish and Gentile believers, is really conceived exclusively with regard to

[13]Thus, e.g., Barrett, *A Commentary on the Epistle to the Romans*, 7; Dodd, *The Epistle of Paul to the Romans*, xxv; Knox, "The Epistle to the Romans," 360–63.

[14]If the letter were actually a personal *apologia* and such an extensive piece were required to achieve the noted aims, we would be forced to presume that the Roman community was strongly predisposed against Paul, so much so that only such a letter would suffice to gain the readers' approbation (thus Michel, *Der Brief an die Römer*, 4, and Knox, "The Epistle to the Romans," 362–63). But there is no basis for this presumption, and it cannot be assumed simply from the letter itself.

the collection visit. Indeed, it might be regarded as a "letter to Jerusalem," or at the least as containing major elements of the apologetic speech which Paul was planning to give in Jerusalem.[15] This aspect of Paul's situation and the conclusions drawn from it go a long way toward explaining the nature and content of the Roman letter. But if this view provides a good reason why Paul wrote this *kind* of letter, it is all the more problematic why this letter was sent *to Rome*.

An alternative perspective rejects the assumption that Romans can be understood in abstraction from the concrete situation of the Roman church and insists that not only was Paul acquainted with the circumstances of the church but that in Romans he addresses those circumstances directly. This view places Romans on a par with the rest of the letters, locating its occasion primarily in the community addressed.[16] To the extent that this view assumes that Paul knew something of the Roman situation, then at first glance our conclusion that ch. 16 is an integral part of the letter seems to support that assumption. But this is not necessarily the case; the question whether Paul had any acquaintances in Rome, or whether he knew anything in particular about the Roman community, is not the same as the question whether in Romans Paul means to speak to specific issues in the Roman community. A positive answer to the first question does not automatically require a positive answer to the second. Nevertheless, these two concerns cannot be entirely separated, and in the light of our investigation their mutuality must be more clearly perceived.

Why is it commonly concluded that the Roman letter has no direct bearing on, or occasion within, the Roman community and its internal situation? The grounds for this are several. First among them is the obvious fact that Paul did not establish this church and had never visited it. Therefore it is assumed that Paul had no knowledge—at least no specific information—about the actual conditions of the Roman church and, consequently, cannot in his letter have spoken to those conditions. He had to speak only in general terms; it was a matter of "expounding" instead of "applying" his gospel. Second, there is an appeal to the character of the Roman letter itself, which, by comparison with the other letters, seems to lack the explicit directness, the references to individual persons, groups and perspectives, and the sense of dialogue elsewhere typical. And third, there is the textual observation that there are forms of the letter in the tradition which are entirely general and do not refer to Rome at all, a fact sometimes taken to show that Paul sent the letter to other communities also. A letter made available to more than one community could hardly be concerned with unique circumstances. All of these factors converge to

---

[15]This view was early adumbrated by Ernst Fuchs, *Hermeneutik* (Bad Cannstatt, 1954) 191. See now especially Jervell, "Der Brief nach Jerusalem; Über Veranlassung und Adresse des Römerbriefes," 61–73; Suggs, " 'The Word is Near You,' " 289–312; and to some extent Bornkamm, *Paul*, 92–96.

[16]Among recent advocates of this view, and for a variety of reasons, are H. Preisker, "Das historische Problem des Römerbriefes," *Wissenschaftliche Zeitschrift, Jena* 2 (1952–53) 25–30; G. Harder, "Der konkrete Anlass des Römerbriefes," *Theologia Viatorum* 6 (1959–60) 13–24; E. Trocmé, "L'Epître aux Romains et la méthode missionaire de l'apôtre Paul," *NTS* 7 (1961–62) 148–153; K. H. Rengstorf, "Paulus und die älteste römische Christenheit," *Studia Evangelica* II/1 (ed. F. L. Cross; TU 87; Berlin, 1964) 447–464; H. W. Bartsch, "Die historische Situation des Römerbriefes," 281–291; *idem,* "Die antisemitischen Gegner des Paulus im Römerbrief," in *Antijudaismus im Neuen Testament? Exegetische und systematische Beiträge* (ed. W. Eckert, N. P. Levinson and M. Stöhr; Munich, 1967) 27–43; Marxsen, *Introduction to the New Testament,* 92–104; and Donfried, "A Short Note on Romans 16." Many of these develop arguments from the substance of the letter body without making any appeals to ch. 16.

suggest that the Roman letter is conceived, apart from its framework, without pointed relevance to Rome.

Yet each of the premises fostering this conclusion is problematic. To proceed from Paul's lack of firsthand acquaintance with the Roman church to the assertion that therefore he had no knowledge about its internal condition is a *non sequitur*. If ch. 16, which suggests close relationships between Paul and those addressed, must have been an integral part of the letter, then despite the absence of a visit Paul may very well have possessed specific knowledge of the community. As to the supposedly general substance of the letter we are on no firmer ground, since the argument assumes what is still to be proved. That Paul has not visited the church, that he had not previously exerted his authority there and that the community as such had not acknowledged his authority—these, not any lack of information about the church, may be the real reasons why the letter seems to have an oblique cast. Then too, the letter does revolve around a limited number of concerns; like the other letters, it presents only aspects of Paul's thought. But why these particular concerns and aspects? What "principle of selection," what specific aim, dictated that the letter should have the substance that it does? Moreover, we find in Romans at least one section which we would not be surprised to find in any other of his letters, namely the very "practical" and pointed admonitions concerning the "strong" and the "weak" in faith (14:1–15:6). If this section were found in another letter it would not be regarded as merely "theoretical" or paradigmatic; it would be understood in a highly specific way. There is, further, the continuing enigma how the tortuous effort in chs. 9–11 to comprehend and explicate the unbelief of Israel fits into the letter structurally and thematically; that problem is all the more intractable if it has no relevance to the Roman church. In short, it is altogether possible that we have mistaken an obliqueness of approach for a generality of content. As to the third argument for the generality of the letter, we have already shown that the existence of generalized forms of the text gives no indication that the letter was ever intended by Paul to have general applicability.

We are left, then, with a letter sent exclusively, so far as we can tell, to the Roman church and with the knowledge that specific information about the situation of that church could have been available to Paul through his close acquaintances there. The critical principle for the interpretation of the other letters—the necessity of correlating the content of the letter with the situation of the recipients—must remain in force for the Roman letter also. The task of reconstructing that situation is beyond our present intentions, and may be hampered by a paucity of evidence. Yet one important element in a solution may be available: the possible effects of the so-called edict of Claudius of *ca.* 49. The motive, scope and practical import of this decree have yet to be clarified in detail, but a large-scale expulsion of Jews from Rome seems beyond doubt. If Roman Jewish-Christians fell under this ban (cf. Acts 18:1ff.), then the concerns of the Roman letter would be of the greatest relevance to the situation which may have obtained once the proscription was rescinded and the Jewish-Christian constituency sought to reestablish itself in Rome. A study of the edict and its consequences is therefore a logical beginning point for reconstituting the situation of Roman Christianity when Paul wrote.[17] As important as a study of

---

[17]Heavy emphasis is placed upon the edict by Bartsch, "Die antisemitischen Gegner des Paulus im Römerbrief," and Marxsen, *Introduction to the New Testament*. Firm deductions require that the edict

the Roman background of the letter may be, it is still necessary to keep Paul's own situation in view and to grasp the epistolary situation as a whole. With Paul on the verge of embarking for Jerusalem, we might expect to discover a remarkable coincidence and convergence of Paul's preoccupations and the issues confronting the Roman community. But at the least, it is clear that no interpretation of Romans will be adequate if it fails to make sense of the fact that in Romans we have a letter addressed to a specific community and, as it appears, only to that community.

Literary Criticism, Style Criticism, and Textual Criticism

Of the undisputed letters of Paul only Philemon has as yet escaped the scalpel of critical literary partition, that is, attempts to discover in what is transmitted as the text of a single letter parts of more than one originally independent letter. These efforts have a long history behind them, but have come increasingly into vogue of late.[18] Since we have dealt specifically with this issue in relation to Romans, it is appropriate in retrospect to give some attention to partition theories generally, not least because the partitioning of Romans, together with that of 2 Corinthians, has been invested with the greatest likelihood and so has helped justify the development of similar approaches to other letters. Of course, it would be completely unwarranted to impugn literary analysis for other letters only because we have found it to be unsatisfactory for Romans, for the literary problems attendant on Paul's letters are not the same from one letter to the next and each has to be accorded literary evaluation on its own terms. Our investigation does not challenge the principle that criticism of the letters need not and cannot take their integrity for granted. Nevertheless, this study has at least by implication raised questions about the adequacy of the *methods* which have served this critical principle, and these problems of method deserve explicit consideration in conclusion.

Perhaps the greatest methodological problem in the literary analysis of the epistles is simply the determination of relevant evidence and the way such evidence is evaluated. A review of literary-critical work makes it plain that partition theories consistently depend on the same *type* of evidence. One aspect of this evidence is purely literary, and though the specifics of literary difficulties vary from letter to letter, the general nature of the problems remains much the same. We may mention, for example, abrupt changes of subject matter, interruptions in an otherwise continuous train of thought, seeming inconsistencies or even contradictions within a given letter, the presence of certain formulae in supposedly inappropriate or uncustomary contexts, redundancy, etc. Another aspect of such evidence consists of perceived changes in "tone" or "style" (rather elusive categories) and the apparent assumption by the writer of different circumstances on the part of the addressees

---

itself (nature, time, and consequences) be more clearly understood. A good bit of progress in this matter has been made by Wiefel, "Die jüdische Gemeinschaft im antiken Rom und die Anfänge des römischen Christentums."

[18]For a thorough survey of earlier partition theories see Carl Clemen, *Die Einheitlichkeit der paulinischen Briefe, an Hand der bisher mit Bezug auf sie aufgestellten Interpolations- und Kompilationshypothesen* (Göttingen, 1894). More recent studies are too numerous to name: see the bibliographies to 1 and 2 Corinthians, Philippians and 1 Thessalonians in Kümmel, *Introduction to the New Testament*. The most thoroughgoing advocate of partition theories is Schmithals, most of whose proposals are available in *Paul and the Gnostics*.

within what is presented to us as a single letter. To be sure, there is an element of subjectivity in observations of both sorts (more in the second than the first), but this is necessary and acceptable. Even those who do not concur in judgments against integrity occasioned by these difficulties are usually willing to acknowledge the difficulties as such. The issue is not so much whether we can discover literary problems in the *Corpus,* but only how we may best account for these problems.

The interpreter seeks to explain these difficulties in a rationally coherent way, and one means of doing this is to formulate theories of partition which posit as the cause of literary problems the editorial compilation of one letter from originally discrete and independent parts. There is nothing inherently impossible about this, for we know little indeed about the early history of Paul's letters prior to their incorporation into the canon of the NT. The field is open to conjectures and theoretical reconstructions, yet theories must be held accountable to their interpretations of evidence. The phenomena considered in literary analysis—abrupt changes of subject matter, broken trains of thought, shifts in tone or style, and the like—constitute evidence for partition only to the extent that they are seen as departures from a preconceived "norm": that is, it is assumed that Paul's letters should be characterized by logical and consistent progression, smooth transitions, close organization and so on. If this assumption is reasonable enough on its own terms, we must still ask to what extent these criteria are legitimately derived from the materials at hand and to what extent they are really imposed from the outside. Paul is not usually commended for the rigor of his logic, the precision of his terminology, an aptitude for organization, or a placid temperament. Is this only because his letters fail to reveal him truly? Those who in a given case do not hold partition to be a likely explanation of literary problems sometimes appeal to other possible causes—a sleepless night, interruption in dictation, the arrival of new information *in medias res,* Paul's volatile temperament, or his tendency to digress. (Advocates of partition theories tend to dismiss such suggestions as "psychologistic" or "rationalistic," but it should not be obscured that their own assumptions fall into the same category.) If these alternative causes often appear to be naive or contrived, they are at least useful in preserving the recognition that any number of contingent factors may have conspired to produce the perceived result, even if we can now know little or nothing of the immediate circumstances surrounding the composition of the letters. There is no need for us to take a side in this debate; it is important, however, to point up the problem of defining and evaluating evidence for partition. If the methodological impasse is to be overcome, and even if the issue is to be rightly posed, there are several prerequisites with which the critic must reckon.

First, before any conclusions can be drawn about how Paul "should" or "must" have expressed himself, it is necessary to discover as much as possible about how he "does" in fact express himself in the letters as we have them. The question of partition is usually raised prematurely, that is, before learning all that can be learned about the form and style of the letters as they have been transmitted to us. Epistolary form and style are, after all, part of the objective data which are available and ought to be taken into account as important evidence for or against literary-critical operations. If in the end the Pauline letters can be seen to exhibit a considerable degree of structural and stylistic consistency among themselves, then it will be important whether this feature or that is characteristic of the letters generally or represents a clear departure from the norm. From the point of view of method, a thorough formal and stylistic description of the Pauline letter must provide a basis for judgments about literary integrity. Otherwise, theories of partition will be unnecessarily arbitrary and lacking adequate formal controls.[19] The implications of such analysis for literary questions were recognized and to some extent demonstrated by Schubert[20] and have been developed more broadly by Bjerkelund, who gives particular attention to partition theories and in several cases finds that the evidence of epistolary style, once brought to light, weighs heavily against partition theories.[21] Also, we have tried to show that the evidence of the style of the conclusions speaks decisively against separating Rom 16 from the rest of the letter. The style of the conclusions has special relevance in the case of Romans, less for other letters whose integrity is in question (though it does speak to the problem of the literary character of Philippians).[22]

But if literary analysis must be subject to the controls provided by prior analysis of the form and style of the Pauline letters, this is only one part of its obligation. Partition theories must also be attentive to the larger issues which they inevitably raise. These include questions about the motives, occasions and agents of redaction, but also—by implication—the whole problem of the early history of the *Corpus Paulinum*.[23] These questions are ordinarily neglected by advocates of partition theories, as though it were sufficient to discover literary reasons for suspecting the text of a letter to be composite without asking why, when, and by whom such redaction might have been undertaken. There has been only one systematic attempt to come to terms with these issues, and it is to the credit of W. Schmithals that he has at least recognized the broad implications of his own theories, even if few have found his comprehensive scheme adequate. Supporters of partition theories must not only see the relevance of these larger problems, but must also seek their solution. The plausibility of a given theory depends *equally* on how well it explains the literary features of a text *and* on how well it is capable of comprehending the redactional effort as such.

There is, generally, no necessity that particular partition theories be brought into close connection with the emergence of the collected letters of Paul. G. Bornkamm, for example, has attributed the compilation of Philippians and 2 Corinthians to different editors whose intentions did not embrace any letters beyond those to a single community. The motive in each case was not to "collect" Paul's letters, but to work into convenient form letters already at hand.[24] Nevertheless, the

---

[19]A clear illustration of uncontrolled redactional analysis is provided by Schmithals, whose cumulative statement of his theories amounts to a virtual *reductio ad absurdum* of the whole enterprise. See his essay, "On the Composition and Earliest Collection," esp. 245–253. Schmithals enumerates no fewer than sixteen letters (or letter fragments) embedded in the received text. Equally astonishing is the way in which he supposes these diverse items were conflated. He makes the *Corpus* a veritable pastiche of disparate elements almost indiscriminately thrown together.

[20]*Form and Function of the Pauline Thanksgivings,* 26 on 1 Thessalonians (". . . the thanksgiving itself constitutes the main body of I Thessalonians") and 76–77 on Philippians (showing the close functional correspondence between the thanksgiving of 1:3ff. and 4:10–20, and judging the latter "much more than an incidental appendix").

[21]*Parakalô, passim.* (See on 2 Corinthians, 147–155, on 1 Thessalonians, 125–140, on Romans, 158–160.)

[22]See Appendix II.

[23]This was rightly pointed out by W. Michaelis, "Teilungshypothesen bei Paulusbriefen: Briefkompositionen und ihr Sitz im Leben," *TZ* 14 (1958) 321–26.

[24]"Der Philipperbrief als paulinische Briefsammlung," in *Neotestamentica et Patristica* (Cullmann Freundesgabe; Leiden, 1962) 200–202.

idea that different letters were independently redacted by various individuals in far-flung communities and at different times becomes increasingly tenuous with the number of letters for which redaction is proposed. If in addition to 2 Corinthians and Philippians we were also to consider Romans a redactional product, then Schmithals would be very much to the point when he suggests that in this case there must have been a remarkable and unparalleled "editorial neurosis" (*Kompositions-psychose*) in early Christianity.[25] For his own part, Schmithals, with merciless single-mindedness, carries the argument for partition through to what is, relatively speaking, a more satisfactory conclusion. He proposes that the redaction of the Pauline letters was undertaken by a single individual at one time under the constraint of a compelling motive: to provide a collection of seven Pauline letters which could be commended to the church catholic as a weapon against the gnostic threat.

As evidence for this grandiose conception Schmithals draws upon both the "raw materials" of redaction (the supposed components of the transmitted letters) and the final product, the primitive collection of Paul's letters. By comparing the earliest canon lists he abstracts what he believes to be the content and order of the earliest *Corpus:* Corinthians (1–2), Galatians, Philippians, Thessalonians (1–2) and Romans. He finds the interest of the redactor expressed in the ecumenical address of the first letter (1 Cor 1:2b), in the fact that he strived in his redaction for exactly seven letters (again suggesting the ecumenicity of the collection), in the fact that each letter was made to contain some anti-gnostic polemic, and in the doxology of Rom 16:25–27, provided as a conclusion to the whole.

On its own premises Schmithals' construction hangs together well enough; at least it is self-consistent. But, problematically, all of the premises are dubious, and the stringing together of doubtful premises rarely makes for a convincing argument.[26] The entire scheme is vulnerable both from the side of his literary analysis of the individual letters, which by any standard is quite arbitrary, and from the side of his understanding the formation of the *Corpus*. It is not our aim here to offer a thorough critique of Schmithals' views, but to indicate that while he has rightly recognized the far-reaching questions which partition theories raise, his own answers carry little probative force.

Finally, it remains to suggest the need to bring issues of literary analysis into relation, not simply with the history of the canon, but with textual criticism. In reality, no strict separation can or should be made between the history of the formation of the *Corpus* and the history of the text of Paul's letters. That being the case, literary-critical theories must come to terms with the significance of textual evidence in relation to them, and this study has shown the necessity and fruitfulness of this interaction in the case of Romans. Of course, if the formation of the *Corpus*, taken as a momentary event, is seen as the occasion for the redaction of the letters (e.g., Schmithals)[27] and if a pre-*Corpus* circulation of the letters is ruled out (Goodspeed and others), or if an individual letter is supposed to have entered the tradition separately only in composite form (e.g., Bornkamm), then partition

---

[25] "On the Composition and Earliest Collection," 271.

[26] For a general critique of Schmithals' hypothesis see my essay, "The Redaction of the Pauline Letters and the Formation of the Pauline Corpus."

[27] As this is applied to Romans, see above, 43–45. In the case of Romans it is virtually mandatory for those who deny the integrity of the letter to suppose that the redaction of the letter took place in connection with the formation of the *Corpus*, for in this letter we would have to reckon with a combination, unparalleled in other partition theories, of writings to two *different* communities.

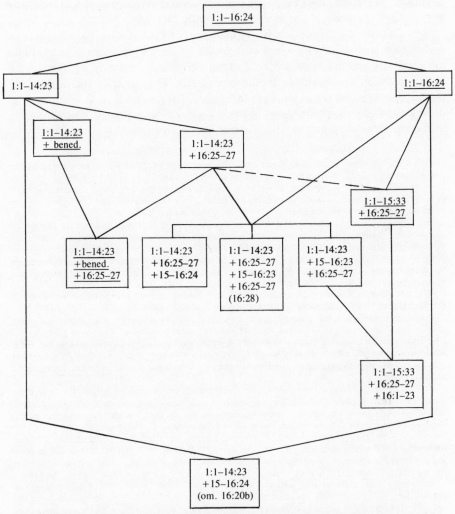

Schema of the Development
of the Textual Forms of Romans

Underlined forms of the text are not attested, but are conjectured on the basis of the attested forms.

theories are naturally placed beyond the pale of text-critical investigation. On such assumptions textual evidence is not anticipated. From these various points of view, the presence of other forms of the letter in the textual tradition of Romans—indeed, of what would have to be called a "pre-redactional" form (Rom 1–15)—is itself a strong argument against the assumption that the textual history of this letter began only with the publication of the *Corpus*. We have tried to show that the shorter forms of Romans could have arisen only during the early period, when the Roman letter circulated independently. If, on the other hand, it is admitted that the letters did circulate individually before the collected letters were "published" as a group,[28]

[28]This has recently been allowed as a possibility even by Schmithals ("On the Composition and Earliest Collection," 273–74), but seemingly without a sense of the real consequences of the insight

this means that we have every right to look for and to expect some textual traces, however obscure, of such pre-*Corpus* forms of the letters. Once a pre-*Corpus* circulation is granted, then the absence of any textual evidence in support of partition theories comprises a formidable limitation to their plausibility.[29]

In sum, the literary analysis of the letters of Paul as it has been carried out suffers methodologically for a lack of rigor and a failure to grasp the problem in its total and essential dimensions.[30] Until these difficulties are remedied, theories of literary partition will inevitably appear to be, and will be, arbitrary and inadequate, providing interesting conjectures but little more.[31] It may well be that we owe the present form of some of the letters of Paul to editorial compilation. Whether that is in fact the case has yet to be demonstrated with conviction.

---

either for the question of textual evidence or for his own view of the redaction of the letters as a thoroughgoing process. He explains that at the time the letters did not have "canonical status" and thus could be freely handled by a redactor. Even though the letters certainly did not have "canonical status" in the proper, later sense, it seems quite likely that texts already known, used, and valued in one form could not with impunity be singlehandedly recast in another form.

[29]See the pointed reflections of Aland on the significance of textual criticism for theories of interpolation, redaction, etc. in his essay, "Glosse, Interpolation, Redaktion und Komposition in der Sicht der neutestamentlichen Textkritik," esp. 48: "Eingriffe in den Text einer Schrift, welche sich von ihrem Verfasser gelöst und nach den Gesetzen literarischen Überlieferung ihre Eigendasein begonnen hat, bleiben nicht ohne deutlich sichtbare Spuren. Sind solche Spuren nicht nachweisbar, kann daraus geschlossen werden, dass die Struktur des Textes ungestört blieb. Wer für die von ihm behauptete Glosse, Interpolation, Redaktion, Komposition oder was dergleichen immer sein mag, keinen Beleg in der handschriftlichen Überlieferung zu bringen vermag, gefährdet seine These von vornherein." This objection can be circumvented, it seems, in only two ways: either by denying that the letters in question enjoyed any independent early circulation (which does not seem possible for Romans or likely for the other letters), or by contending that a given letter entered the tradition only in composite form. But in the latter case one must face the problem of having to specify probable motives and occasions for redactional activity—a problem which becomes progressively intractable with the number of letters thought to be editorial products.

[30]Beyond the problems noted earlier, yet another needs to be mentioned, namely the necessity of clarifying not only the motives, occasions and agents of compilation, but also the *method* of redaction. Schmithals' redactor would appear to have worked with no "method" at all in the ordering of the disparate fragments which Schmithals postulates. For 2 Corinthians, G. Bornkamm (*Die Vorgeschichte des sogenannten zweiten Korintherbriefes* [Sitzungsberichte der Heidelberger Akademie der Wissenschaften, phil.-hist. Klasse, Jahrgang 91, Abhandlung 2; Heidelberg, 1961] 24–28) has tried to show that the letter thought to be contained in chs. 10–13 was placed at the end of the whole compilation because of the "formal law" of early Christian literature that warnings against false teachers should have a concluding position. Yet we may well wonder whether this was any more a law of redaction than of composition.

[31]The remarks of James Price about the partition debate on 2 Corinthians is a fitting commentary on the whole question: "For over fifty years the same arguments pro and con have been repeated, with only slight amendment and—one may suspect—some increase in certainty as a result of their repetition in critical introductions and commentaries. Occasionally champions of partitioning theories have implied that only conservative biases obscure the demonstrative force of the internal evidence in their favor; while writers defending the letter's unity sometimes have decried the wresting of texts by theologically suspect critics, in the interest of their ingenious hypotheses, and always insisted upon the patent exegetical support for their counter-arguments.

"One can, of course, discount the exaggeration and the ad hominem elements in polemical statements. Yet, after this dross has been sifted it cannot be said that the critical residue decisively weights the argument on either side of this long-standing debate" ("Aspects of Paul's Theology and Their Bearing on Literary Problems of Second Corinthians," in *Studies in the History and Text of the New Testament* [Festschrift for K. W. Clark, ed. B. L. Daniels and M. J. Suggs; Studies and Documents 29; Salt Lake City, 1967] 95).

Hopefully, some of the considerations we have suggested will help bring the issues into clearer focus and move the debate to a more productive level.

THE EPISTOLARY CONCLUSIONS
AND THE EARLY LITURGY

There has been a recurrent tendency in the study of the Pauline letters to speak of liturgical influences on their style and of liturgical elements embedded in them, and such influences and elements have been seen among other places in the epistolary conclusions, where benedictory and doxological formulae appear with regularity and concentration. Thus it is sometimes suggested that Paul conceived his final words with a view to the reading of his letters in the liturgical assemblies of the communities addressed. On this basis the characteristic features of the epistolary conclusions are supposedly understood.

Especially important to this point of view is 1 Cor 16:20–23. The elements encountered here, consisting of the kiss-greeting, a ban-formula, an invocation, and a benediction, have been thought to reproduce "the earliest Christian liturgical sequence."[1] Support for this suggestion has been sought in alleged parallels, especially Did 10:6 and Rev 22:20–21. If this hypothesis is correct, it could be argued that Paul intended his letter to lead directly into the eucharistic celebration of the Corinthian community. It is impossible to substantiate such possibilities as these; the evidence adduced is extremely tenuous.[2] Nevertheless, it is a frequent assumption that the benedictory and doxological elements of the letters are drawn directly from the early Christian liturgy and are to be understood on that basis.[3]

It is beyond the purpose of the present study to deal in detail with the possible relationship between the Pauline letters and early Christian worship, but two points must be emphasized so far as benedictory and doxological elements in

---

[1]See above, Chapter III, n. 89.

[2]All of the suggested parallels are partial and pertain to different elements in the series. One item common to 1 Cor 16, Rev 22, and Did 10 is the grace-benediction, but in Did 10:6 this has a different form altogether and an earlier position than in the other two texts. An invocation is also present at each point. Otherwise there is no similarity among the texts. If Paul does take up traditional formulae in 16:22, that does not in itself suggest that the conclusion is deliberately given a liturgical orientation. When all is said, 1 Cor 16:20–23 has its greatest similarities to the other Pauline conclusions—a fact which cannot, in the absence of further evidence, be taken to show the liturgical cast of the conclusions.

Equally troublesome for the hypothesis is the assumption made to explain why Paul should have used a series of liturgical phrases to bring his letter to a close, namely, that he wished to provide within the letter an immediate transition to the eucharistic celebration. This presumes both that Paul knew in advance in what context the letter would be read, and that the eucharist was a regular part of the primitive service of worship. But none of this is self-evident (for the view that the eucharist was a regular component of the service see Oscar Cullmann, *Early Christian Worship* [SBT 10; London, 1959], but for the opposite opinion see Delling, *Worship in the New Testament*).

[3]See, for example, the study of Champion, *Benedictions and Doxologies in the Epistles of Paul;* in addition, this is generally the approach of Cullmann, *Early Christian Worship;* Delling, *Worship in the New Testament;* and G. P. Wiles, *The Function of Intercessory Prayer in Paul's Apostolic Ministry With Special Reference to the First Epistle to the Thessalonians* (dissertation; Yale University, 1965), who speaks of a "liturgically oriented closing pattern" in Paul's letters.

the conclusions are concerned. The first is simply that we know all too little about the early Christian liturgy to make judgments about such specific elements in the letters. That benedictory and doxological formulae had a place in the liturgy is scarcely to be doubted, but that this or that particular benediction or doxology in the letters is derived from or intended for a liturgical setting cannot be verified or even made likely, and little is gained by such conjectures. W. C. van Unnik has rightly cautioned against a " 'pan-liturgism' which sees everywhere in the Pauline epistles the background of the liturgy whenever a simple parallel . . . is found."[4] Though the issue may never be satisfactorily illumined—the materials are too sparse—a rapid and uncritical resort to a hypothetical liturgical context ought to be avoided.

Instead, most necessary is a stricter attention to the *epistolary* contexts and functions of benedictory and doxological items, and other supposedly "liturgical" formulae, deferring the possibility of another and prior context and function. A liturgical *form* may indeed be derivative, but in the letters may perform a strictly epistolary *function*.[5] This clearly seems to be the case for the peace-wish, kiss-greeting and final benediction, and is likely for other elements at earlier points in the letters.[6] To the extent that such formulae can be seen to serve purely epistolary needs and/or to possess contextual relationships, and thus to be integral to the letters *as letters,* there is no reason to seek out a non-epistolary rationale for their use.

[4]"*Dominus Vobiscum*: The Background of a Liturgical Formula," 272. For a sober estimate of liturgical arguments and their results, see G. W. H. Lampe, "The Evidence in the New Testament for Early Creeds, Catechisms and Liturgy," *ExpT* 71 (1959–60) 359–363.

[5]This distinction is essential. A failure to make use of it is a major problem in Champion's study and in many others.

[6]This applies especially to Paul's introductory epistolary greeting, which Ernst Lohmeyer suggested was a liturgical formula ("Probleme paulinischer Theologie, I: Briefliche Grussüberschriften," *ZNW* 26 [1927] 158–173; see, however, the critique by Gerhard Friedrich, "Lohmeyers These über das paulinische Briefpräskript kritisch beleuchtet," *ZNW* 46 [1955] 272–74), but also to benedictory, doxological and other prayer-wish formulae at intermittent points throughout the letters which appear to mark the conclusions of discrete parts of the letters and/or serve as transition devices.

SOME NOTES ON THE LITERARY PROBLEMS IN PHILIPPIANS

Recent studies have called into question the integrity of Philippians, suggesting that the letter in its transmitted form is a conflation of several pieces of Paul's correspondence with the Philippian community.[1] Two sections of the present letter have been found to present literary problems. First, there is an apparent break between 3:1 and 3:2 marked by a shift in subject and a change of tone, the section beginning at 3:2 comprising a polemical statement which extends to 4:1. Moreover, the τὸ λοιπόν of 3:1 might be regarded as a *locutio properans ad finem,* a possibility supported by the following χαίρετε, which could be rendered "farewell" as easily as "rejoice," and by the presence in the preceding context (2:25–30) of such remarks as might be expected in a letter-conclusion. Further, it is possible to understand 4:4–7 as the natural continuation of 3:1, completing the conclusion there begun. Secondly, it has often been considered impossible, or at least many have found it incomprehensible, that Paul's expression of thanks for the Philippians' gift should appear only at the end of the whole letter—and indeed that the acknowledgment of the gift was not made earlier in time, immediately on receipt instead of after the recovery of Epaphroditus. Thus 4:10–23 is often thought to have been a separate letter.[2] Our observations on the style and structure of the epistolary conclusions are only partially applicable to these difficulties, but still not without value.

We observed earlier the close structural correspondence between Romans and Philippians in their concluding portions.[3] In each case the main part of the letter can be seen to close with the formulaic wish of peace (Rom 15:33; Phil 4:9). This is followed in both letters by extended sections (Rom 16:1–19; Phil 4:10–18) which have nothing in common by way of content but which are closed off with formally similar prayer-wishes (Rom 16:20a; Phil 4:19). In each case also a brief section of greetings and the grace-benediction follow, bringing the letters to an end. Of course the possibility cannot be excluded altogether that the structural correspondence between the conclusions of these two letters is a consequence of secondary redaction. But this seems rather unlikely given both the distinctive features of these two letters and their correspondence with the other Pauline conclusions in the use of

---

[1] See Schmithals, "The False Teachers of the Epistle to the Philippians," 65–122; J. Müller-Bardorff, "Zur Frage der literarischen Einheit des Philipperbriefes," *Wissenschaftliche Zeitschrift, Jena* 7 (1957–58) 591–604; B. D. Rahtjen, "The Three Letters of Paul to the Philippians," *NTS* 6 (1959–60) 167–173; Bornkamm, "Der Philipperbrief als paulinische Briefsammlung," 192–202; H. Köster, "The Purpose of the Polemic of a Pauline Fragment," *NTS* 8 (1961–62) 317–332; A. F. J. Klijn, "Paul's Opponents in Philippians 3," *NovT* 7 (1965) 278–284.

[2] We have briefly summarized observations made by Schmithals, "The False Teachers of the Epistle to the Philippians," 78–81, and Rahtjen, "The Three Letters of Paul to the Philippians."

[3] See above, 88, 94.

concluding elements and the way those elements are structured. The correspondence can be well accounted for by regarding the final portion of Philippians (4:10–20) as autographically written, even though this is not explicitly stated. This would provide a sound explanation why the expression of thanks stands at the end, for in the autographic conclusion the writer is in immediate touch with the readers and can speak most personally.[4] And not to be overlooked here is the similarity of this section, at least in function, to commercial receipts, that is, legal acknowledgments of payment, which required autographic certifications. The ἀπέχω of 4:18 is the basic technical term of receipts among the papyri.[5]

Regarding the more strictly literary observations made in the interest of partition, several comments are appropriate. The τὸ λοιπόν of 3:1 cannot be called an immediate transition to the epistolary conclusion. Despite the similarity to 2 Cor 13:11, the use of this phrase is not at all common to the Pauline conclusions, whereas it is used several times in contexts which precede by a considerable space the epistolary conclusions as such.[6] As for the χαίρετε of 3:1, apart from the fact that "rejoicing" is a constant theme of the letter as it stands, χαίρειν is not used as a *final* wish among ancient letters or in the letters of Paul. In terms of the conclusion proper, what we have found to be characteristic of the letters generally is equally evident in Phil 4:9–23. The wish of 4:9b cannot be construed as a final element which might have served as the original conclusion of an independent letter, any more than can 4:7.[7] The wish of peace found in common form in 4:9 is elsewhere always penultimate; the grace-benediction is Paul's constant concluding formula. Thus from the perspective of epistolary style there appear to be no substantial reasons for viewing Phil 4:10–23 as (part of?) an originally independent letter.

All the problems of Philippians are not thereby solved by any means. Whether Phil 3:2ff. actually presupposes a situation different from that of the earlier part of the letter is still an open question.[8] Yet the literary features of 3:1 and 4:4–9 cannot be used to support the isolation of 3:1–4:9 or 3:2–4:3+4:8–9 as an independent letter.

[4] Of course this observation does not explain why a note of thanks was not sent earlier, but the assumption that this should have been the case is gratuitous.

[5] Cf. Preisigke, *Wörterbuch der griechischen Papyrusurkunden,* I, 162–63, *s.v.*

[6] Cf. 1 Thes 4:1, 2 Thes 3:1, Phil 4:8 (also Eph 6:10), as noted by B. S. Mackay, "Further Thoughts on Philippians," *NTS* 7 (1961) 161–170, esp. 163–64. Not surprisingly, Schmithals ("The False Teachers of the Epistle to the Philippians," 71 n. 36) embraces the objection and turns it to his profit by holding the other occurrences before conclusions to be the result of redaction.

[7] Schmithals (ibid., 75, 77) takes 4:9b as the conclusion of his letter C and 4:7 as the conclusion of his letter B.

[8] On the other problems see the remarks of T. E. Pollard, "The Integrity of Philippians," *NTS* 13 (1966–67) 57–66; Robert Jewett, "The Epistolary Thanksgiving and the Integrity of Philippians," *NovT* 12 (1970) 40–53; and Victor Paul Furnish, "The Place and Purpose of Philippians 3," *NTS* 10 (1963) 80–88.

SELECTED BIBLIOGRAPHY

Aland, Kurt. "Glosse, Interpolation, Redaktion und Komposition in der Sicht der neutesta-mentlichen Textkritik." *Studien zur Überlieferung des Neuen Testaments und seines Textes*. Arbeiten zur neutestamentlichen Textforschung 2. Berlin, 1967.

Anderson, Charles P. "The Epistle to the Hebrews and the Pauline Letter Collection." *HTR* 59 (1966) 429–438.

Bacon, Benjamin W. "The Doxology at the End of Romans." *JBL* 18 (1899) 167–176.

Bahr, Gordon J. "Paul and Letter Writing in the First Century." *CBQ* 28 (1966) 465–477.

———. "The Subscriptions in the Pauline Letters." *JBL* 87 (1968) 27–41.

Bardy, Gustav. "Le texte de l'épître aux Romains dans le commentaire d'Origène-Rufin." *RB* 17 (1920) 229–241.

———. "Marcionites (prologues)." *Dictionnaire de la Bible, Supplement*. Vol. V.

Barnett, Albert E. *Paul Becomes a Literary Influence*. Chicago, 1941.

Barrett, C. K. *A Commentary on the Epistle to the Romans*. Harper's New Testament Commentaries. New York, 1957.

Bartsch, Hans-Werner. "Die antisemitischen Gegner des Paulus im Römerbrief." *Anti-judaismus im Neuen Testament? Exegetische und systematische Beiträge*. Edited by W. Eckert, N. P. Levinson and M. Stöhr. Abhandlungen zum christlich-jüdischen Dialog 2. Munich, 1967.

———. "Die historische Situation des Römerbriefes." *Studia Evangelica* IV. Edited by F. L. Cross. TU 102. Berlin, 1968.

Bauernfeind, Otto. *Der Römerbrieftext des Origenes, nach dem Codex von der Goltz, unter-sucht und herausgegeben*. TU 44. Leipzig, 1924.

Berger, Samuel. *Histoire de la Vulgate pendant les premiers siècles du moyen âge*. Paris, 1893.

Bjerkelund, Carl J. *Parakalô. Form, Funktion und Sinn der parakalô-Sätze in den paulinischen Briefen*. Bibliotheca Theologica Norvegica 1. Oslo, 1967.

Blackman, Edwin Cyril. *Marcion and His Influence*. London, 1948.

Bornkamm, Günther. "The Anathema in the Early Christian Lord's Supper Liturgy." *Early Christian Experience*. New York, 1969.

———. "The Letter to the Romans as Paul's Last Will and Testament." *AusBR* 11 (1963) 2–14.

———. *Paul*. New York, 1971.

———. "Der Philipperbrief als paulinische Briefsammlung." *Neotestamentica et Patristica* (Cullmann Freundesgabe). Supplements to Novum Testamentum 6. Leiden, 1962.

———. *Die Vorgeschichte des sogennanten zweiten Korintherbriefes*. Sitzungsberichte der Heidelberger Akademie der Wissenchaften, phil.-hist. Klasse, 91, 2. Heidelberg, 1961.

Bruyne, Donatien de. "La finale marcionite de la lettre aux Romains retrouvée." *RBen* 28 (1911) 133–142.

———. "Les deux derniers chapitres de la lettre aux Romains." *RBen* 25 (1908) 423–430.

———. "Prologues bibliques d'origin marcionite." *RBen* 24 (1907) 1–14.

———. *Sommaires, divisions et rubriques de la Bible latine*. Namur, 1914.

Buck, Charles Henry. "The Early Order of the Pauline Corpus." *JBL* 68 (1949) 351–57.

Campenhausen, Hans von. *The Formation of the Christian Bible*. Philadelphia, 1972.

Chadwick, Henry. "Rufinus and the Tura Papyrus of Origen's Commentary on Romans." *JTS* N.S. 10 (1959) 10–42.

Champion, L. G. *Benedictions and Doxologies in the Epistles of Paul.* Oxford, 1934.

Corssen, Peter. *Epistularum Paulinarum codices Graece et Latine scriptos Augiensem, Boernerianum, Claromontanum examinavit inter se comparavit ad communem originem revocavit.* Programmae gymnasii Ieverensis. 2 vols. Kiel, 1887–89.

———. "Zur Überlieferungsgeschichte des Römerbriefes." *ZNW* 10 (1909) 1–45.

———. "Zur Überlieferungsgeschichte des Römerbriefes, Nachtrag." *ZNW* 10 (1909) 97–102.

Cullmann, Oscar. *Early Christian Worship.* SBT 10. London, 1959.

Dahl, Nils A. "The Particularity of the Pauline Epistles as a Problem in the Ancient Church." *Neotestamentica et Patristica* (Cullmann Freundesgabe). Supplements to Novum Testamentum 6. Leiden, 1962.

———. "Welche Ordnung der Paulusbriefe wird vom muratorischen Kanon vorausgesetzt?" *ZNW* 52 (1961) 39–53.

Deichgräber, Reinhard. *Gotteshymnus und Christushymnus in der frühen Christenheit; Untersuchungen zu Form, Sprache und Stil der frühchristlichen Hymnen.* Studien zur Umwelt des Neuen Testaments 5. Göttingen, 1967.

Deissmann, Adolf. *Light from the Ancient East; the New Testament Illustrated by Recently Discovered Texts of the Graeco-Roman World.* 2nd ed. London, 1927.

Delling, Gerhard. *Worship in the New Testament.* Philadelphia, 1962.

Dodd, C. H. *The Epistle of Paul to the Romans.* Moffatt New Testament Commentary. London, 1932.

Donfried, Karl P. "A Short Note on Romans 16." *JBL* 89 (1970) 441–49.

Doty, William G. "The Classification of Epistolary Literature." *CBQ* 31 (1969) 183–199.

———. *Letters in Primitive Christianity.* Philadelphia, 1973.

Dupont, Jacques. "Pour l'histoire de la doxologie finale de l'épître aux Romains." *RBen* 58 (1948) 3–22.

Emmet, C. W. "Romans XV. and XVI.: A New Theory." *Expos,* EIGHTH SERIES 11 (1916) 275–288.

Erbes, K. "Die Bestimmung der von Paulus aufgetragenen Grüsse, Röm. 16,3–15." *Zeitschrift für Kirchengeschichte* 22 (1901) 224–231.

———. "Zeit und Ziel der Grüsse Röm. 16,3–25 und der Mittheilungen II Tim. 4,9–21." *ZNW* 10 (1909) 128–147, 195–218.

Exler, F. X. J. *The Form of the Ancient Greek Letter. A Study in Greek Epistolography.* Washington, 1923.

Feine, Paul, and Behm, J. *Einleitung in das Neue Testament.* 9th ed. Heidelberg, 1950.

Finegan, Jack. "The Original Form of the Pauline Collection." *HTR* 49 (1956) 85–104.

Fitzmyer, Joseph A. "Some Notes on Aramaic Epistolography." *JBL* 93 (1974) 201–225.

———. "The Letter to the Romans." *The Jerome Biblical Commentary.* Edited by R. E. Brown, J. A. Fitzmyer and R. E. Murphy. 2 vols. in 1. Englewood Cliffs, N.J., 1968.

Frede, Hermann Josef. *Altlateinische Paulus-Handschriften.* Vetus Latina. Die Reste der altlateinischen Bibel. Aus der Geschichte der lateinischen Bibel 4. Freiburg, 1964.

———. "Die Ordnung der Paulusbriefe und der Platz des Kolosserbriefs im Corpus Paulinum." *Vetus Latina. Die Reste der altlateinischen Bibel,* XXIV/2; *Epistulae ad Philippenses et Colossenses.* Freiburg, 1969.

Funk, Robert W. *Language, Hermeneutic and Word of God; the Problem of Language in the New Testament and Contemporary Theology.* New York, 1966.

———. "The Apostolic *Parousia:* Form and Significance." *Christian History and Interpretation: Studies Presented to John Knox.* Edited by W. R. Farmer, C. F. D. Moule and R. R. Niebuhr. Cambridge, 1967.

Gamble, Harry. "The Redaction of the Pauline Letters and the Formation of the Pauline Corpus." *JBL* 94 (1975) 403–418.

Georgi, Dieter. *Die Geschichte der Kollekte des Paulus für Jerusalem.* Theologische Forschung 38. Hamburg, 1965.

Goguel, Maurice. *Introduction au Nouveau Testament*. 4 vols. Paris, 1922–26.
Goodspeed, Edgar J. *Introduction to the New Testament*. Chicago, 1937.
———. "Editio princeps of Paul." *JBL* 64 (1945) 193–204.
———. "Phoebe's Letter of Introduction." *HTR* 44 (1951) 55–57.
———. "Ephesians and the First Edition of Paul." *JBL* 70 (1951) 285–291.
Gyllenberg, R. "De inledande hälsningsformlerna i de paulinska breven." *SEA* 16 (1951) 21–31.
Harder, Günther. "Der Konkrete Anlass des Römerbriefes." *Theologia Viatorum* 6 (1959–60) 13–24.
———. *Paulus und das Gebet*. Neutestamentliche Forschungen 10. Gütersloh, 1936.
Harnack, Adolf von. "κόπος (κοπιᾶν, οἱ κοπιῶντες) im frühchristlichen Sprachgebrauch." *ZNW* 27 (1928) 1–10.
———. *Marcion: das Evangelium vom fremden Gott. Eine Monographie zur Geschichte der Grundlegung der katholischen Kirche*. 2nd ed., rev. TU 45. Leipzig, 1924.
———. "Über I Kor. 14,32ff. und Röm. 16,25ff. nach der ältesten Überlieferung und der marcionitischen Bibel." *Studien zur Geschichte des Neuen Testaments und der Alten Kirche, I, Zur neutestamentlichen Textkritik*. Berlin, 1931.
Hartke, W. *Die Sammlung und die ältesten Ausgaben der Paulusbriefe*. Bonn, 1917.
Hatch, W. H. P. "On the Relationship of Codex Augiensis and Codex Boernerianus of the Pauline Epistles." *Harvard Studies in Classical Philology* 60 (1951) 187–199.
Hitchcock, F. R. M. "A Study of Romans XVI." *CQR* 121 (1935–36) 187–209.
Hofmann, Karl M. *Philema Hagion*. Beiträge zur Forderung christlicher Theologie 38. Gütersloh, 1938.
Hort, F. J. A. "On the End of the Epistle to the Romans." *Journal of Philology* 3 (1871) 51–80.
Jervell, Jacob. "Der Brief nach Jerusalem; Über Veranlassung und Adresse des Römerbriefes." *ST* 25 (1971) 61–73.
Jewett, Robert. "The Form and Function of the Homiletic Benediction." *ATR* 51 (1969) 18–34.
Kamlah, Ehrhard. *Traditionsgeschichtliche Untersuchungen zur Schlussdoxologie des Römerbriefes*. Dissertation, Tübingen University, 1955.
Käsemann, Ernst. *An die Römer*. HNT 8a. 3rd ed. Tübingen, 1974.
Kenyon, F. G., ed. *The Chester Beatty Biblical Papyri. Descriptions and Texts of Twelve Manuscripts on Papyrus of the Greek Bible*. London, 1936–37.
Keyes, C. W. "The Greek Letter of Introduction." *American Journal of Philology* 56 (1935) 28–44.
Kim, Chan-Hie. *Form and Structure of the Familiar Greek Letter of Recommendation*. Society of Biblical Literature Dissertation Series 4. Missoula, Montana, 1972.
Klein, Günther. "Der Abfassungszweck des Römerbriefes." *Rekonstruktion und Interpretation. Gesammelte Aufsätze zum Neuen Testament*. Beiträge zur evangelischen Theologie 50. Munich, 1969.
Knox, John. "A Note on the Text of Romans." *NTS* 2 (1955–56) 191–93.
———. *Marcion and the New Testament; An Essay in the Early History of the Canon*. Chicago, 1942.
———. *Philemon Among the Letters of Paul*. Chicago, 1935.
———. "The Epistle to the Romans; Introduction and Exegesis." *The Interpreter's Bible* IX. Edited by George A. Buttrick. New York, 1954.
Koskenniemi, Heikki. *Studien zur Idee und Phraseologie des Griechischen Briefes bis 400 n. Chr.* Annales Academiae Scientiarum Fennicae, series B, CII, 2. Helsinki, 1956.
Kümmel, Werner Georg. *Introduction to the New Testament*. Rev. ed. Nashville, 1975.
Lake, Kirsopp. *The Earlier Epistles of St. Paul*. London, 1911.
———, and New, Silva, eds. *Six Collations of New Testament Manuscripts*. Harvard Theological Studies 17. Cambridge, Mass., 1932.
Leenhardt, Franz J. *The Epistle to the Romans*. Cleveland, 1961.
Lietzmann, Hans. *An die Korinther I–II*. HNT 9. 4th ed., expanded by W. G. Kümmel. Tübingen, 1949.

————. *An die Römer*. HNT 8. 4th ed. Tübingen, 1933.

————. "Einführung in die Textgeschichte der Paulusbriefe." *Kleine Schriften, II, Studien zum Neuen Testament*. Edited by K. Aland. TU 68. Berlin, 1958.

————. "Zwei Notizen zu Paulus." *Kleine Schriften, II, Studien zum Neuen Testament*. Edited by K. Aland. TU 68. Berlin, 1958.

Lightfoot, J. B. *Biblical Essays*. London, 1893.

Lönnermark, Lars-Göran. "Till frågan om Romarbrevets integritet." *SEA* 33 (1968) 141–48.

Lührmann, Dieter. *Das Offenbarungsverständnis bei Paulus und in paulinischen Gemeinden*. WMANT 16. Neukirchen-Vluyn, 1965.

McDonald, J. I. H. "Was Romans XVI a Separate Letter?" *NTS* 16 (1970) 369–372.

Manson, T. W. "St. Paul's Letter to the Romans—and Others." *Studies in the Gospels and Epistles*. Edited by Matthew Black. Manchester, 1962.

Marxsen, Willi. *Introduction to the New Testament*. Philadelphia, 1968.

Michaelis, Wilhelm. *Einleitung in das Neue Testament*. 3rd ed. Bern, 1961.

————. "Teilungshypothesen bei Paulusbriefen: Briefkompositionen und ihr Sitz im Leben." *TZ* 14 (1958) 321–26.

Michel, Otto. *Der Brief an die Römer*. Meyer 4. 4th ed. Göttingen, 1966.

Moule, C. F. D. *Worship in the New Testament*. London, 1961.

Mowrey, Lucetta. "The Early Circulation of Paul's Letters." *JBL* 63 (1944) 73–86.

Mullins, Terence Y. "Greeting as a New Testament Form." *JBL* 87 (1968) 418–426.

Oepke, Albrecht. *Der Brief des Paulus an die Galater*. Theologische Handkommentar zum Neuen Testament 9. 2nd ed. Berlin, 1957.

Preisigke, F. *Wörterbuch der griechischen Papyrusurkunden*. Ed. by E. Kiessling. 3 vols. Berlin, 1925–31.

Riggenbach, Eduard. "Die Kapitelverzeichnisse zum Römer- und Hebräerbrief im Codex Fuldensis der Vulgata." *Neue Jahrbücher für Deutsche Theologie* 3 (1894) 350–363.

————. "Die Textgeschichte der Doxologie Röm. 16,25–27 im Zusammenhang mit den übrigen, den Schluss des Römerbriefs betreffenden, textkritischen Fragen." *Neue Jahrbücher für deutsche Theologie* 1 (1892) 526–605.

Roller, Otto. *Das Formular der paulinischen Briefe; ein Beitrag zur Lehre vom antiken Briefe*. BWANT 4/6 (58). Stuttgart, 1933.

Sanday, W. and Headlam, A. C. *A Critical and Exegetical Commentary on the Epistle to the Romans*. ICC. 2nd ed. New York, 1926.

Schelkle, Karl Hermann. "Römische Kirche im Römerbrief." *Wort und Schrift; Beiträge zur Auslegung und Auslegungsgeschichte des Neuen Testaments*. Kommentare und Beiträge zum Alten und Neuen Testament. Düsseldorf, 1966.

Schenke, Hans-Martin. "Aporien im Römerbrief." *TLZ* 92 (1967) 881–84.

Schlier, Heinrich. *Der Brief an die Galater*. Meyer 7. 4th ed. Göttingen, 1965.

Schmidt, Hans Wilhelm. *Der Brief des Paulus an die Römer*. Theologischer Handkommentar zum Neuen Testament 6. 2nd ed. Berlin, 1966.

Schmithals, Walter. *Paul and the Gnostics*. Nashville, 1972.

————. "On the Composition and Earliest Collection of the Major Epistles of Paul." *Paul and the Gnostics*. Nashville, 1972.

————. "The False Teachers of Romans 16:17–20." *Paul and the Gnostics*. Nashville, 1972.

Schubert, Paul. *Form and Function of the Pauline Thanksgiving*. BZNW 20. Berlin, 1939.

Schumacher, Rudolf. *Die beiden letzten Kapitel des Römerbriefes. Ein Beitrag zu ihrer Geschichte und Erklärung*. NTAbh 14/4. Münster, 1929.

Suggs, M. Jack. "'The Word is Near You': Romans 10:6–10 within the Purpose of the Letter." *Christian History and Interpretation: Studies Presented to John Knox*. Edited by W. R. Farmer, C. F. D. Moule and R. R. Niebuhr. Cambridge, 1967.

Thraede, Klaus. *Grundzüge griechisch-römischer Brieftopik*. Zetemata: Monographien zur klassischen Altertumswissenschaft 47. Munich, 1970.

Unnik, W. C. van. "*Dominus Vobiscum;* The Background of a Liturgical Formula." *New Testament Essays in Memory of T. W. Manson*. Edited by A. J. B. Higgins. Manchester, 1959.

Vogels, H. J. "Der Einfluss Marcions und Tatians auf Text und Kanon des Neuen Testaments." *Synoptische Studien, Alfred Wikenhauser zum siebzigsten Geburtstag dargebracht.* Munich, 1953.

Wendland, Paul. *Die urchristlichen Literaturformen.* HNT 1/3. Tübingen, 1912.

Wiefel, W. "Die jüdische Gemeinschaft im antiken Rom und die Anfänge des römischen Christentums. Bemerkungen zu Anlass und Zweck des Römerbriefes." *Jud* 26 (1970) 65–88.

Williams, C. S. C. "P46 and the Textual Tradition of Romans." *ExpT* 61 (1949–50) 125–26.

Wordsworth, J., White, H. J., *et al.*, eds. *Novum Testamentum Domini nostri Iesu Christi Latine secundum editionem sancti Hieronymi.* 3 vols. Oxford, 1889–1954.

Zahn, Theodor von. *Der Brief des Paulus an die Römer.* Kommentar zum Neuen Testament 6. Leipzig, 1910.

_____. *Geschichte des neutestamentlichen Kanons.* 2 vols. Erlangen, 188–92.

_____. *Introduction to the New Testament.* 3 vols. New York, 1909.

Ziemann, F. *De epistularum Graecarum formulis sollemnibus: quaestiones selectae.* Dissertationes philologicae Halenses 18. Halle, 1911.

Zuntz, G. *The Text of the Epistles; A Disquisition upon the Corpus Paulinum.* The Schweich Lectures of the British Academy 1946. London, 1953.